ENCYCLOPEDIA OF
Paden City Glass

IDENTIFICATION
AND
VALUES

Carrie
and
Jerry Domitz

COLLECTOR BOOKS
A Division of Schroeder Publishing Co., Inc.

On the Cover

Front Cover:
Top Row —
   Ruby #881 Gadroon vase, Trumpet Flower etching
   Ebony genie vase, Ardith etching
   Cheriglo #1 ashtray, "Souvenir of Paden City, W. V."
Bottom Row —
   Green #300 mayonnaise set, Cupid etching
   Ebony #210 ice bucket, Black Forest etching

Back Cover:
Left — Cheriglo #182 elliptical vase, Peacock & Rose etching
Right — Green #61 vase, Zinnia & Butterfly etching

Cover design: Beth Summers
Book design: Joyce A. Cherry

Collector Books
P.O. Box 3009
Paducah, KY 42002-3009

www.collectorbooks.com

Copyright © 2004 by Carrie & Jerry Domitz
gedom@comcast.net

The current values in this book should be used only as a guide. They are not intended to set prices, which vary from one section of the country to another. Auction prices as well as dealer prices vary greatly and are affected by condition and demand. Neither the authors nor the publisher assumes responsibility for any losses which might be incurred as a result of consulting this guide.

Searching For A Publisher?

We are always looking for people knowledgeable within their fields. If you feel that there is a real need for a book on your collectible subject and have a large comprehensive collection, contact Collector Books.

Contents

Dedication

Sherryl and Dick Ponti

This book is dedicated to the memory of Sherryl Ponti, who lost her battle with breast cancer on October 28, 2000. Sherryl was one of the nicest people we've ever known. She loved collecting Paden City, she loved her friends, and she loved her husband Dick most of all. Whenever asked, Sherryl was willing to share her vast knowledge of Paden City, speaking at events and conventions. Even after she was very ill, she never lost her sense of humor and she made every effort to raise the spirits of her friends, who were suffering as they watched watched her grow more and more ill. It was an honor to have known her, so we will take the liberty of naming the beautiful and rare rosebud etching on the Gadroon vase "Sherry's Rose," so that everyone will remember the beautiful spirit she had.

Acknowledgments

When we decided to take on the very difficult project of writing a comprehensive book about Paden City, we knew that we would have the support of Dick Ponti, Ted and Judy Johnson, Steve and Rhonda Stone, and Bruce and Bonnie Catton. We had no idea that we would find support from people we didn't know very well. Listing their names doesn't begin to tell you the value of their help.

Our daughter, Greta Davis, is a professional photographer and we couldn't have done this book without her help. She set us up with the right equipment, showed us how to place the lights so that the etchings would stand out, and shot all the cover photos for us.

Dick Ponti loaded our van with sixty boxes of his collection, without the slightest worry that something could happen to that glass. Well, maybe he worried, but he didn't tell us. He provided us with the backbone of this book. Because the glass was at our house, we didn't have to rush and were able to measure every piece. We can't begin to tell you how helpful that was. We're not sure we could have done this without his help. Bob Carlson, who we didn't really know prior to this project, not only gave us the benefit of photographing his collection, but was an enormous help with researching our Primrose and Imperial Molly questions. John and Cindy Frank gave us a place to stay while we photographed their beautiful collection of Gothic Garden, as well as other patterns. Bruce and Bonnie Cattan opened their house to us even though Bruce was recovering from surgery. Ted and Judy Johnson allowed us to photograph every piece of their extensive collection, even though we had to take over their house for two days. Jim and Carlotta Roecker brought over some of their rarest pieces. Steve and Rhonda Stone gave me two tries when my first pictures were terrible. Gordan and Darlene Cochran allowed us to photograph at their house during the holidays, and we're certain they had many other things to do at the time. We were worried that we wouldn't be able to find enough Popeye and Olive for the book, but our friend Dale Mitchell let us photograph his collection. Mary Jacobs sent me a DVD with many of her rare pieces, because we ran out of time to go to her house. Marjory and Arlen Stokes contributed the reamer photos. We were amazed that, with all the glass each collector had, we didn't find a lot of repetition.

We owe a special thanks to Frank Fenton, who allowed us access to his research room and allowed us to use the drawings we found there. Gene Florence has answered the many questions we have had and is letting us use photos from several books he wrote. Kenn and Margaret Whitmyer took time away from working on their own books to take photos of their collection.

We also had support from many show dealers, as you will see from the huge list of contributors. Several shows allowed us to set up our lights and take photos during the show hours. They are the Sacramento Depression Glass Club Show, Palmer Wirf Shows, EK Glass Show, the Portland Rain of Glass, Heavenly Productions, and the Green River Depression Glass Show.

Individuals from Washington, Oregon, and California who helped us are Dennis Canavan, Bill Harmon, Galen Temple, Vi Kennedy, Carolyn Urbanski, Iris Natividad, Susan Hill, Robert Henicksman, Larry Hamilton, Gordon Boggs, Elisabeth Ventura, Judy Sowell, Jennifer and Don Vatne, Jane Kennedy, Cathy Tunnell, Ann Christianson, Allen and Diana Schafer, Leegh and Michael Wyse, Becki Ray, Terry and Bea Martin, Carolyn Crow, Jay and Nadine Downhan, Kate Winkle, Charley and Nancy Swehla, Erick and Georgia Paul, Steve and Karen Thacker, Linda and Dennis Sexton, Paula Spencer, Lynne Denman, Elva Fernandez, James and Deborah Mize, Carol Bess White, John Ojeda, Anne Eichner, John Peterson, Charles Griggs, Ron and Donna Miller, Tom and Karen Sanders, Karen Rau, Frank and Margaret Maxwell, Jerry and Beth Willey, Jeanenne Granger, Tracy Towry, Jay and Mary Atzbach, Cecil and Sharon Taylor, Bob Van Aiken, and Tom Smith of Indiana.

Those from the internet who helped are Dale Stillman of Mountian Home, Arkansas; Sandra Bentley Knee of Hillsboro, New Hampshire; Jeff and Shannon Cheek of Indiana, Beverly Kappenman of Nebraska, Tracy Towry of Oregon, Ed Goshe of Ohio, Nancy Stender of West Virginia, and Dave Green of California.

Introduction

I began collecting glass about 33 years ago, when a friend showed me her collection of covered animal dishes. From that time forward, I bought everything my weekly allowance of $15 dollars would buy. There was so little information available at the time that I bought a lot of brand-new pieces which were sold to me as old. Luckily, by the time I decided to sell them, they were worth more than I had paid. It's amazing what twenty years or so will do to the value of glass. I'm telling you this story because it's a typical story of a beginning collector. Don't be afraid to make a mistake or two, and buy every book you can find that relates to your collection. Even a bad book will have something of value to you.

We began selling glassware on a part time-basis twenty years ago, but I became a full-time antiques dealer five years later. Jerry is a mail carrier in Ballard, Washington, but helps me when he can. We decided to write this book last May, because I discovered new information about Paden City and I had no outlet for those new facts. This book has taken on a life of its own. I won't be able to list and price everything I know Paden City made, because this book would be so thick that you would need a wheelbarrow to carry it. In the future, I plan to write separate books, one for etchings and one for patterns. Some of the patterns will suffer in this book; I just don't have enough room to do them justice. I will try to fit as much information as I can within these pages.

When Jerry and I married 23 years ago, he encouraged me to do the thing that I enjoyed the most, research. We have tracked down out-of-print books and traveled to museums in search of information, but it is the time that I've spent with Frank Fenton that has taught me the most about research. Frank has taught me to not make rash decisions, but to follow the evidence where it takes me. I can't begin to count the hours we sat in his office arguing about an attribution, or the months it has taken me to prove that I'm right. More than half of the times, Frank has proven that I just didn't follow the evidence far enough. I spent two years trying to prove that a hobnail bottle I gave him for the museum was Fenton. Finally, Frank told me that it couldn't possibly be Fenton because Fenton couldn't have made it in the four-part mold used for my bottle. Of course, he could have told me that right away, but I learned more in my search for that answer than if he had made it easy for me. There is a lot of research in this book that directly contradicts the information provided by other authors, but I hope you will take the time to read about the steps I took to come to these conclusions.

Why Should I Collect Glass?

The answer to that question is easy if you look at the fluctuations of the stock market. Glassware is the fastest growing collectable on eBay and at antique shows. The best way to increase the value of a collection is to buy when prices are low, so that you will be able to make a profit later. The best way to buy low is to collect a category of glass that isn't well known, but has great potential. Glass made by Paden City is in that category right now. While patterns like Crow's Foot and etchings such a Cupid are well known and bring high prices, patterns like Party Line and Rena are still at prices low enough to be affordable. There are beautiful etchings, such as Gothic Garden, Ardith, and Eden Rose, that are still in the medium price bracket, and new pieces in every etching are being found every day. Now is the time to start collecting Paden City.

Pricing and Listing

You will find that the prices within this book are in the moderate range. I did this with the knowledge that many of the same items have sold on eBay for exorbitant prices. Some of those prices were so high that it would be irresponsible to place that value on the item, because a second one may only bring half of that amount. This is a strange time in the history of glass collecting. More and more collectors are skipping traditional shows and are spending their money buying online through auctions or other websites. I believe that by skipping shows, collectors are missing many bargains. But to go back to my philosophy of pricing, I tried to list items at prices that will appeal to the collector and that will allow dealers to sell mer-

chandise in a timely manner. There will always be collectors who are willing to pay much higher prices, but sometimes those collectors are hard to find. My price guide is set for the average seller selling to the average collector and is not meant to set prices. These prices reflect the retail value of the items, not the amount a dealer may pay. There are also price variations due to regional differences. Always bear in mind that dealers have no place to buy wholesale and sometimes they have to pay high prices to have quality merchandise to offer collectors. Pay the amount you feel comfortable spending.

Measurements

Measurements are inexact, because this is handmade glassware that was also shaped by hand. The same mold was used to produce several shapes; therefore, a 12" bowl can be cupped to make it much smaller or flared to make it much bigger. A comport can measure as much as 2" taller or shorter than its mold, depending on the way the bowl is shaped, so keep that in mind when you are looking at the list of pieces made. It would be impossible to list all the variations, but as a rule, the price remains the same for all of them.

History

Paden City, located in Paden City, West Virginia, began producing glass in November of 1916. David Fisher, who had previously been the manager of the New Martinsville Glass Company, was hired to manage the new plant. He had enjoyed great success when he managed New Martinsville, and it was hoped that he could repeat that success with this new company. The company started quite small, with about 300 workers, but it was truly "the little company that could."

Paden City produced hand made glassware that was of the highest quality. Its glass was either pressed or blown into a mold. Its owned many molds that had been used by the Higbee Glass Company, but was quick to supplement those with designs of its own. Because it had no design department, many of the new designs were adaptations of other companys' products. That wasn't unusual in the glass business. Companies were quick to react to the success of a design, color, or etching. Only a few details had to change to avoid encroaching upon another company's patented design, and there are several examples of that in this book. You only need to look at the items that were believed to be Imperial's Molly for so long to see that there are differences that set them apart from the genuine Molly pieces.

David Fisher ran the company until his death on May 21, 1933. Because he had been grooming his son, Samuel, to take over after he retired or died, the leadership was passed on in a very orderly fashion. Samuel Fisher was responsible for building Paden City into a fierce competitor that produced a high quality product, but he was reluctant to issue catalogs. That has made identification of Paden City pieces very difficult.

It appears that most of Paden City's business came from selling its glass to decorating companies such as Lotus and National Silver, as well as to other sales organizations such as the Rubel Company, Edward Paul, and L. G. Wright. Like most companies of that time period, its glass wasn't marked but came with a paper label, and many of the molds it used provided large areas on the pieces that would serve the needs of decorating companies well.

In 1949, a decision was made to buy the American Glass Company factory, which was automated. That appears to have been a mistake that would lead to the closing of both factories. Samuel Fisher held his leadership role until the very end of business. He had led the company to great successes but, in the end, his leadership also caused the failure of Paden City. It closed its doors on September 21, 1951.

Paden City Line Drawings

The line drawings and letters shown in this book came from Frank Fenton's files of communications between glass factories and the National Association of Manufactures of Pressed and Blown Glassware. When a factory planned to produce pieces from a new mold, it sent a line drawing of the piece to the union, which then told them how much to pay each of its workers. These communications have greatly improved my knowledge of American glassware. I will never be able to thank Frank Fenton enough for his generosity in allowing me to reprint them here.

There were many surprises in store for me when I began pulling all the Paden City information from those files. I was particularly happy to be able to identify the Ruby-colored Cherry Smash dispenser and the Thirst Extinguisher cocktail shakers as Paden City products, but there was much more. You will see many new and interesting pieces identified in this book.

Edward Paul Company

The Edward Paul Company was an importer that, like many others during World War II, suddenly became unable to buy European glassware. To remain in business, it turned to many American glass factories willing to help it fill its orders. I was able to find a three-page catalog of pieces made by Paden City for the Edward Paul Company in the 1940s. The catalog information is backed up by many line drawings of pieces found placed between the catalog pages. There is also a notation in the catalog, "all Paden City," that appears to have been written by someone from the union.

The first page of the catalog shows many pieces that, at first glance, appear to be pieces of Duncan's Sylvan and American Way patterns. When I compared them to pieces shown in the Duncan and Miller catalogs, I found a few distinct differences that set them apart from the Duncan pieces. The Paden City 3-part leaf-shaped relish has nine sections. The 3-part Sylvan piece has 15 sections. The pieces that resemble Duncan's American Way pattern have 12 swirls. The same Duncan American Way piece has only nine swirls.

The candlesticks shown were a big surprise, but unfortunately, I was not able to photograph a pair for the book. The candy is very similar to Heisey's Crystolite. In the bottom right-hand corner, one can see a spoon and fork set inside a salad bowl. It looks very much like the set that has been identified as being made by Cambridge. This would indicate that it was made by Paden City. I was most impressed by the two pages of perfumes, powders, and trays. Without the line drawings, they would never have been identified as being made by Paden City, because they are intricate and look more like Czechoslovakian products than American. I've seen the trays for years, and they have always been mistaken for Imperial's Candlewick. Those items can be found in the Vanity section, page 376.

Edward Paul Company catalog page.

Those Confusing Look-alikes

One of my first experiences with glass collecting was with carnival glass. During that era in glass making, it was a common practice for factories to copy one another's popular patterns. Often they made small changes that are hard to find, but armed with the information that these changes exist, it is easy to ferret them out. Coming from that understanding, I approach look-alikes differently than other authors. When you see pieces with popular patterns, the first approach should be to look for differences among them, not assume that the pieces were made or etched by only one company.

During the depression era and the 1950s, all the factories were fighting for every dollar that was to be made on glassware. Hand-made glassware was already more expensive than machine-made pieces were. Each factory had the expenses that came from paying its workers and from everyday maintenance. The cost of a blank included not only the cost of materials used to make it, but also a portion of these wage and maintenance expenses. It was cheaper to just buy a piece that was attractive and have a mold made that would be a close, but not exact, copy of it. All of the glass factories did that. If the design was patented, a factory had to change a few elements of the design, but if the design had no patent, a company could make a copy so close that it would be hard to find the differences.

Many sales companies, e.g., Edward Paul or L .G. Wright, owned their own molds and contracted with glass factories to produce glass sold under the names of the sales companies. In that case, it was common for molds to move from factory to factory. Each company placed a bid to produce glass from those molds. Whoever had the lowest bid made the glass. If a sales company discovered that it was losing money on that bid, as was often the case, a new bid would be sought and the molds would move on to another company.

Many decorating companies, such as the Lotus Decorating Company, bought blanks to decorate and sell under their own names. Occasionally, you can find sets with a pitcher from one factory and tumblers from another. Decorating companies could afford to buy blanks, because they didn't have the expense of maintaining glass furnaces and the many other expenses that a factory has every day, open or not.

Paden City seemed to be particularly adept when it came to diversifying its product line, so it would really have no need for another company's blanks. There are many examples of items and etchings that bear a close resemblance to that of another company. The photo below includes, from left to right, Paden City's #184 vase, Cambridge's #402 vase, and Fenton's #184 vase. As you can see, all three are almost identical.

Paden City #184 vase, Cambridge #402 vase, and Fenton #184 vase.

Imperial Molly

Although a few authors maintain that glass companies lent molds or sold blanks to each other, I can, at least, prove that Imperial Molly blanks were never used by Paden City.

It was easy to determine that the pieces thought to be Molly blanks simply couldn't be. Most of the Paden City pieces don't match the same size Molly blanks. Paden City's small bowls and plates have ten sides; Imperial's have six. The Imperial plate measures 6"; the Paden City one is 6½", with much smaller handles. You only have to look at them side by side to see the enormous disparity in the size of the pieces, the handles, and the center well. Also, the large Cupid-etched bowl shown in *Paden City Glassware* by the Torsiellos and the Stillmans has a flat base and is octagonal. The same bowl made by Imperial has ten sides. The only large octagonal Molly bowl is footed, not flat. A photo of that bowl can be seen on page 124. The heart-shaped center-handled server is the only piece that is an exact duplicate of one of Imperial's Molly pieces. The only one that we know for certain was made by Paden City is the piece in the Cupid section, but I'm certain there are more that have cuttings or silver overlay

that makes them harder to identify. I would have been happier if I could have found a piece I know to be Imperial to compare to the Cupid-etched center-handled tray, but I couldn't locate one. I was able to photograph a comparison of the #701 handled tray. As you can see in the photos, the Paden City piece is larger, 10¾" to Molly's 10⅜". Even though the Molly piece is smaller in diameter, the handles are larger: the #701 handles are 2½", Molly handles are 2⅝". The center of the #701 tray is 4⅝", the center of the Molly tray is 3¾". Paden City's center has a rim where the curve joins the flat area; the Molly center gradually slopes into the flat area and has no definition.

The reason that many other researchers were certain that Paden City bought Imperial blanks instead of using its own is that the catalog page for the #701 line doesn't show the lines or optics in those pieces. Paden City was in the habit of changing molds constantly, to freshen its product line, and this was the case here. Creams and sugars in the #701 line came with and without optics, as did the large, flat candy boxes. Lines or optics are put in glassware by using a different plunger to force the glass into the mold and are easy to change.

Imperial Molly comparison. Imperial Molly is on the right; Paden City Ardith is on the left.

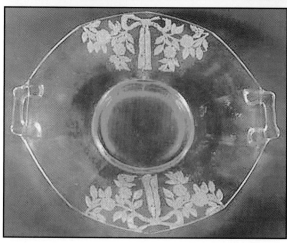

Paden City #701 Eden Rose.

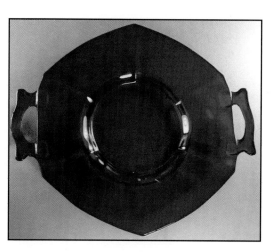

Imperial Molly.

Primrose

One of the first questions I asked each collector I spoke to when I began to write this book was, "What color do you believe to be Primrose? Is it an Amber with a red tint, or is it a brownish version of Cheriglo?" I got a different answer from every single person. I was so puzzled by the responses that I wasn't certain I could find the correct answer, but Bob Carlson found the answer for me. He went back to Jerry Barnett's *Paden City, the Color Company* and found a published article (page 56) promoting Paden City's Penny Line. In that ad, there is a list of colors in which Penny Live was being produced. Those colors were green, Amber, Royal Blue, Ruby, Cheriglo, and PRIMROSE. If Amber had been listed one year and canceled and replaced by Primrose the next, it would be possible that the company had reworked its amber color, but it simply doesn't make sense that it would make two different amber colors for the same line at the same time. Bob checked the dictionary and found that one definition of primrose is "a delicate shade of yellow." After he told me what he had found, I did more research on *primrose*. Primroses bloom in the spring, not the fall. It wouldn't make sense for Paden City to have used a name associated with a spring flower for Amber, a fall color.

Soon after Bob told me his theory, I had the chance to photograph a collection of Penny Line high-footed cocktails. The collection, bought as a set, includes all the colors listed in the advetisement: green, Amber, Royal Blue, Ruby, Cheriglo, and YELLOW (Primrose). This color is very light. I think that the reason collectors haven't commonly noticed this version of yellow is that they have believed it to be a bad batch of crystal. You only need to set it next to a yellowed crystal to discover that it is darker and more consistent than it would be if it was a mistake. I was able to find both a Primrose Ardith vase and a bird, the latter still on the piece glass companies call the bust-off. I also found that there are some pieces of Delilah Bird and Sasha Bird that use that same very pale yellow. It should be priced the same as the darker Topaz color that was used for the #411 Mrs. B. pattern.

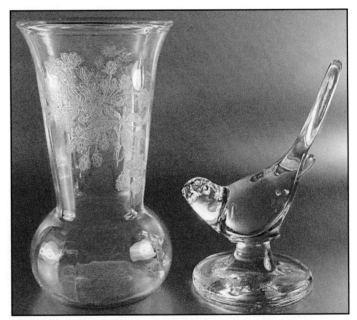

Primrose #184 Ardith vase and Primrose long-tailed bird on stand.

Etchings

Anna

A beautiful sunflower has been used for this etching. For quite some time, no one was certain that Paden City was the correct attribution, but two pieces were found that confirm Paden City as the maker, a #182 elliptical vase and a #180 cylinder vase. What we can't say for certain is whether the etching was done by Paden City or by a private decorator. Pieces have been found with a plain top edge or with an etched gold border. I think that these pieces are hard enough to find that the price should be the same whether or not there is a border.

Close-up showing border detail on #184 vase.

Description	Line	Size	Amber	Green/Pink
vase	180	12"		$225-250
vase	180	8"		$300-350
vase	184	10"	$200-225	$200-250
vase	184	12"	$225-250	$250-275

Green #184 10" vase. $200.00 – 250.00.

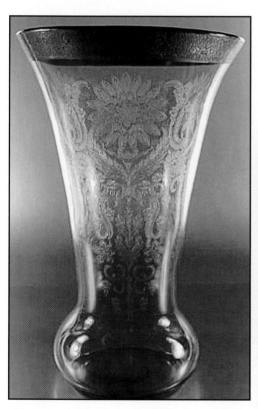

Cheriglo #184 12" vase. $250.00 – 275.00.

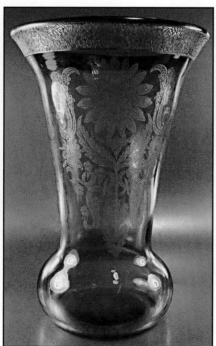

Amber #184 10" vase. $200.00 – 225.00.

Ardith

Ardith is a very pleasing etching that looks very good on most of Paden City's pressed and blown ware. It's also easier to find than most of Paden City's etchings, but there are a few very rare and exciting pieces to be found. The cherub-held decanter is spectacular and the blown pitchers are beautiful. I was very surprised to see the 10" #210 dinner plate, because many believe that it just doesn't exist. The proof is in the viewing. Several cracker jars have been found with plain lids, but recently an etched lid was discovered. That lid increases the value by 50%. Gold, silver, or other color inlays increase the value by 25%. Ruby or Cobalt Blue pieces are very rare and are expensive when found. I combined the two colors because they have the same value, but I'm not certain all pieces found in one color are also found in the other. I'm sure the listings will increase with each new edition.

Description	Line	Size	Amber	Cheriglo/ Green	Cobalt/ Ruby	Crystal	Ebony	Yellow
bar bottle		10½"				$50-75		
bowl	210	11"		$75-95		$45-50	$65-75	$65-75
bowl, center handled	411	9"		$75-95		$45-50	$60-75	$75-95
bowl, center handled	701	9¼"x10¾"		$90-100			$60-75	
bowl, console	211	12½"				$65-75		
bowl, console	411	12"		$95-125		$50-65	$75125	$75-125
bowl, console	412	12"		$125-150	$175-225		$125-150	
bowl, console	555	9"				$50-75		

Ebony #210 8½" vase. $150.00 – 200.00.

Ebony #411 10" cracker plate. $65.00 – 95.00.

Ebony #411 14" oval, handled tray. $55.00 – 60.00.

Description	Line	Size	Amber	Cheriglo/ Green	Cobalt/ Ruby	Crystal	Ebony	Yellow
bowl, console	701	12"		$85-100		$45-55	$75-100	$75-100
bowl, flat edge or rolled	411	11"		$85-100			$60-75	$75-95
bowl, handled	411	9"		$125-150				$125-150
bowl, handled	701	9¼"x11"					$64-75	
bowl, lily	900	13"				$50-75		
bowl, oval, handled	411	11¼"x3¼"	$100-125			$50-75	$75-90	
bowl, ftd. (comport)	412	9" x4½"		$125-150	$175-225	$50-60	$125-150	$125-150
bowl, ftd.(comport)	411	9"		$150-175		$50-65	$150-165	$150-165
cake plate	300	9½"						$150-175
cake plate	411	9½"		$150-185			$95-125	$150-165
candlestick, rd., center	555	6"				$40-50 ea.		
candlestick, winged	555	6"				$40-50 ea.		
candlestick	210	4½"x2½"		$35-45 ea.			$35-45 ea	$35-45 ea.
candlestick	412			$50-65 ea.	$75-95 ea.	$25-40 ea.	$45-60 ea.	$45-60 ea.
candlestick	701	4½"		$55-75 ea.		$35-55 ea.	$45-60 ea.	$45-65 ea.
candlestick, keyhole	411			$55-75 ea.		$35-45 ea.	$55-60 ea.	$50-60 ea.
candlestick, rolled up edge	411	4"		$65-85 ea.		$60-75 ea.	$65-85 ea.	$65-85 ea.
candlestick, mushroom	411	4½"x2½"	$55-70 ea.		$45-65	$95-125 ea.	$55-65 ea.	
candy box	210			$250-275		$125-150	$225-250	$225-250
candy box	411	6¼"		$100-125		$45-50	$100-125	$100-125
candy box	412	6⅞"		$100-125		$40-50	$100-125	$100-125
candy box, ftd.	555	10"				$65-70		
candy box, cloverleaf	412	7"		$75-95		$50-65	$75-95	$75-95
candy, w/round base	411	6½"		$150-$200		$75-100	$150-200	$150-200
candy, ½ lb lid 411, base 701		8"	$250-275			$200-250	$250-275	
candy, flat	701	7¾"x4¼"		$150-200		$65-95	$150-200	$150-200
candy, flat	890	5¾"x5¾"		$150-200	$250-300	$100-125		$150-200
candy, ftd, round finial 411 lid, 503 base		6½"x6"		$250-325				
candy, keyhole lid 411 lid, 503 base							$250-325	
cheese & cracker set	412	10¼"		$175-225	$250-350	$65-95		$150-175
cheese & cracker plate	411	10"		$100-150		$65-95		$100-150
comport	411	7½"		$75-95		$45-50	$45-55	$75-95
comport	412	7"x6½"			$150-175	$50-60		
comport, cheese (plain)	411	5"		$20-25		$15-20	$20-25	$20-25

Decription	Line	Size	Amber	Cheriglo/Green	Cobalt/Ruby	Crystal	Ebony	Yellow
comport, cheese (plain)	412	5"x2"		$20-25	$50-65	$15-20	$20-25	$20-25
comport	300							$125-150
creamer	300			$50-65				$50-65
creamer	411			$50-60		$20-30	$45-55	$35-45
creamer	412			$40-45		$25-35		$40-45
cup	411	2½"x3¾"		$45-50	$85-100			$45-50
cup	412				$85-100			$65-75
decanter	410	14"				$150-175		
decanter, pinch		10¼"		$250-275				$225-250
decanter, cherub holder		8"x10½"		$450-600				
gravy, ftd.	412			$75-95				$75-95
ice bucket	902		$100-125	$125-150		$55-75	$125-150	$100-125
ice bucket/cracker jar				$450-600			$250-350	$300-450
Ivy Ball	411	4¼"					$95-120	
jug, batter	11	7"				$125-150		
mayonnaise, ftd.	411	6"x3½"		$65-75	$75-95			$125-135
mayonnaise liner	411	7¼"		$25-35	$35-45			$25-35
pitcher, optic or plain		7¾	$375-450					$375-450
pitcher	210	10"		$300-375				
plate	215	9¼"				$18-22		
plate	412	8¾"			$75-95			$45-50
plate, cracker	411	10"		$75-125		$45-75	$65-95	$75-125
plate, cracker	412	10"		$150-200	$200-250			$125-150
plate, dinner	210	10"					$100-125	
plate,* handled	701	6½"		$40-50		$20-35		$40-50
plate, handled	411			$75-90			$55-65	$75-85
plate, luncheon,	411	8½"		$75-90	$75-85			$40-50
plate,* turned up	701	5½"					$50-75	$75-85
saucer	411			$20	$25-35			$20
saucer	412			$20	$25-35			$20
sugar	300			$45-50				$45-50
sugar	411			$50		$20-30	$50	$40
sugar	412			$35-50		$20-30		$35-50
tray, center handled	411	10½"		$100-125	$225-275			$65-75
tray, center handled	412	10¼"		$75-125	$225-275			$75-95
tray, handled	411	11" at handles		$75-95			$55-60	$65-85
tray, oval, handled	411	14"x10"		$75-95			$55-60	$65-85
tumbler	191			$75-85				$65-75
tumbler	991	3¾"		$35-45				
tumbler, ice tea (blown)	2108	12 oz.	$75-125	$75-125				$75-125
tumbler, whiskey	215	3 oz.					$75-95	
vase	191½	3"					$175-200	
vase	210	10"					$175-200	
vase	210	6½"		$75-95				$75-95
vase **	184	8"		$150-175				$125-150
vase, elliptical	182	5½"				$75-95	$100-125	
vase, elliptical	182	8"		$175-225		$125	$175-200	$175-200
smoke stack	210	8½"		$175-225			$150-200	
vase, various tops, genie		6¼"-7"		$195-225			$195-225	$195-225
vase, various tops, ribbed	300	6¼"-7"					$275-350	

* ribbed
**Primrose, $150-200

Ebony #210 11" console bowl. $65.00 – 75.00.

Ebony #182 5½" elliptical vase. $100.00 – 125.00.

Ebony 7" genie vase. $195.00 – 200.00.

Ebony #411 12" x 10¼" x 3" handled bowl. $125.00 – 150.00.

Ebony 7" genie vase. $195.00 – 200.00.

Ebony #701 ribbed, handled plate. $40.00 – 50.00.

Ebony #411 center-handled tray. $70.00 – 80.00.

Ebony ice bucket with a wicker handle (should have lid). $250.00 – 350.00 with lid.

Ebony #210 10¼" cracker plate. $45.00 – 65.00.

Ebony #411 flat candy (with lid; base is crystal). $95.00 – 115.00.

Ebony 6¼" vase with ribbed sides. $275.00 – 350.00.

Ebony #210 10½" dinner plate. $100.00 – 125.00.

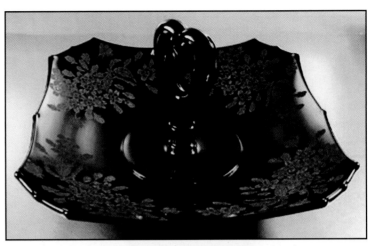

Ebony #411 center-handled tray with cupped edges. $75.00 – 85.00.

Ebony #701 9¼" x 10¾" x 2¾" handled bowl. $65.00 – 75.00.

Ebony #411 handled plate. $55.00 – 65.00.

Ebony #411 keyhole candlestick. $55.00 – 60.00.

Ebony #210 6½" vase. $75.00 – 95.00.

Ebony #411 rolled-edge comport. $45.00 – 55.00.

Crystal #555 10" gold-encrusted footed candy.
$80.00 – 85.00.

Crystal #411 6¼" flat candy. $45.00 – 50.00.

Crystal #412 6¼" x 3½" comport. $50.00 – 60.00.

Crystal #412 square candy with ivory inlaid etching.
$50.00 – 65.00.

Crystal #411 keyhole candlestick. $35.00 – 45.00.

Crystal #11 8" batter pitcher. $125.00 – 150.00.

Crystal #11 7" milk pitcher. $125.00 – 150.00.

Crystal #410 13½" bell-shaped decanter.
$150.00 – 175.00.

Crystal #411 creamer. $20.00 – 30.00.

Crystal #182 elliptical vase in ormolu holder. $125.00 – 150.00.

Crystal #902 ice bucket.
$55.00 – 75.00.

Cheriglo 10 oz. flat decanter and six shot glasses, in a silver holder. $450.00 – 600.00.

Cheriglo 10¼" pinch decanter. $250.00 – 275.00.

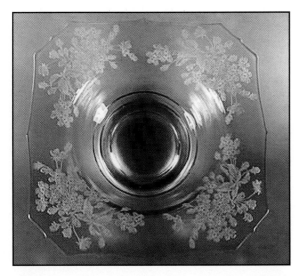

Cheriglo #411 11" flat-edged bowl. $85.00 – 100.00.

Cheriglo #411 9" handled bowl. $125.00 – 150.00.

Cheriglo #210 6½" vase. $75.00 – 95.00.

Cheriglo #411 7½" cupped-edge comport. $75.00 – 95.00.

Cheriglo #411 keyhole candlestick. $55.00 – 75.00.

Cheriglo #411 center-handled server.
$100.00 – 125.00.

Cheriglo cookie jar with wicker handle. $450.00 – 600.00.

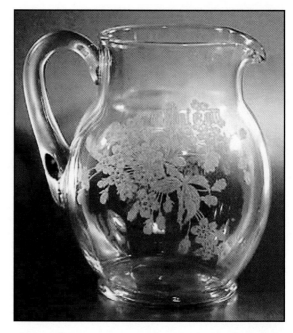

Cheriglo #411 cheese and cracker; note that the cheese is not etched. $100.00 – 150.00.

Yellow 7¾" blown rib optic jug. $375.00 – 450.00.

Cheriglo #701 flat candy.
$150.00 – 200.00.

Yellow #411 10" center-handled server.
$65.00 – 75.00.

Yellow #411 flat candy. $100.00 – 125.00.

Yellow #411 9½" x 4½" footed bowl (comport).
$150.00 – 165.00.

Yellow #411 cream and sugar. $75.00 – 85.00.

Yellow #411 9½" cake salver. $150.00 – 165.00.

Yellow #300 11¼" cake salver. $150.00 – 175.00.

Yellow #412 center-handled tray. $75.00 – 95.00.

Yellow #412 8½" plate. $45.00 – 50.00.

Yellow #412 cup and saucer. $85.00 – 95.00.

Yellow #184 8" vase. $125.00 – 150.00.

Yellow #411 mushroom candlestick. $55.00 – 65.00.

Yellow #411 mayonnaise set. $150.00 – 175.00.

Yellow #411 7¼" tall footed candy (#701 base).
$250.00 – 325.00.

Yellow #701 tab-handled plate. $40.00 – 50.00.

Yellow #991 7 oz. tumbler, 3¾".
$35.00 – 45.00.

Yellow #300 comport. $125.00 – 150.00.

Yellow #411 10" oval bowl. $75.00 – 90.00.

Yellow #412 cream and sugar. $75.00 – 95.00.

Yellow #411 footed bowl. $150.00 – 165.00.

Royal Blue #412 saucer. $25.00 – 35.00.

Royal Blue #890 candy with crystal base.
$200.00 – 250.00.

Green #411 7½" x 4¼" oval, cupped comport.
$75.00 – 95.00.

Green #411 center-handled tray. $100.00 – 125.00.

Green #411 keyhole candlestick. $55.00 – 75.00.

28

Green #411 footed candy with #513 base. $250.00 – 300.00.

Green #991 3¾" tumbler. $35.00 – 45.00.

Top view of green #411 footed candy. $250.00 – 300.00.

Green #411 8½" plate. $60.00 – 75.00.

Green #411 cup and saucer. $65.00 – 70.00.

Green #411 console bowl. $95.00 – 125.00.

Green #411 center-handled bowl. $75.00 – 95.00.

Green #2108 5¼" blown ice tea tumbler. $75.00 – 125.00.

Ruby #412 7" comport. $150.00 – 175.00.

Green #412 footed gravy. $75.00 – 95.00.

Ruby #412 10" cracker plate. $100.00 – 150.00.

Ruby #412 9" footed bowl. $175.00 – 225.00.

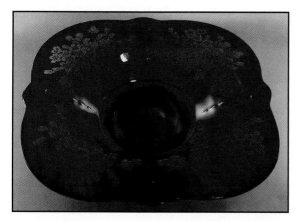

Ruby #412 12" console bowl. $175.00 – 225.00.

Amber #2108 5¼" blown ice tea tumbler.
$75.00 – 125.00.

Aster

The etching plate for this pattern was found at an L. G. Wright sale, so Aster was a Paden City etching rather than one done by a decorating company such as Lotus. A complete listing for this pattern isn't possible at this time, but please e-mail me if you have seen other pieces. To price pieces that you may find that I have not listed, as a rule of thumb use a 25% increase in the value of that piece if it were plain.

Description	Line	Size	Crystal
bowl, Plume	888	6"	$18 – 20
platter	700	13"	$45 – 50

Crystal #888 6" bowl. $18.00 – 20.00.

Baby Orchid

It is very easy to tell the difference between Orchid and Baby Orchid (Paden City original name). Orchid is a deep plate etching, and Baby Orchid is a deep carved pattern that feels similar to cut glass or to the 1950s sand-carved decorations done by Dorothy Thorpe or Tiffin. I've only found this etching used on blanks from these lines: #555, #444 Vale, and #211 Spire. Because #555 wasn't introduced until sometime in 1940 or 1941, it is likely that all the Baby Orchid pieces were produced after that date. The #444 candlestick is often mistaken for Imperial's popular Candlewick pattern. Evidently Paden City used only crystal for this design, but I wouldn't rule out other colors.

Crystal #555 10" handled bowl. $50.00 – 60.00.

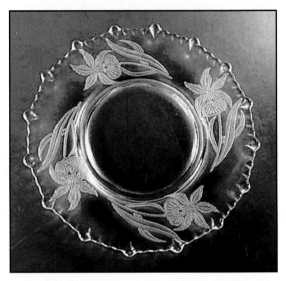

Crystal #555 8" plate. $25.00 – 35.00.

Crystal #555 cup and saucer. $42.00 – 45.00.

Crystal #555 footed, covered candy jar. $75.00 – 100.00.

Description	Line	Size	Crystal
bowl	444	9"x2½"	$40-50
bowl	555	9"x3"	$40-50
bowl, handled	555	10"x3"	$50-60
bowl	555	12"x4 "	$50-60
bowl, handled	900		$75-125
candlestick,	444	6"	$30-40 ea.
candlestick	900		$30-40 ea.
candlestick, duo	555		$35-50 ea.
candy, covered	555	7"	$75-100
creamer	444		$30-35
creamer	555		$25-30
cup	555		$30
mayonnaise, 2 pc.	444		$65-75
mayonnaise, 2 pc	555		$65-75
plate	555	8"	$25-35
plate, handled	555	12½"	$65-85
platter	211	15"	$75-95
platter*	555	15"	$75-95
saucer	555		$12-15
server, center handled	555	11"	$85-100
sugar	444		$25-30
sugar	555		$20-25

*found with both large and small orchids

Crystal #555 cream and sugar. $45.00 – 55.00.

Crystal #211 15" Spire platter. $75.00 – 95.00.

Crystal #555 9" bowl. $40.00 – 50.00.

Crystal #555 11" center-handled server. $85.00 – 100.00.

Crystal #444 single candlestick.
$30.00 – 40.00.

Crystal #555 15" platter. $75.00 – 95.00.

Crystal #444 9" bowl. $40.00 – 50.00.

Crystal #900 9" console bowl, $75.00 – 125.00, and #900 5"
candlesticks, $30.00 – 40.00 each.

Basket Flowers

The etching plates for Basket Flower were found at the L. G. Wright auction, so this is a Paden City creation, not one from a decorating company. It's a fairly obscure etching, so a complete listing cannot be done at this time. For items found but not listed here, find the pattern in the Pattern section and add 20% to the value listed there. Please e-mail me if you have seen other pieces.

Crystal #412 gold-encrusted flat candy. $28.00 – 37.00.

Crystal #555 footed cake salver. $40.00 – 45.00.

Description	Line	Size	Crystal	Crystal w/Gold
cake plate, ftd.	555	12"	$40-45	$45-50
candy, 3-part	412	6⅞"	$25-35	$28-37
creamer	555		$20-22	$22-24
plate	555	11"	$25-30	$30-34
sugar	555		$18-20	$20-22

Birch Tree/Deerwood

When pieces of Paden City started showing up with the Deerwood etching, collectors assumed that Tiffin had bought the blanks from Paden City. Of course, Tiffin had plenty of blanks of its own, so I felt that I needed to look closer at these etchings. They are so alike that, unless you compare them detail to detail, they appear to be the same. I asked Tiffin researcher and writer Ed Goshe to help me, and he generously agreed to do so. He compared photos I sent him to the comparable Tiffin piece and came to the same conclusion I did. These are different etchings done by different companies. Four of the pieces shown here were made and etched by Paden City. The candlestick is Tiffin's Deerwood. To differentiate one from the other, I'm going to call the Paden City version Birch Tree, which has always been used as an alternate name for Deerwood.

The plate shown here is 8½", a full inch bigger than the Tiffin counterpart. On Paden City's 8½" plate,

there is only one buck with its head turned; the 7½" Tiffin plate has two. On the 10" cake plate and the center-handled server, the Tiffin version has a large open area where the doe and fawn are grazing. The tree branches don't touch above them. On the Paden City version, the etching is placed evenly around the edge with only a tiny gap in the tree branches over the grazing deer. A dealer who knew I was trying to find a piece of Tiffin's Deerwood to photograph for comparison brought the ebony with gold cracker plate to me. We were both surprised to find that it was also made by Paden City. The sequence of the etching matches all the other Paden City pieces and is wrong

for Tiffin's Deerwood. Again, there is only one buck with a turned head, while even the smallest plates made by Tiffin have two. This plate has a cheese stand that is not etched, as do most other Paden City cheese and crackers. Because it was plain, she didn't bring it in to be photographed, but it will be in the second edition. From this experience, I now believe that there is as much Paden City Birch Tree out there as there is Tiffin Deerwood. Watch the blanks carefully and don't assume that all the gold-encrusted ebony pieces were made by Tiffin. I've only seen #300 Archaic and #700 Simplicity items, but there may be others.

Cheriglo #700 center-handled tray. $100.00 – 150.00.

Description	Line	Size	Amber/Crystal	Pink/Green	Ebony
cake plate	700	10"	$100-125	$150-200	$150-200
candy	198		$75-95	$125-150	$125-150
cheese and cracker	700		$75-100	$150-175	$175-200
creamer	300			$25-35	
nappy, covered,					
3-part (flat candy)	300		$75-125	$150-200	
plate	700	8½"	$25-35	$ 50-75	
server, center handled	700	10"	$50-75	$100-150	$100-150
sugar	300			$20-22	

Cheriglo #700 8½" plate. $50.00 – 75.00.

Cheriglo #700 high-footed cake salver.
$150.00 – 200.00.

Ebony #700 10¼" gold-encrusted cracker plate.
$125.00 – 150.00.

TIFFIN Ebony Deerwood candlestick (for comparison only).

UNITED STATES GLASS COMPANY, PITTSBURGH, PA., U. S. A.
ETCHED "DEERWOOD" DESIGN.
Furnished on Green or Pink Glass.
The Prices given are per Dozen, List.

Factory "GES"
150-12-2-29

No. 2809
Goblet
$10.00

No. 2809
Sau. Champ.
$10.00

No. 2809
Wine
$9.50

No. 2809
Cocktail
$9.50

No. 2808-Footed
Ice Tea Tumbler
$10.00

No. 2808-Footed
Table Tumbler
$10.00

No. 9395-Cup and Saucer
$19.00

No. 8133-Breakfast Dish
$16.00

No. 151-Celery Tray
$22.20

Note: For other items listed in this Design, See Plate No. 354

No. 8859-10' Dinner Plate
$23.75

No. 8836-7½' Salad Plate
$11.80

No. 8836-5½' Plate
$10.60

No. 6471-10' Vase
$23.75

Printed in U. S. A.

Plate No. 35

This Tiffin catalog reprint was generously furnished by the Tiffin Collectors Club, for comparison of Birch Tree and Deerwood. The 10" plate has the gap above the gazing deer. To the right of those deer there is a small bush, then a buck with his head turned. On the Paden City version, there is a large tree, a rabbit, and a large bush before the buck with his head turned.

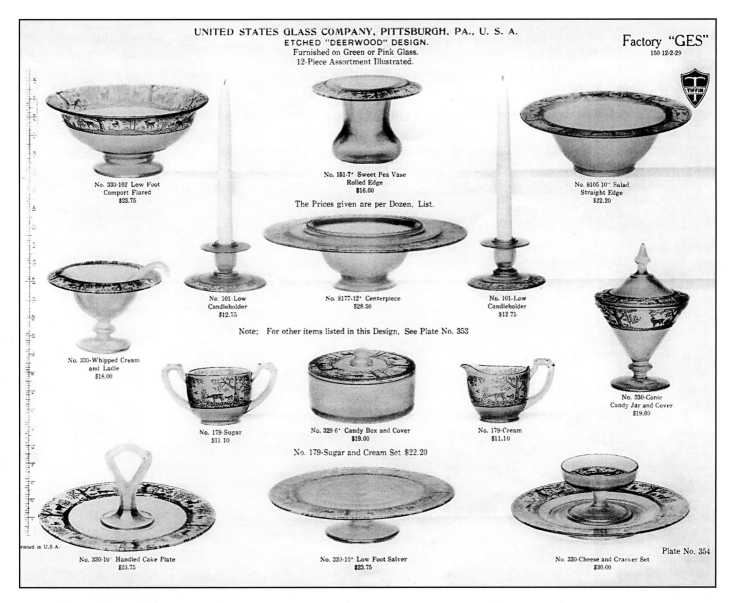

UNITED STATES GLASS COMPANY, PITTSBURGH, PA., U. S. A.
ETCHED "DEERWOOD" DESIGN.
Furnished on Green or Pink Glass.
12-Piece Assortment Illustrated.

Factory "GES"
150-12-2-29

No. 330-102 Low Foot
Comport Flared
$23.75

No. 151-7' Sweet Pea Vase
Rolled Edge
$16.00

The Prices given are per Dozen, List.

No. 8105 10" Salad
Straight Edge
$22.20

No. 101-Low
Candleholder
$12.75

No. 8177-12' Centerpiece
$28.50

No. 101-Low
Candleholder
$12.75

No. 330-Whipped Cream
and Ladle
$18.00

Note: For other items listed in this Design, See Plate No. 353

No. 179-Sugar
$11.10

No. 329 6' Candy Box and Cover
$19.00

No. 179-Cream
$11.10

No. 330-Conic
Candy Jar and Cover
$19.00

No. 179-Sugar and Cream Set $22.20

No. 330-10" Handled Cake Plate
$23.75

No. 330-10' Low Foot Salver
$23.75

No. 330-Cheese and Cracker Set
$30.00

Plate No. 354

This Tiffin catalog reprint was generously furnished by the Tiffin Collectors Club. The cake plate in this catalog reprint is very simular to the Paden City cake plate, but Tiffin's is low footed and Paden City's is high footed. As with the other pieces, the pattern sequence is different.

Black Forest

Black Forest is a very popular pattern but, for the most part, the prices of the common pieces have remained affordable. When Hazel Marie Weatherman wrote her book, *Colored Glassware of the Depression Era, Book 2*, she included an advertisement for the Black Forest etching sold by the Frank L. Van Deman and Son Company of New York City. At that time, she wasn't aware that the glass advertised by that merchandising company had actually been made by Paden City. There is no way to know whether or not Black Forest was made as an exclusive for Van Deman, but if it was, the company must have been very successful to have ordered and sold the enormous amount of Black Forest available. It is possible, but not easy, to collect a dinner set in this pattern.

Most of the time, Black Forest is found on the #210 Regina pattern blanks, but pieces on Party Line have been found, and other kinds of blanks with Black Forest may exist. It's hard to list all the rarities in this pattern, but some of the stand-outs are the covered footed relish, the #210 night set, the #210 pitchers with a lid, all the blown tumblers, the whip cream pail, the #184 vase, and the #210 perfume. I've priced the pitcher both with and without the lid. Look at that lid closely, because it would be easy to pass it by without knowing it belongs on the #210 pitcher. The only piece of crystal I've found with this etching is a #210 cup paired with a #191 saucer. Combining two patterns wasn't unusual for Paden City, so I think it was probably sold that way.

The #210 pitcher shown here is a brown-toned pink that has been mistaken for Primrose (now known to be pale yellow, not Amber with a red tone). Pink, or Cheriglo, was a hard color to control, thus the many shades found. Some chemicals were difficult to find and demand for glassware was high. Frank Fenton once told me that during World War II, the company could sell anything it made, so it wasn't important that every piece matched. The Cheriglo color ranges from a delicate pink to a color that is more orange than pink. Because of that, I photographed tumblers in two differenct shades so that you can compare them. If you are looking for a matched set, you will need to check the color carefully before buying on eBay or using other types of mail-order.

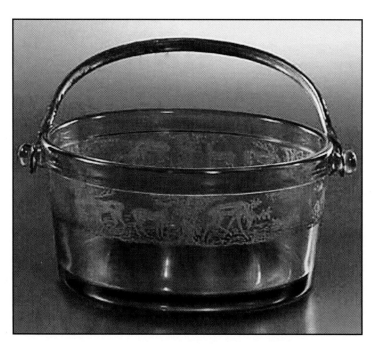

Amber 6" x 3" metal-handled whip cream pail.
$125.00 – 150.00.

Amber #191 7¾" footed candy and lid.
$125.00 – 150.00.

Amber #210 10" tab-handled bowl. $95.00 – 120.00.

Description	Line	Size	Amber	Ebony	Crystal	Cheriglo/Green	Ruby
batter jug	11	8"	$175-200	$175-200		$175-200	
bowl, closed tab handled	210	10"x8¾"		$50-75		$75-95	
bowl, console	210	10¼"x4"		$75-95		$75-90	
bowl, handled	210	10½"x9"x3¼"	$95-120	$140-175		$100-125	
bowl, rolled edge	210	12"		$95-115		$85-95	
bowl, rolled edge	210	13"		$100-125		$150-175	
cake plate	210	11"x2"		$125-150		$150-175	
candlestick	118	1½"x3⅝"				$55-60 ea.	
candlestick, mushroom	210	4½"x3"		$45-55 ea.		$50-55 ea.	
candy jar, flat	210	6½"		$200-250		$225-275	
candy jar, ftd., w/lid	191	7¾"	$125-150			$150-175	
candy jar, ftd.	210	6⅜"x6¼"		$200-250		$225-275	
comport	210	9¾"x3½"		$125-150		$150-175	
comport, high ftd.	210			$75-95		$100-120	
creamer	210	3⅝"		$25-30		$35-45	
cup	191						$150-200
cup	210			$55-60	$65-75	$55-60	
decanter, w/stopper	210	10"				$400-500	
decanter, genie		8½", 28 oz.				$750-850	
eggcup	210					$150-175	
guest set	210						
ice bucket	210	5¼"x4"	$100-125	$100-125		$125-150	
ice bucket*	300						
mayonnaise comport	210	7"x3¼"	$50-70	$65-85		$75-95	
perfume bottle	210			$150-175	$200-225	$175-200	
pitcher, w/lid, ice tea	210	12½"				$850-950	
pitcher, w/o lid	210	10½"				$650-750	
pitcher	210	10½", 72 oz.				$550-750	

Description	Line	Size	Amber	Ebony	Crystal	Cheriglo/Green	Ruby
pitcher, milk	11	7"	$150-175	$150-175			
plate, dinner	210			$75-100			
plate, handled	220	10"			$50-75		
plate, handled	210	13⅛"x11¼"x1¼"		$60-75		$60-75	
plate, liner	210	7½"		$20-25		$25-35	
plate, luncheon	210	8¼"		$65-85			
plate, tab handled	210	10"		$60-65		$60-75	
relish, ftd.	210 base	9"x11¼"				$500-650	
saucer	191				$20-35		$50-75
saucer	210			$20-22	$15-18	$20-22	
sugar	210	4"		$20-25		$30-35	
syrup	11	5¼"	$125-165	$125-165			
tray, center handled	210	11"		$75-100		$100-120	
tray, center handled	900	11"		$65-95		$100-125	
tumbler		5¾"				$65-75	
tumbler, shot, hourglass		2½", 2 oz.				$125-150	
tumbler, blown	192	3⅞", 2½ oz.				$65-85	
tumble-up	210	8¼"				$600-750	
vase	184	10"				$150-225	
vase	210	10"		$150-200		$175-225	
vase	210	6½"		$100-125		$100-125	
vase**	184	12"				$175-250	
vase, straight sided	210	9"		$175-225		$200-250	
whip cream pail		6"x3"	$125-150				

* Aqua, $450-600
** top turned down, $450-600

L. G. WRIGHT

goblet, ftd., Amber & crystal, $45
goblet, ftd., Aqua & green, $65

**Amber #503 candy, missing lid.
$125.00 – 150.00 complete.**

**Amber #11 7" milk jug, missing lid.
$150.00 – 175.00 complete.**

Ebony #210 6½" vase. $100.00 – 125.00.

Ebony #700 11" center-handled tray. $65.00 – 95.00.

Ebony #210 10" bowl. $75.00 – 95.00.

Ebony #210 6¼" tall candy and lid. $200.00 – 250.00.

Ebony #210 8¼" luncheon plate. $65.00 – 85.00.

Ebony #210 10" dinner plate. $75.00 – 100.00.

Ebony #210 gold-encrusted tab-handled ice bucket. $150.00 – 175.00.

Ebony #210 12" rolled-edge console bowl. $95.00 – 115.00.

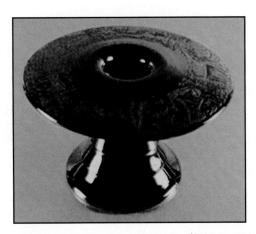

Ebony #210 mushroom candlestick. $45.00 – 55.00.

Ebony #210 9" straight-sided vase.
$175.00 – 225.00.

Ebony #210 10" vase. $150.00 – 200.00.

Ebony #210 cup and saucer. $75.00 – 85.00.

Green #210 cream, sugar, and tray. $90.00 – 125.00.

Green #210 6½" vase. $100.00 – 125.00.

Green #210 3-piece mayonnaise set.
$100.00 – 130.00.

Green #210 decanter. $400.00 – 500.00.

Green #210 mushroom candlestick.
$50.00 – 55.00.

Green #210 tumble-up as it was used.
$600.00 – 750.00.

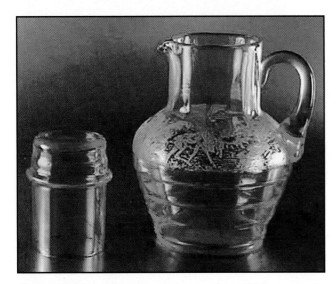

Green #210 tumble-up pitcher and tumbler; note the
ring around the base of the tumbler. $600.00 – 750.00.

Green #210 loop-handled plate.
$100.00 – 120.00.

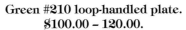

Green #210 11" x 2" low-footed cake salver. $150.00 – 175.00.

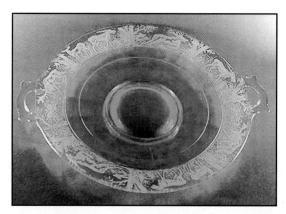

Green #210 tab-handled plate. $60.00 – 75.00.

Green #184 10" vase with flattened top. $400.00 – 600.00.

Top view of green #184 vase. $400.00 – 600.00.

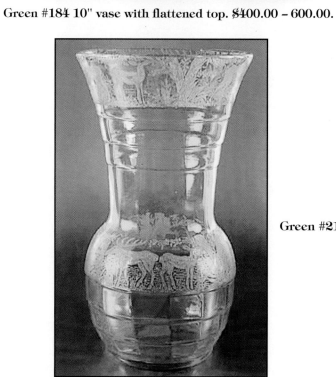

Green #210 10" vase. $175.00 – 225.00.

Green #210 5-part footed, covered relish. $500.00 – 650.00.

Green #210 footed candy. $225.00 – 275.00.

Green #210 tab-handled bowl. $75.00 – 95.00.

Green #902 ice bucket. $125.00 – 150.00.

Cheriglo #192 3⅞" blown whiskey, 2½" oz. $65.00 – 75.00.

Cheriglo #210 decanter set. $860.00 – 990.00.

Cheriglo #210 decanter only.
$600.00 – 650.00.

Cheriglo #210 cup and saucer. $75.00 – 82.00.

Cheriglo #210 6½" vase. $100.00 – 125.00.

Cheriglo #118 candlestick. $20.00 – 22.00.

Cheriglo #700 12" rolled-edge console bowl. $85.00 – 95.00.

Cheriglo #210 11" center-handled server. $100.00 – 120.00.

Cheriglo #210 mayonnaise set. $100.00 – 130.00.
Spoon $35.00 – 50.00.

Cheriglo #210 handled bowl. $100.00 – 125.00.

Cheriglo #210 5¾" blown ice tea.
$65.00 – 75.00.

Cheriglo #210 footed cake salver. $150.00 – 175.00.

Cheriglo #210 12" rolled-edge console bowl.
$150.00 – 175.00.

Cheriglo color range.

Cheriglo #210 mushroom candlestick with
satin etching. $50.00 – 55.00.

Cheriglo #210 creamer. $35.00 – 45.00.

Cheriglo #210 flat candy. $225.00 – 275.00.

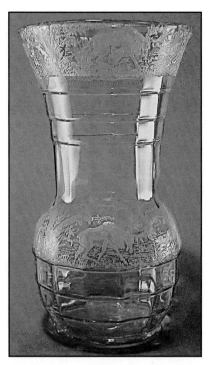

Cheriglo (darker shade) #210 10" vase.
$175.00 – 225.00.

Cheriglo #210 mushroom candlestick with shiny etching.
$35.00 – 45.00.

Cheriglo lid for #210 lemonade pitcher. $200.00.

Cheriglo #210 lemonade pitcher with lid.
$850.00 – 950.00.

Aqua L. G. Wright goblet. $65.00.

Crystal L. G. Wright goblet. $45.00.

Amber L. G. Wright goblet. $45.00.

Green L. G. Wright goblet. $65.00.

Bridal Bouquet

This is a Lotus etching that has only been found on crystal pieces. Because it's a Lotus etching, not every piece you may find will have necessarily been made by Paden City. The Paden City blanks used were #444 Vale, #211 Spire, #1503, and #221 Maya, but there may be others. The candlestick is a mystery. It's been listed as #555 and #221, but the Paden City Glass Society describes it as a fill-in candlestick. Because it would go with so many different console bowls, I think they are right, so I'm listing it as such. It's often found with gold inlay; this inlay raises the value about 10%. The prices here are for plain crystal pieces.

Crystal #444 footed, gold-encrusted, covered candy. $50.00 – 55.00.

Description	Line	Size	Crystal
candlestick, fill in		5"	$25-35 ea.
candy, high ftd.	444	9½"	$45-50
candy, low ftd.	211		$50-65
cheese & cracker	211	11"x13"	$65–85
cheese & cracker, covered	221		$120-150
plate, footed	211	14¼"	$35-45
plate, turned up	1503	7⅜"	$20-25

Crystal #444 footed covered candy. $45.00 – 50.00.

Crystal #1503 handled dish. $20.00 – 25.00.

Crystal #555 candlestick.
$25.00 – 35.00.

Bridal Wreath

Bridal Wreath is a perfect name for an etching of cascading flowers. This etching is most common in crystal, but a few pieces in Ruby or that have been Ruby flashed have been found. Add 20% for gold inlay (encrusted) or Ruby-flashed pieces. Although flashed pieces will appear to be Cranberry, they actually have a fired paint finish that, if perfect, is beautiful.

Description	Line	Size	Crystal	Ebony	Ruby
bowl	890	12"	$40-50		
bowl, cereal, Nerva		6½"x2¼"			
cake plate, Nerva		12½"x4"	$125-150		
candlestick, duo, Nerva		5¾"	$35-50 ea.		
candy	890/895	5½"	$60-65		
candy, ftd.	444	9½"	$45-65		$100-120
candy, Nerva		7⅛"	$75-100		
cheese & cracker, w/lid	211			$200-225	
comport, cheese		5"	$12-15		
comport, Nerva		9½"x6¾"	$50-75		
cracker plate	895	10½"	$40-55		
creamer	890		$20-25		
creamer, Nerva			$20-25		
shot glass, Glades	215		$50-65		
sugar	890		$20-22		
sugar, Nerva			$20-22		
vase, elliptical	182	8"	$75-95		

Ruby #444 gold-encrusted covered candy.
$100.00 – 120.00.

Crystal #890 11" flared, footed console bowl. $40.00 – 50.00.

Top view of #895 candy.

Crystal #895 covered candy with #890 base. $60.00 – 65.00.

Crystal Nerva cream and sugar. $40.00 – 50.00.

Crystal Nerva covered candy. $75.00 – 100.00.

Crystal #215 shot glass.
$50.00 – 65.00.

Crystal Nerva double candlestick.
$35.00 – 50.00.

Crystal #182 elliptical vase.
$75.00 – 95.00.

Crystal Nerva 6½" cereal bowl. $35.00 – 40.00.

Crystal Nerva footed cake salver. $125.00 – 150.00.

California Poppy

Recently, a California Poppy vase was found with a Lotus Decorating Company sticker, indicating that it was decorated by Lotus. While there is no catalog proof that Lotus decorated these pieces, it is very likely the design came from Lotus etching plates. The two vases, listed but not illustrated, are so rare that I have no photo of them. The vase I listed as #444 Vale has the same ball foot that is common to that line. The flip vase, #2121, is shaped like a very large drinking glass. I hope to be able to include photos of these vases in a later edition. Add 15% to vases found with gold detail.

Cheriglo #184 10" vase.
$200.00 – 250.00.

Green #184 10" vase.
$200.00 – 250.00.

Description	Line	size	Crystal	Ebony	Pink/Green
vase	184	10"	$125-150	$250-275	$200-250
vase	184	12"	$150-175	$275-325	$200-250
vase	444	11"	$125-150		
vase, flip	2121	14"	$150-200		

Carousel Pony, a.k.a. Pegasus Carousel

This etching is so rare that I was only able to photograph a cream and sugar. It appears to have been etched on crystal #412 blanks, but other patterns may have been used. I am limiting the listing to pieces I know were made, so please write me if you have other pieces.

Crystal #412 sugar bowl.
$20.00 – 25.00.

Crystal #412 creamer.
$25.00 – 30.00.

Description	Line	Size	Crystal
candlestick, keyhole	412	5"	$45-$55 ea.
comport	412	6"	$50-65
creamer	412		$25-30
sugar	412		$20-25

Cosmos

Cosmos is a border design that is used alone or with another etching. This page lists the pieces that have no other etching. Where Cosmos is used as a border, it will be priced under the primary etching. This listing will, by no means, be complete. I will add pieces as I discover them but, in the meantime, if you find a piece with only the Cosmos etching, you can add 10% to the value of the piece plain. This should help until a more complete listing can be made.

Description	Line	Size	Aqua/Blue/Mulberry	Cheriglo/Green/Ebony	Crystal/Amber
candlestick,	191	4"		$35-40 ea.	
candlestick,	211	5"			$18-22 ea.
candy	503/198			$65-75	
candy	701	5¼"x8½"	$65-75		
candy	191,	4½", ½ lb.		$55-70	
candy, covered	555	9¾"	$55-65		
creamer,	210			$18-22	
creamer,	503			$18-22	
pitcher	189, 60 oz.	11"	$125-150		
plate		12"		$50-65	
cheese & cracker, oval	700		$125-150	$100-125	
server, center handled, oval	700				$75-95
sugar	210			$18-20	
sugar	503			$18-20	
tumbler		3½"	$25-35		

Green #191 candlestick. $35.00 – 40.00.

Copen Blue #555 covered candy.
$55.00 – 65.00.

Top view of #555 covered candy.

Cheriglo #503 gold-encrusted creamer. $18.00 – 22.00.

Neptune Blue #189 60 oz. pitcher. $125.00 – 150.00.

Cheriglo #191 plate. $50.00 – 65.00.

Crystal #211 single candlestick.
$18.00 – 22.00 each.

Green #198 covered candy with #503 base.
$65.00 – 75.00.

Cheriglo #191 ½ lb. candy jar. $55.00 – 70.00.

Courting Peacocks

Courting Peacocks is one of the more elaborate Paden City etchings, as well as one of the most beautiful. There is always a chance of finding a bargain, but this etching is so rare that you should expect to pay a premium for any piece you find. Of course, there are more collectors willing to pay the lower range of the prices below. On pieces with a wide etching surface, both peacocks are used, but when the surface is too small, the pattern is reduced to just one peacock. Some collectors feel that a different name should be assigned for the single bird, but I am leaving it as Paden City probably intended.

Description	Line	Size	Cobalt Blue	Ebony	Crystal
vase	184	10"	$900-1200		
vase	182	8"		$600-850	
vase	412	10"		$600-850	$500-700
vase, flip	2121	14"			$500-700

Royal Blue #184 10" vase.
$900.00 – 1,200.00.

Ebony #182 8" elliptical vase. $600.00 – 850.00.

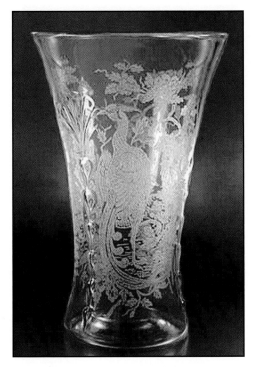

Crystal #890 10" flared vase. $500.00 – 700.00.

Cupid

When Paden City is mentioned, Cupid is the etching that often comes to mind. So much Cupid has disappeared into collections that it's now very hard to find and is usually very expensive. Some of the rarities in this pattern are casseroles in any color, the #300 butter tub, the #300 candy, the #184 vase, and the night set, of which only the pitcher has been found. Pink and green are the most common colors. Amber is hard to find, and crystal, Light Blue, and Ebony are so rare that only a few pieces have been found in those colors. The casserole lid shown in this section is crystal, but the ridge and handles are rimmed with yellow. It doesn't appear to be paint, so it may be an experimental piece on which the colored glass has been applied to the edge. Samovars have been found in green, crystal painted orange, and Peacock Blue. The orange samovar pictured in this section is a lot less attractive than the photo would have you believe.

I'm listing the pieces that have previously been identified as Imperial Molly as they should be listed, as #701. Several different items in this shape have been found: the mayonnaise sets, a flat console bowl, and a center-handled tray and bowl. The console bowls that have been found are all octagonal; the Imperial Molly flat bowl has ten sides, so the Paden City blank doesn't match any Molly blank. While we have no catalog information about the heart-handled servers, there is also no reason to believe that Paden City didn't make them. For more information on the confusion between companies, refer to page 11. Some of the pieces with the gold are closer to yellow than Amber, so I'm listing the colors together.

All but one of the Cupid pieces with silver overlay were made in Germany. Those pieces may have been the inspiration for this pattern. There is no track record of prices for these pieces, so I'm including a few for comparison only.

Ebony #184 12" gold-encrusted vase. $1,000.00 – 1,500.00.

Shape	Line	Size	Amber/ Yellow	Aqua/ Blue	Crystal	Ebony	Green/Pink
bowl, console, w/gold	701	12"	$400-450		$300-350		$425-550
bowl, flared, ftd.	300	11"	$275-350		$175-200		$275-300
bowl, ftd. oval	300	8¼"			$150-175		$250-300
bowl, low ftd.	300	10"			$200-250		$450-500
bowl, center loop handled	300	11"			$150-175		$250-300
bowl, heart handled	701	10½"	$350-500				
bowl, oval	300	9"			$150-175		$250-300
bowl, rolled edge	300	14"	$150-200	$200-250	$100-125	$500-600	$150-200
bowl, salad	300	9"	$150-200	$200-250	$100-125		$125-150
butter tub	300	5"					$750-950
cake plate	300	10"					$175-200
candlestick	300	3"	$50-75 ea.	$100-125 ea.	$30-35 ea.		$45-55 ea.
candlestick, w/gold	701	5¼"					$150-125 ea.
candy, flat	300	6½"					$500-600
candy, low ft.	300	6"					$275-300
casserole		12" x 9"	$850-1000		$750-950	$1200-1500	$850-1000
casserole base		12" x 9"	$125-150		$125-150	$200-225	$150-200
casserole lid		10¼" x 7"	$725-850		$625-800	$1000-1275	$700-800
cheese & cracker	300	10"			$150-200		$350-400
comport	300	7"	$250-300	$450-550	$150-175		$200-250
comport, mayonnaise	701	7" x 4"	$200-250		$150-200		$200-250
creamer	300			$150-175	$50-65		$65-75
creamer, ribbed or plain	701	4"					$65-75
creamer, w/gold	505						$150-175
ice bucket	300	5½" x 4⅝"					$200-250
ice bucket	902						$225-275
mayonnaise set, 3-pc.	300		$250-300	$350-400	$200-250		$200-250
mayonnaise set, 3-pc.	701		$350-450		$300-350		$350-450
pitcher, guest set	179						$550-700
plate, cracker	300	10"		$250-300	$125-150		$150-175
plate, handled	701	10¾"					$125-175
plate, oval	300	10½" x 7½"					$250-300
samovar,* large				$650-850			$650-850
samovar,** small				$450-575			$550-650
sugar	300				$40-45		$50-60
sugar, plain or ribbed	701						$65-75
sugar, w/gold	505						$150-175
tray, heart handled	701	12"	$350-500				
tray, loop handled	300	11"			$250-300		$175-225
vase	184	10"					$600-800
vase	184	12"				$1000-1500	$650-900
vase, elliptical	182	8"					$450-550
vase, fan	300	8½"					$750-900
vase, silver overlay	180	12"					$450-550

*crystal with orange paint, $400-475

** crystal with orange paint, $350-450

Neptune Blue large, footed samovar, $650.00 – 850.00, with original cups, $18.00 – 22.00 each.

Neptune Blue large, flat samovar. $650.00 – 850.00.

Silver overlay on a slag vase; vase is signed "Made in Germany." $100.00 – 125.00.

Green #300 3-piece mayonnaise set. $200.00 – 250.00.

Green #701 creamer with no optic, $65.00 – 75.00, and sugar with ribbed optic, $65.00 – 75.00.

Green #300 12" console bowl. $150.00 – 200.00.

Green #300 mushroom candlestick with satin etching. $45.00 – 55.00.

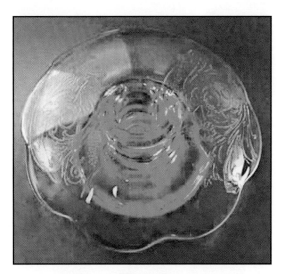

Green #300 mushroom candlestick with glossy etching. $45.00 – 55.00.

Green #300 8¼" oval, footed bowl. $250.00 – 300.00.

Green #902 ice bucket. $225.00 – 275.00.

Green #180 12" vase with silver
overlay pattern. $450.00 – 500.00.

Green #300 flared, footed bowl. $450.00 – 500.00.

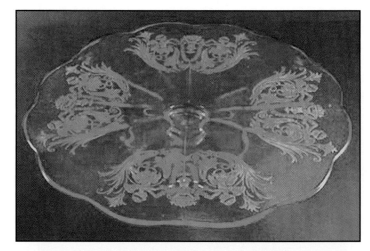

Green #300 low-footed cake plate. $125.00 – 150.00.

Green #300 loop-handled tray. $175.00 – 225.00.

Green #300 ice bucket. $200.00 – 250.00.

Green #701 sugar and creamer with ribbed optic.
$130.00 – 150.00 set.

Green #300 sugar and creamer. $110.00 – 135.00.

Green #300 comport. $200.00 – 225.00.

Green large samovar. $650.00 – 750.00.

Green 2-piece casserole with flowering urn border.
$850.00 – 1,000.00.

Green #182 elliptical vase. $450.00 – 550.00.

Green #300 flat candy. $600.00 – 700.00.

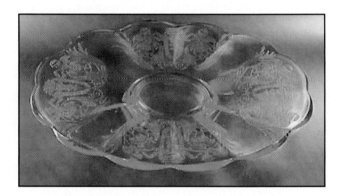

Green #300 oval plate. $250.00 – 300.00.

Green #300 loop-handled bowl. $250.00 – 350.00.

Green #300 footed candy.
$275.00 – 300.00.

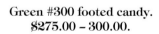

Cheriglo #300 cream and sugar. $110.00 – 135.00.

Cheriglo #701 mayonnaise set with flowering urn and Cupid etchings. $350.00 – 450.00.

Top view of Cheriglo #701 mayonnaise set.

Cheriglo #300 comport.
$200.00 – 250.00.

Cheriglo #701 mayonnaise liner. $100.00 – 125.00.

Cheriglo #182 8½" elliptical vase.
$450.00 – 550.00.

Cheriglo #902 ice bucket. $225.00 – 275.00.

Cheriglo #701 ribbed sugar and creamer. $165.00 – 195.00.

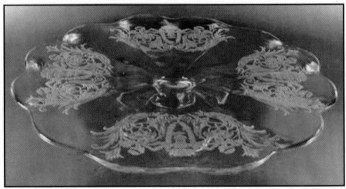

Cheriglo #300 11" low-footed cake plate. $175.00 – 200.00.

Cheriglo #300 13" flared salad bowl with 2-ring base.
$125.00 – 150.00.

Cheriglo 2-piece casserole with flowering urn border.
$850.00 – 1,000.00.

Cheriglo #300 butter dish. $750.00 – 950.00.

Different view of the Cheriglo #300 butter dish.

Cheriglo #300 6½" flat candy. $500.00 – 600.00.

Cheriglo #300 loop-handled bowl. $250.00 – 350.00.

Cheriglo #300 ice bucket. $200.00 – 250.00.

Cheriglo #300 flared salad bowl with 3-ring base, made from the #300 oval bowl mold. $125.00 – 150.00.

Cheriglo #300 mushroom candlestick. $45.00 – 55.00.

Cheriglo #701 sugar and creamer with no optic.
$165.00 – 195.00.

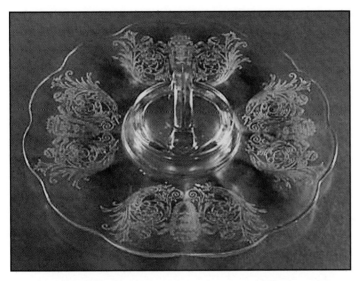

Cheriglo #300 loop-handled tray or server. $175.00 – 225.00.

Cheriglo #300 footed candy. $275.00 – 300.00.

Cheriglo #300 3-piece mayonnaise set. $200.00 – 250.00.

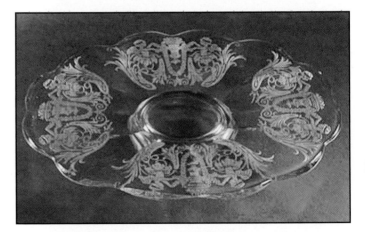

Cheriglo #300 oval tray. $250.00 – 300.00.

Cheriglo #300 oval bowl. $250.00 – 300.00.

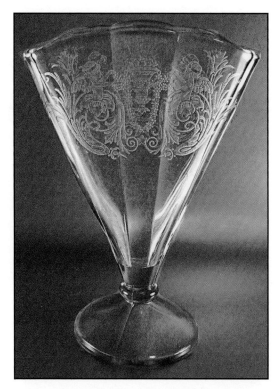

Cheriglo #300 fan vase. $750.00 – 950.00.

Cheriglo #300 12" rolled-edge console bowl.
$150.00 – 200.00.

Cheriglo #300 cheese and cracker; note that the cheese
comport is not etched. $350.00 – 400.00.

Cheriglo #701 handled plate. $125.00 – 175.00.

Amber #300 rolled-edge comport. $250.00 – 300.00.

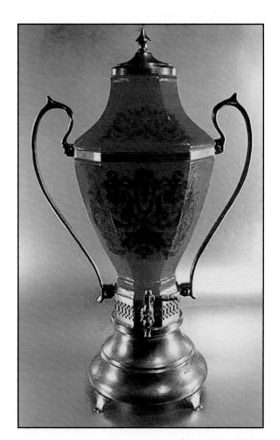

Orange-painted small samovar. $350.00 – 450.00.

Amber 2-piece covered casserole with flowering urn border.
$850.00 – 1,000.00.

Amber #300 mushroom candlestick. $50.00 – 75.00.

74

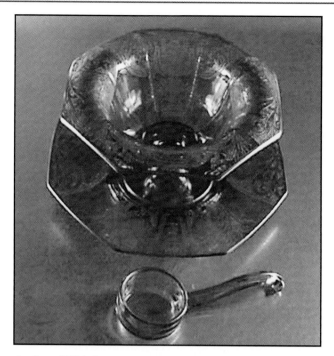

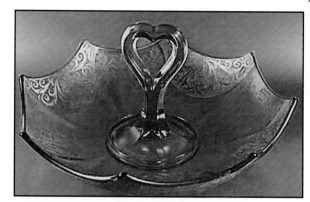

Amber #701 heart-handled server with flowering urn secondary etching. $350.00 – 500.00.

Amber #701 3-piece mayonnaise set with flowering urn secondary etching. $350.00 – 450.00.

Purple urn with Cupid silver overlay, marked "Made in Germany." $100.00 – 125.00.

Close-up of etchings.

Crystal #300 loop-handled tray. $250.00 – 300.00.

Crystal casserole lid with unusual Amber handles. $275.00 – 300.00.

Daisy

While I have found mostly vases with this etching, the plate indicates that it was also used on dinnerware. The vases are found with or without the Cosmos border.

Description	Line	Size	Blue	Crystal	Green\Pink
plate	700	14½"		$50-65	
vase, cylinder	180	12"			$150-175
vase, elliptical	182	8¼"			$150-175
vase	184	10"			$125-150
vase	184	12"	$200-250		$150-175

Green #184 12" vase.
$150.00 – 175.00.

Green #182 8" elliptical vase.
$150.00 – 175.00.

Crystal #700 14" plate. $50.00 – 65.00.

Cheriglo #180 12" cylinder vase with Cosmos-etched border. $150.00 – 175.00.

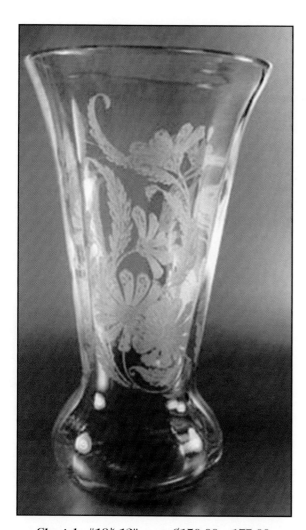

Cheriglo #184 12" vase. $150.00 – 175.00.

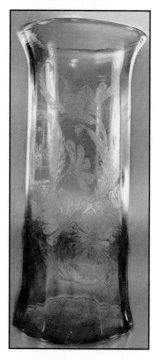

Cheriglo #180 12" cylinder vase with plain border. $150.00 – 175.00.

Daisy Cross

This is the only example I have to illustrate this etching, but I'm sure Daisy Cross can be found on most of the Crow's Foot Square pieces. The bowl I photographed looks like the #412 pattern, but it has no fans in the curved area. That may also be true of the other pieces I've listed or it may be an anomaly.

Description	Line	Size	Crystal	Yellow
bowl	#412 variation	12"	$65-80	$75-95
comport	#412	6"½x3½"	$65-80	$75-95
mayonnaise, ftd.	#412	6"x3"	$70-85	$100-125
mayonnaise liner	#412	7½"	$18-22	$ 20-25

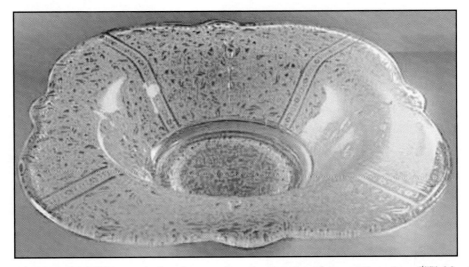

Yellow #412 variant 12" console bowl; note that there are no fans on the edge. $75.00 – 95.00.

Delilah Bird, a.k.a. Peacock Reverse

Delilah Bird is just as beautiful as Courting Peacocks, but prices are more reasonable because it is more available. While it can't be considered rare, it's not that easy to find. It's particularly beautiful in Ruby or Cobalt Blue, and these colors command the highest prices. Some of the yellow pieces are the Primrose color, but the difference is subtle. Most of Delilah Bird is found on #412 Crow's Foot blanks, but there are a few pieces in #411 Mrs. B., #991 Penny Line, #701 Octagonal, and the #182 elliptical vase. Gene Florence, in his *Collector's Encyclopedia of Depression Glass* book, 13th edition, shows a blue sugar, but so far, no creamer has appeared. That really isn't an uncommon situation. Sugars are often left sitting on the table, but creamers are regularly picked up to be emptied and washed, so they are the first pieces to break. I'm listing the creamers because I'm certain they are out there; as a rule, I don't want to list "fantasy" pieces. Please let me know if I've missed something.

Ebony #182 5½" elliptical vase. $225.00 – 275.00.

78

Description	Line	Size	Ebony	Blue/Ruby	Crystal	Green/Pink	Amber/Yellow/Primrose
bowl, berry	412	4½"		$75-85	$25-35	$50-65	$45-60
bowl, console	412	12"		$300-400	$125-150	$250-350	$200-250
bowl, ftd.	412	11"x4½"		$350-450	$150-250	$325-425	$300-400
bowl, sq.	411	10"				$150-200	$150-200
bowl, sq., w/handles	412	12"		$275-375	$135-165	$250-300	$200-275
cake plate, low ft.	412		$175-200	$275-325	$125-150	$225-300	$150-175
candlestick, any top	411	4½"				$50-100 ea.	$40-80 ea.
candlestick, keyhole	411	5"		$100-125 ea.		$75-100 ea.	$65-95 ea.
candlestick, keyhole	412	5"		$100-125 ea.	$50-75 ea.	$75-100 ea.	$65-95 ea.
candlestick, mushroom	412	2½"		$75-100 ea.	$25-40 ea.	$50-75 ea.	$40-60
candy, flat	198	6½"				$175-225	
candy, flat	411	6¼"		$300-350		$250-300	$200-250
candy, flat	412	6½"		$300-400			
candy, flat, rd. base	411	6½"				$275-325	$225-275
candy, flat, ribbed or plain	701	7"				$250-300	$200-225
candy. ftd	503	6"				$175-250	
cheese & cracker set	412	10" plate		$250-300	$100-125	$200-250	$175-200
comport, high ftd.	412	7"x6¼"		$225-275	$75-95	$150-200	$125-175
comport, low ftd.	412	7"x3¾"		$150-200	$50-75	$125-150	$100-125
comport, mayo	412	6¼"x3"		$175-220	$50-75	$125-150	$100-125
cracker jar w/lid		5⅝"	$450-500			$450-500	$400-500
creamer	412	2¾"		$60-80	$20-25	$35-45	$30-40

Ebony #412 11" low-footed bowl.
$275.00 – 325.00.

Close-up of pattern on #412 low-footed bowl.

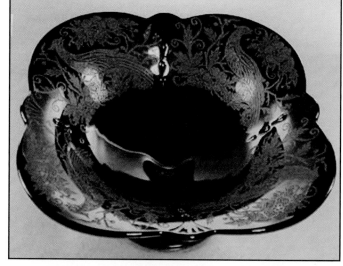

Description	Line	Size	Ebony	Blue/Ruby	Crystal	Green/Pink	Amber/Yellow/Primrose
cup	412					$65-85	$50-75
gravy, ftd.	412	7½"x4⅞"x4¼"		$250-300	$125-150	$200-250	$175-225
mayo liner	412	6"		$25-30	$15-20	$20-25	$20-25
mayonnaise set, 2-pc.	412			$200-250	$65-85	$150-175	$125-150
plate	412	7½"		$45-60	$18-22	$25-35	$25-35
plate, cracker	412	10"		$200-250	$75-100	$175-225	$150-175
plate, handled	412	10"	$100-125	$200-250	$75-100	$175-225	$150-175
plate, luncheon	701	8½"				$50-65	
saucer	412	6"				$20-25	$18-22
sherbet, high ftd.	991	4⅞"		$100-125			
sugar	412	2¾"		$50-70	$18-22	$30-40	$25-35
tray, center handled	412	10"	$125-175	$150-200		$125-175	$100-150
tumbler	991, 9 oz.	4"		$125-150			
vase	210	6"	$225-275	$350-450		$300-400	$250-300
vase, elliptical	182	5½"	$225-275		$125-175		
vase, smoke stack	210	8½"	$375-450				

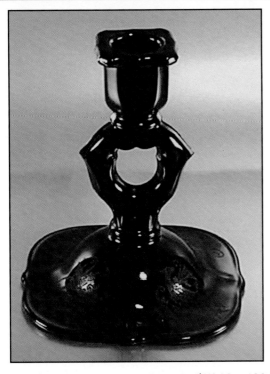

Ebony #412 5" keyhole candlestick. $85.00 – 100.00.

Crystal #412 mushroom candlestick. $25.00 – 40.00.

Crystal #412 low-footed bowl.
$150.00 – 250.00.

Crystal #412 high-footed comport. $75.00 – 95.00.

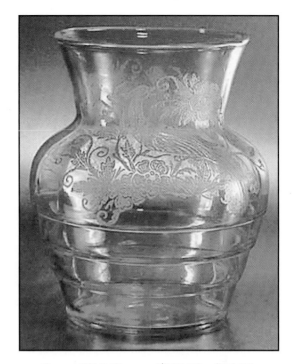

Green #210 6" vase. $300.00 – 400.00.

Green #412 5" keyhole candlestick.
$75.00 – 100.00.

Green #412 7½" plate. $25.00 – 35.00.

Green #701 flat candy with ribbed lid.
$250.00 – 300.00.

Green #503 6" footed candy. $175.00 – 250.00.

Ruby #412 low-footed comport. $150.00 – 200.00.

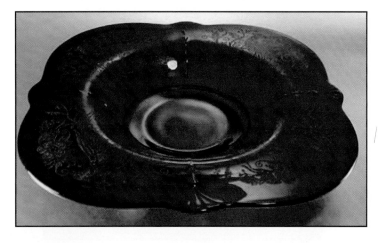

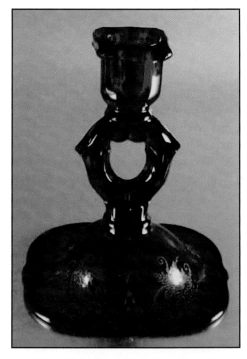

Green cracker jar/ice bucket without lid. $450.00 – 500.00 complete.

Ruby #412 5" keyhole candlestick. $100.00 – 125.00.

Ruby #412 12" console bowl. $300.00 – 400.00.

Ruby #412 footed bowl. $350.00 – 450.00.

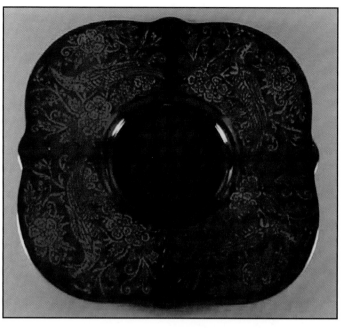

Ruby #412 7½" plate. $45.00 – 60.00.

Ruby #412 10" cracker plate. $200.00 – 250.00.

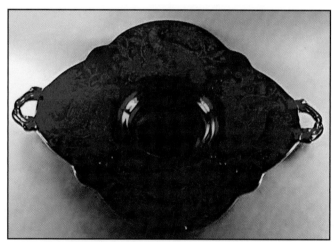

#412 Ruby 10" handled plate. $200.00 – 250.00.

Primrose #412 10" ruffled bowl.
$300.00 – 400.00.

Primrose #412 candy with round base. $225.00 – 275.00.

Primrose #412 5" keyhole candlestick.
$65.00 – 95.00.

Royal Blue #412 10" handled plate. $200.00 – 250.00.

Royal Blue #412 5" keyhole candlestick.
$100.00 – 125.00.

Cheriglo #411 flat candy.
$250.00 – 300.00.

Eden Rose

While Eden Rose is generally a reasonably priced etching, there are some very unusual pieces that exist. The hats and the decanter are not only pretty, but also very hard to find. There is a decanter, like the one pictured here, that is taller because the base is a music box that plays "How Dry I Am." It is very rare and commands a higher price than other pieces. I was surprised to see a utilitarian item like the han-dled #210 tray, but it is very attractive. The square 2-part relish is very unusual and is a part of the Glades #215 line. Guest sets, or tumble-ups, exist in several colors, all of which are rare. Many Eden Rose pieces are found with color inlaid to enhance their beauty, and those pieces sell for 15 – 20% higher than the plain pieces.

Shape	Line	Size	Ebony	Crystal	Neptune Blue	Pink/Green	Yellow/Amber
bowl	503	7"		$40-50			
bowl, handled	1503	6⅝"		$45-50			
cake plate	210	10¾"x2"	$100-125			$100-125	
candleholder, mushroom	701	2½"				$45-65 ea.	
candleholder, mushroom	210	2¾"x4¾"	$35-50	$25-35		$45-65 ea.	
candy, flat	210	6½"	$125-150			$150-200	
candy, ftd.	503	7" x6¼"				$150-175	
comport	211	6¼"		$45-65			
creamer	503					$60-80	
decanter		11½"				$450-650	
decanter, plays "How Dry I Am"						$550-750	
mayonnaise bowl, handled	701	4½"	$35-45	$25-35		$45-50	
mayonnaise set	701	6½" plate	$50-65	$35-45		$50-65	
pitcher, guest set	179	6¼"			$175-225	$150-200	$125-175

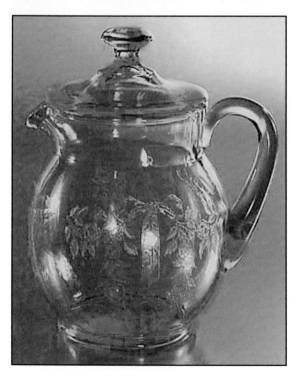

Neptune Blue 6¼" covered pitcher from guest set.
$175.00 – 200.00.

Neptune Blue #499 tumble-up, or guest set.
$300.00 – 350.00.

Shape	Line	Size	Ebony	Crystal	Neptune Blue	Pink/Green	Yellow/Amber
plate, 2-handled, any shape	701	6½"	$15-20	$10-15		$15-20	
plate, handled	1503			$18-22			
relish, 3-part	300					$125-175	
relish, sq., divided	215	7"		$45-65			
sugar	503					$55-75	
top hat, large		5"x8" brim		$125-150			
top hat, medium		3¾"x6⅜" brim		$65-95			
top hat, small		3½"x5¼" brim		$50-75			
tray, rectangle	210	13¼"x7¾"				$175-200	
tumble up/guest set	499	7⅜"			$300-350	$275-350	$200-250
vase	210	10"	$100-125			$150-175	
vase	184	12"	$125-150			$150-200	
vase, smoke stack	210	9"	$175-200			$200-250	

Crystal 3½" tall small hat with 5¼" brim.
$50.00 – 75.00.

Crystal 3¾" tall medium hat with 6⅜" brim. $65.00 – 95.00.

Crystal #211 Spire comport.
$45.00 – 65.00.

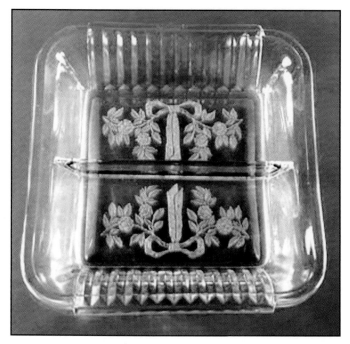

Crystal #215 Glades 7" square relish. $45.00 – 65.00.

Crystal #503 7" bowl. $40.00 – 50.00.

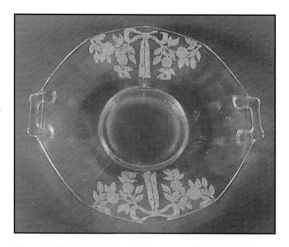

Green #701 6½" handled plate. $45.00 – 50.00.

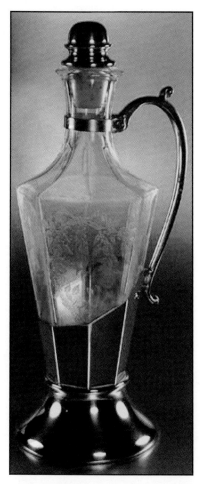

Green decanter with chrome holder. $450.00 – 650.00. With music box, $550.00 – 750.00.

Green #701 mayonnaise set. $50.00 – 65.00.

Cheriglo #210 mushroom candlestick.
$45.00 – 65.00.

Green #701 6½" turned-up plate. $15.00 – 20.00.

Cheriglo #701 5" handled mayonnaise bowl. $45.00 – 50.00.

Cheriglo #503 footed candy. $150.00 – 175.00.

Cheriglo mushroom candlestick.
$45.00 – 65.00.

Cheriglo #210 10" vase. $150.00 – 175.00.

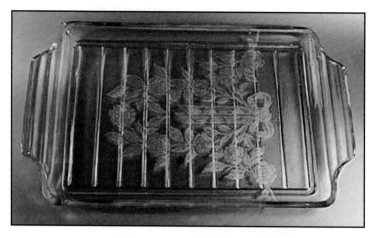

Cheriglo #210 13¼" x 7¾" handled tray. $175.00 – 200.00.

Ebony #184 10" vase. $125.00 – 150.00.

Cheriglo #210 flat candy. $150.00 – 200.00.

Cheriglo #210 low-footed cake salver.
$100.00 – 125.00.

Ebony #184 12" vase.
$150.00 – 175.00.

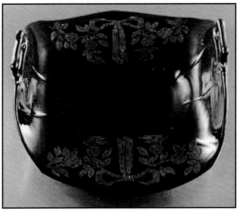

Ebony #701 6½" turned-up plate.
$15.00 – 20.00.

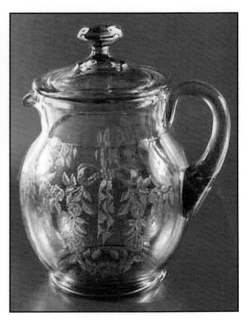

Amber #179 6¼" covered pitcher from
guest set. $125.00 – 175.00.

Eleanor

Eleanor and Ardith are very similar and easily confused. The flowers of Eleanor are larger and spread apart, showing branches and leaves. On the Ardith etching, the flowers are clumped in a spray, with only one spray of leaves. Duncan also did an etching that can be mistaken for Eleanor, but the blanks are different, so you shouldn't have a problem telling one from the other. Eleanor isn't a heavily collected pattern, so this is another pattern that is at a price point that is perfect for beginning collectors. Add 10% for items that are flashed or decorated in either gold or silver.

Description	Line	Size	Crystal	Ruby
bowl, console	220	12"		$150-175
candy, heart-shaped	555	7½"x8½"	$100-125	
decanter	410	13¾"	$125-150	
decanter, horseshoe	211	9"	$ 60-75	

Crystal #555 gold-encrusted heart-shaped
3-part candy. $100.00 – 125.00.

Ruby-flashed #410 14" decanter.
$125.00 – 150.00.

Ruby #220 12" console bowl. $150.00 – 175.00.

Floral Medallion

At first glance, Floral Medallion looks like Cambridge's Rose Point. The Floral Medallion etching plates were found at the L. G. Wright auction and are now in the West Virginia Museum of American Glass.

Floral Medallion a very attractive pattern that has only been found on crystal so far. Most of the blanks are #888 Plume and #900 Nadja. Add 10% to the value when the design is in gold.

Description	Line	Size	Crystal
bowl	888	12"	$50-65
candlestick	900	4½"	$20-25 ea.
comport, low ftd.	888	10"	$45-65
cream	888		$18-20
relish, 4-part	888	10"	$65-75
sugar	888		$15-18

Crystal #888 12" Plume crimped
console bowl. $50.00 – 65.00.

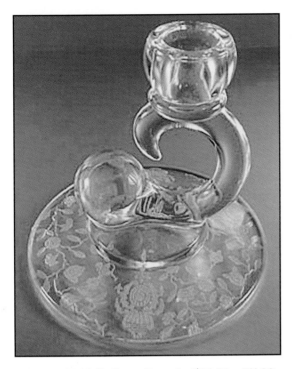

Crystal #900 4⅞" candlestick. $20.00 – 25.00.

Crystal #900 cream and sugar. $33.00 – 38.00.

Crystal #888 Plume comport. $40.00 – 65.00.

Frost

Frost is an appropriate name for this all-over etching. It's attractive, but doesn't command a high price. I've only seen it used on crystal glass, but there may be a few pieces in color.

Crystal #881 12½" Gadroon console bowl. $50.00 – 65.00.

Crystal 8" round vase. $45.00 – 55.00.

Description	Line	Size	Crystal
bowl	330	12⅝"	$50-55
bowl	881	12½"	$50-65
bowl, console	215	12½"	$55-60
bowl, console	330	12¾"	$45-65
bowl, handled	330	12½"	$55-60
bowl, handled	330	9"	$35-45
candlestick	220	5¼"x7¼"	$20-25 ea.
candlestick, heart shaped	300	6½"	$40-50 ea.
candy, covered	330	7"	$75-100
creamer	215		$10-12
plate, handled	330	10"	$20-22
sugar	215		$10-12
vase, elliptical	182	8"	$65-75
vase, round		8"	$45-55

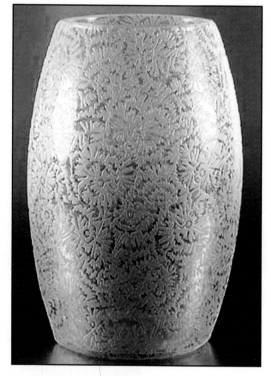

Crystal #182 8" elliptical vase. $65.00 – 75.00.

Crystal #220 double candlestick.
$20.00 – 25.00.

Crystal #215 sugar and creamer. $20.00 – 24.00.

Crystal #330 12½" handled bowl. $55.00 – 60.00.

Crystal #330 handled plate. $20.00 – 22.00.

Crystal #330 13" console bowl. $45.00 – 65.00.

Gazebo

Gazebo can be found on a variety of the later patterns: #555, Vale #444, and Spire #211, but #412 Crow's Foot Square pieces can also be found with this etching. This pattern is so much like the Utopia etching that Paden City may have meant them to be the same pattern, but they will remain separate in this book. Unlike the Peacock and Rose/Nora Bird combination, there is no evidence to prove these two etchings are meant to be the same. Of course, blue pieces command the highest prices, but there are several pieces of crystal Gazebo that rate as rare and expensive. It's still an undervalued line and will increase in value over time. While we can't be certain of Paden City's intent, I am reasonably certain that the blue color was called Copen Blue. Paden City's shade of blue is almost an exact match to Tiffin's blue with the same name.

Copen Blue #555 11" center-handled tray. $75.00 – 85.00.

Copen Blue #555 10½" footed candy. $95.00 – 125.00.

Copen Blue #555 7½" x 10" flared comport. $125.00 – 150.00.

Shape	Line	Size	Copen Blue	Crystal
bowl	211	12"x4½"		$65-75
bowl, console	555	12"	$75-125	$55-70
bowl, fan handled	211	9"		$45-55
bowl, footed. console	211	12"		$45-55
bowl, salad	555	9"	$75-100	$65-85
candlestick	444	6"		$20-25 ea.
candlestick, duo	555			$50-60 ea.
candlestick, fan sides	555, 221	5"		$35-50 ea.
candy, cloverleaf	412	6¾"		$50-65
candy, flat	411	6½"		$65-85
candy, footed	555	10½"	$95-125	$50-65
candy, footed, large size	555	11"		$150-200
candy, heart shaped	555	7½"	$200-250	$100-125
cheese & cracker set	555	12"	$200-250	$125-150
comport, flared	555	7½"x10"	$125-150	$45-50
cream	555		$35-45	$25-35
mayonnaise set	211			$65-85
mayonnaise set	555	4⅝"x2⅝"	$75-100	$45-55
plate	211	11"		$45-55
plate, fan handled	211	12"		$45-55
punch bowl	555			$200-250
punch bowl liner	555	14½"	$65-75	$45-55
punch cup				$8-10
relish, 2-part	555	6¾"x5¼"	$40-50	$25-35
relish, 5-part, rd.	555	10"	$75-95	$60-75*
relish, oblong	555	9½"x7¼"	$75-85	$50-65
sugar	555			$20-25
tray, center handled	555	11"	$75-85	$50-65
tray, handled	211	13"		$55-75
tray, handled	555	12½"		$55-75
tray, swan handled	1504	10"		$100-125
tumbler	2119	3⅜", 3 oz.		$25-35

*ruby stained, $100-125

Copen Blue #555 12" covered cheese and cracker.
$200.00 – 250.00.

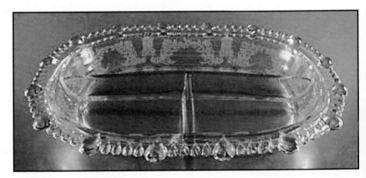

Copen Blue #555 9½" x 7¼" divided relish. $75.00 – 95.00.

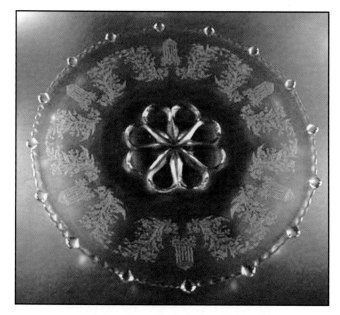

Copen Blue 14½"plate/punch bowl liner. $65.00 – 75.00.

Ruby-stained crystal #555 10" 5-part relish. $100.00 – 125.00.

Crystal #412 cloverleaf candy. $50.00 – 65.00.

Crystal #555 11" center-handled server. $50.00 – 65.00.

Crystal #555 mayonnaise bowl.
$35.00 – 45.00.

Crystal #555 mayonnaise and liner. $45.00 – 55.00.

Crystal #211 12" footed bowl with gold trim. $45.00 – 55.00.

Crystal #555 sugar and creamer. $45.00 – 60.00.

Crystal goose-handled server with gold trim. $100.00 – 125.00.

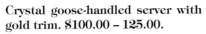

Crystal #2119 3 oz. tumbler. $25.00 – 35.00.

Crystal #555 crimped divided relish. $25.00 – 35.00.

Crystal #211 12" handled platter with gold trim. $45.00 – 55.00.

Crystal punch cup. $8.00 – 10.00.

Crystal #555 14½" punch bowl liner/platter.
$45.00 – 55.00.

Crystal #555 punch bowl. $200.00 – 250.00.

Crystal #555 punch set. $245.00 – 305.00.
Cups, $8.00 – 10.00.

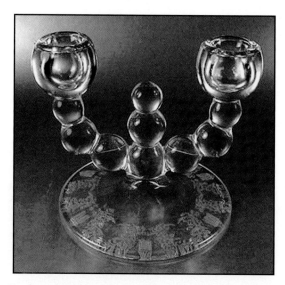

Crystal #444 double candlestick. $50.00 – 60.00.

Crystal #412 cloverleaf candy with gold trim.
$50.00 – 65.00.

Crystal #555 9½" x 7¼" divided relish. $50.00 – 65.00.

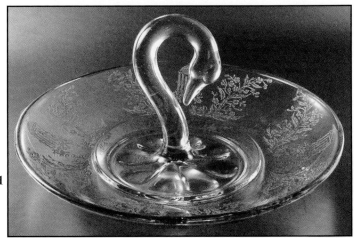

Crystal goose-handled gold-encrusted server. $100.00 – 125.00.

Goddess Etchings and Springtime Silver Overlay

We know for certain that the Salome etching and the Springtime silver overlay were excuted by the Lotus Decorating Company. While we can't say for certain that Aphrodite and Diana were created by Lotus, I think that attribution is more likely than not. The Diana etching and the Springtime patten are very similar. They both have a woman and a Cupid figure, but in Springtime there is a wreath of flowers around the woman, and in Diana the woman is playing a horn. Pieces of etched Springtime have been found on non–Paden City blanks, but there is very strong evidence that those pieces were decorated by a little-known firm, the Maryland Glass Company. The #11 syrup is in the Diana pattern, but it has been decorated with silver overlay rather than give the usual etched treatment.

Aphrodite

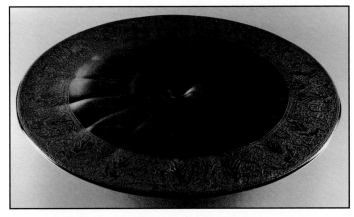

Ebony #210 low-footed cake salver. $200.00 – 225.00.

Close-up showing detail of etching.

Description	Line	Size	Crystal	Ebony
cake salver		11"x2"		$200-250

Diana

Ruby #412 silver-decorated cloverleaf candy.
$200.00 – 250.00.

Close-up showing detail of etching.

Ebony #11 7" milk pitcher with silver overlay design. $350.00 – 400.00 with lid, $250.00 – 300.00 without lid.

Description	Line	Size	Ebony	Ruby/Blue
candy, cloverleaf	412	6½"		$200-250
pitcher, milk	11	7"	$350-400	

101

Salome

Royal Blue #412 silver-decorated cloverleaf candy.
$200.00 – 250.00.

Close-up showing detail of etching.

Description	Line	Size	Crystal	Cheriglo	Ruby/Blue
bowl	411	11"x7"		$125-150	
candy	412	6¾"	$125-150		$200-250
cloverleaf					
tray, center handle	411	10"			$150-200

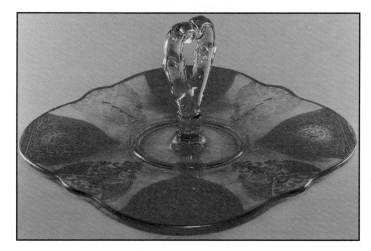

Cheriglo #412 center-handled server with secondary Poppy
etching. $150.00 – 200.00.

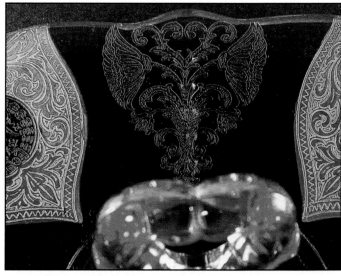

Close-up of the Poppy etching.

Springtime Silver Overlay

The Lotus Decorating Company did this beautiful silver overlay pattern. A Lotus catalog page that illustrates this pattern in Paden City's Opal was reprinted in Hazel Marie Weatherman's *Colored Glassware of the Depression Era, Book 2*. This pattern is found on #412 blanks, but a #411 Mrs B. vase was included in the assortment. While both Ruby and Cobalt Blue examples are rare and beautiful, the Opal pieces are stunning and bring the highest prices. While the Springtime silver overlay and the Diana etching are very similar, there are several differences. If the woman is playing a horn, the pattern is Diana. The woman in the Springtime pattern has a wreath of flowers.

Royal Blue #412 center-handled server with silver overlay.
$150.00 – 175.00.

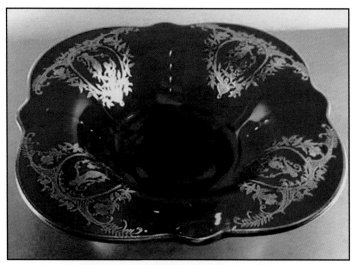

Royal Blue #412 12" console bowl with silver overlay.
$125.00 – 165.00.

Description	Line	Size	Opal	Ruby/Cobalt Blue
bowl, console	412	12"	$125-165	$125-165
candlestick,	412	5"	$75-85 ea.	$65-75 ea.
candy, cloverleaf	412		$350-450	$300-400
candy, flat	412		$350-450	$300-400
cheese & cracker	412	10"	$350-450	$300-400
comport, high ftd.	412	7"	$150-200	$150-200
comport, low ftd.	412	6¼"x3¼"	$125-145	$100-125
creamer	412		$35-45	$30-40
mayonnaise, 2-pc.	412		$175-250	$150-225
sugar	412		$30-35	$25-30
tray, center handled, sandwich	412	10¼"	$175-250	$150-175
tray, handled	412	11¼"x14"	$175-250	$150-175
vase	411	9"	$450-550	$400-500

Royal Blue #412 5" keyhole candlestick with silver overlay. $65.00 – 75.00.

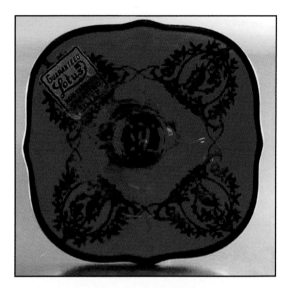

Lotus label on candlestick base.

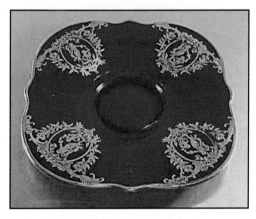

Royal Blue #412 5¼" saucer with silver overlay. $18.00 – 22.00.

Royal Blue #412 mayonnaise set with silver overlay. $150.00 – 225.00.

Ruby #412 mayonnaise liner with silver overlay. $25.00 – 30.00.

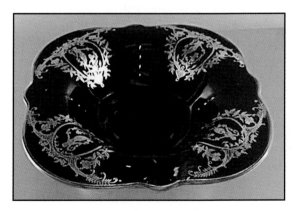

Ruby #412 12" console bowl with silver overlay. $125.00 – 165.00.

Gothic Garden

Gothic Garden was a very popular Paden City pattern when it was made and remains so today. It's possible, but not terribly easy, to put together a complete dinner set in this pattern. Yellow is the most common color for the dinnerware set, but Ebony is in second place. Green and Cheriglo are much harder to find. Most of the pieces will be on the Mrs. B. #411 blanks. Plates were etched two different ways, with the complete etching on each side or with a border etching that goes all around the plate.

The handled decagon pieces have been misidentified as Imperial Molly. They are not. The smaller pieces of Molly have six sides, not ten. It's always a challenge to correctly attribute glassware to the factory in which it was made, but in this case it was easy, because so many Imperial catalog pages are available.

Description	Line	Size	Amber	Ebony	Crystal	Cheriglo/Green	Yellow
bowl	411	6"					$25-35
bowl	411	9"		$55-65		$65-75	$55-65
bowl, console	211	12"			$50-75		
bowl, handled	411	10"				$75-95	$65-85
bowl, handled	411	12¼"x10¼"	$125-150	$150-200		$175-200	$150-200
bowl, handled	701	4¾"		$45-55	$25-35	$65-75	$45-55
bowl, loop handled	300	9¼"					$150-175
bowl, oval	300	4¼"x8½"x7"					$125-150
bowl, rolled or flared	411	12"		$75-125		$100-125	$75-125
bowl, round	300	10"x4"					$125-150
bowl, tab handled	211	9¼"			$45-65		
cake plate	411, 412	9½"x2"				$200-225	

Ebony #411 9½" square vase. $200.00 – 250.00.

Ebony #191 8¼" decanter. $300.00 – 350.00.

Description	Line	Size	Amber	Ebony	Crystal	Cheriglo/Green	Yellow
cake plate, high ftd.	211	12"			$55-75		
candlestick, keyhole	411	5"	$45-50 ea.	$45-55 ea.	$35-45 ea.	$55-65 ea.	$45-55 ea.
candlestick, mushroom	411	2½"					$45-55 ea.
candlestick, oval top	411	4"					$75-95 ea.
candy, flat	211	7¼"			$75-125		
candy, flat	411	6½"		$125-175	$75-95	$175-225	$125-175
candy, flat, rd. base	411	6¼"					$!50-200
candy, ftd.	411/503	6½"					$150-200
cheese & cracker	411	10" plate, 5" comport					
comport	300						$75-95
comport	411	6¾"x6¼"		$55-65	$45-55	$75-85	$55-65
comport	411	9 ½"x4¼"		$75-100		$100-125	$75-100
comport, oval top	411	4½"x7½"x5¼"		$75-100			$75-100
comport, oval top	411	6"x10"x8"		$75-125			$75-125
creamer	300						$50-75
creamer	411	3"			$25-30	$45-50	$35-40
cup	411						$75-85
decanter	191	8½" w/stopper		$300-350			
ice bucket	902	6"				$125-150	
jug, batter	11	8"			$125-150		
mayonnaise	411	6"x3½"		$45-50		$50-65	$45-50
mayonnaise liner	411	7¼"		$10-15		$20-25	$15-18
pitcher	11	7"			$150-175		
plate	211	10½"			$45-65		
plate	411	8½"					$35-55
plate, any shape	701	7"	$18-20	$18-20	$12-16	$18-20	$18-20
plate, candy, loop handled	300	10¼"					$75-125
plate, ftd.	211	14¼"			$45-65		
plate, handled	701	10¾"				$100-125	
plate, handled	211	12"			$50-65		
plate, handled	411	14"x12"					$45-65
rose bowl, any top	411	4¾"		$75-100		$100-125	$75-100
saucer	411						$20-25
snack set	411	10" plate, 6" bowl					$75-125
stem, oyster cocktail		3¼"					$50-65
stem, saucer champagne		5¾"					$65-75
stem, water		8¼", 8 oz.					$100-125
stem, water goblet		7½"					$85-95
sugar	300						$50-60
sugar	411	3"			$20-25	$35-40	$30-35
syrup	11	5¼"			$75-125		
tray, center handled	211	11"			$40-60		
tray, center handled	411	10"		$75-85	$50-65	$100-125	$75-85
tray, ftd., candy	411	7¼"x1½"					$125-175
tray, handled	411	14¼"x10"		$100-150			
vase	184	10"		$150-200			$150-200
vase	184	12"		$175-225			$175-225
vase	184	8"		$125-175		$175-200	$125-175
vase	191	4½"		$200-250			
vase	210	6½"				$125-150	
vase	412	10"				$400-450	
vase, genie		7½"		$150-175		$225-250	$150-175
vase, rectangular	411	9½"		$200-250		$275-350	$200-250
vase, smoke stack	210			$225-275			
vase, Swanson		10½"		$275-350		$400-450	

Ebony and crystal #411 flat candy. $100.00 – 125.00.

Ebony #411 5" keyhole candlestick. $45.00 – 55.00.

Ebony #411 12" x 10" handled bowl. $150.00 – 200.00.

Ebony #411 6" x 10" x 8" low-footed oval-top comport.
$75.00 – 125.00.

Ebony #184 10" vase. $150.00 – 200.00.

Ebony # 411 14½" x 10" handled tray. $100.00 – 150.00.

Ebony #210 8½" straight-sided vase.
$225.00 – 275.00.

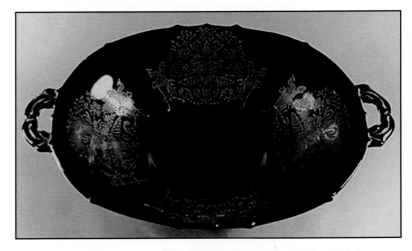

Ebony #411 12¾" x 8½" handled bowl. $150.00 – 200.00.

Ebony #701 7" handled plate with
turned-up edges. $25.00 – 35.00.

Ebony 10½" Swanson vase. $275.00 – 350.00.

Ebony #184 8" vase. $125.00 – 175.00.

Ebony #191 4½" vase. $200.00 – 250.00.

Ebony #411 12" rolled-edge console bowl. $75.00 – 125.00.

Ebony #411 cupped-top footed rose bowl. $75.00 – 100.00.

Ebony #411 flared-top footed rose bowl.
$75.00 – 100.00.

Crystal #211 12" footed cake salver.
$55.00 – 75.00.

Crystal #211 14¼" 4-toed plate.
$45.00 – 65.00.

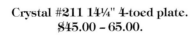

Crystal #211 9¼" tab handled bowl. $45.00 – 65.00.

Crystal # 211 11" center-handled tray. $40.00 – 60.00.

Crystal #211 flat candy. $75.00 – 125.00.

Crystal #411 5" keyhole candlestick. $35.00 – 45.00.

Crystal #11 7" milk pitcher. $150.00 – 175.00.

Crystal #411 sugar bowl. $20.00 – 25.00.

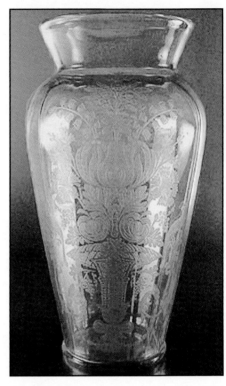

Green 10½" Swanson vase. $400.00 – 450.00.

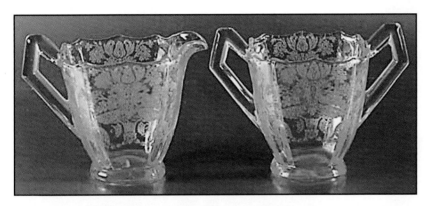

Green #411 cream and sugar. $80.00 – 90.00.

Green #412 9½" footed cake salver. $200.00 – 225.00.

Green #411 footed bowl. $100.00 – 125.00.

Green #411 console bowl. $100.00 – 125.00.

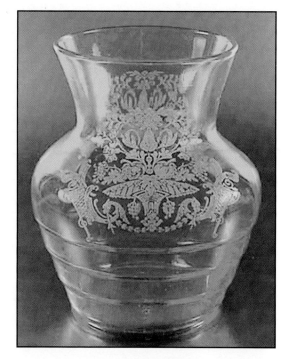

Green # 210 6½" vase. $125.00 – 150.00.

Green #411 12¼" x 8" oval, handled bowl. $175.00 – 200.00.

Green #411 5" keyhole candlestick. $55.00 – 65.00.

Green #412 10" flared-top vase. $400.00 – 450.00.

Green #411 flat 2-part candy. $175.00 – 225.00.

Cheriglo #411 flat candy. $175.00 – 225.00.

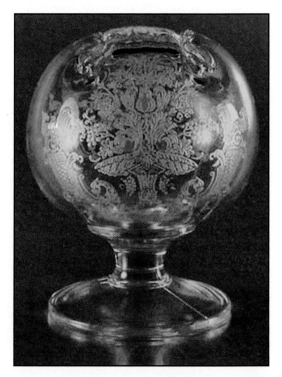

Cheriglo #411 high-footed comport. $75.00 – 85.00.

Cheriglo #411 cupped-top footed rose bowl.
$100.00 – 125.00.

Cheriglo #411 5" keyhole candlestick.
$55.00 – 65.00.

Cheriglo #411 12" console bowl. $100.00 – 125.00.

Cheriglo #411 mayonnaise comport. $85.00 – 95.00.

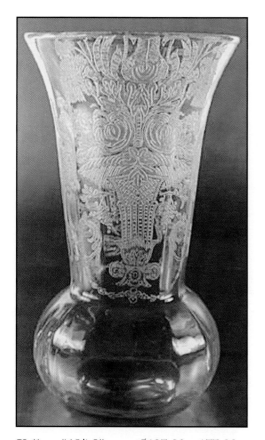

Yellow 5¾" lady leg saucer champagne. $65.00 – 75.00.

Yellow #184 8" vase. $125.00 – 175.00.

Yellow 7½" lady leg water goblet with design on front and back. $85.00 – 95.00.

Yellow #411 7½" footed candy tray. $125.00 – 175.00.

Yellow #411 high-footed comport. $65.00 – 75.00.

Yellow #411 flat candy. $125.00 – 175.00.

Yellow #411 10" center-handled server. $75.00 – 85.00.

Yellow #411 low-footed comport. $55.00 – 65.00.

Yellow #701 handled mayonnaise bowl. $45.00 – 50.00.

Yellow #411 12" rolled-edge console bowl. $75.00 – 125.00.

Yellow #411 cup. $75.00 – 85.00.

Yellow #411 flared-top footed rose bowl. $75.00 – 100.00.

Yellow #411 sugar and creamer. $65.00 – 75.00.

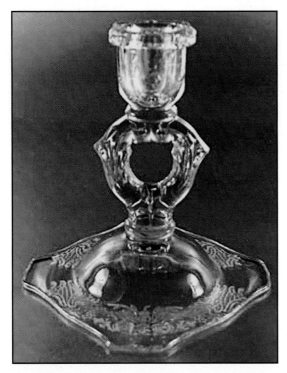

Yellow #411 5" keyhole candlestick. $45.00 – 55.00.

Yellow #411 9" bowl. $55.00 – 65.00.

Yellow #701 plate with turned-up sides. $25.00 – 35.00.

Yellow #411 high-footed, oval-top comport. $75.00 – 125.00.

Yellow #411 10½" center-handled server with turned-up edges. $75.00 – 85.00.

Yellow #411 low-footed gravy. $75.00 – 95.00.

Yellow #300 oval bowl. $125.00 – 150.00.

Yellow #300 10" round salad bowl. $125.00 – 150.00.

Top view of preceding photo.

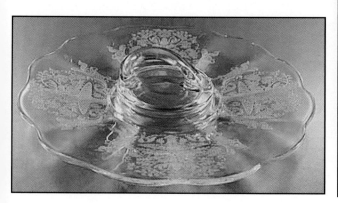

Yellow #300 loop-handled server. $75.00 – 100.00.

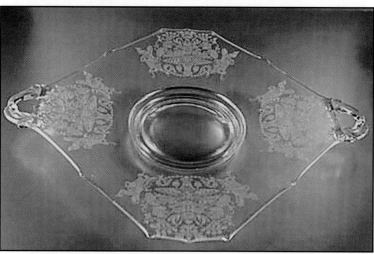

Yellow #411 14" x 12" handled plate. $60.00 – 85.00.

Yellow #411 11" rolled-edge console bowl. $55.00 – 65.00.

Yellow #411 10" handled bowl. $150.00 – 200.00.

Yellow #411 12¼" console bowl. $75.00 – 125.00.

Yellow #411 low-footed bowl with flared edge.
$75.00 – 100.00.

Yellow #411 high-footed comport. $55.00 – 65.00.

Yellow #411 9¼" low-footed cake salver. $125.00 – 150.00.

Yellow #411 mayonnaise set. $80.00 – 95.00.

Yellow #411 6¼" flat candy with keyhole lid and round base.
$150.00 – 200.00.

Yellow #701 5" flared, handled bowl. $45.00 – 50.00.

Yellow #411 9½" square vase. $200.00 – 250.00.

Yellow #411 cupped rose bowl.
$75.00 – 100.00.

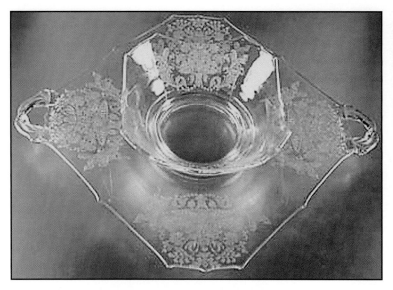

Yellow #300 10" footed bowl. $100.00 – 125.00.

Yellow #411 snack set. $75.00 – 125.00.

Yellow #411 8½" luncheon plate. $35.00 – 55.00.

Yellow lady leg water goblet
with three design medallions.
$100.00 – 125.00.

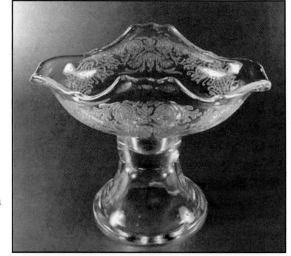

Yellow #411 mushroom candlestick with
oval top. $65.00 – 75.00.

Another view of yellow mushroom candlestick.
$65.00 – 75.00.

Yellow #411 footed candy with keyhole lid and #503 base.
$150.00 – 200.00.

Amber #701 5¼" handled bowl (6¼" across
handles). $18.00 – 20.00.

Amber #411 5" keyhole candlestick. $45.00 – 50.00.

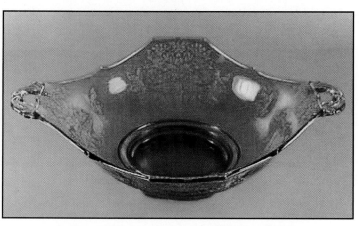

Amber #411 handled bowl. $45.00 – 55.00.

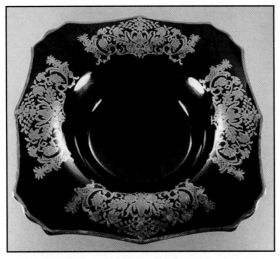

Black bowl made by Diamond, with a sterling overlay similar to Gothic Garden.

Black Imperial Molly 10" footed bowl with Gothic Garden copy; note the differences between it and the #701 octagonal ribbed console bowl.

Harvester

There are two versions of Harvester. The pattern of Amber Harvester shows a plain background, while the green, Ebony, and Cheriglo pieces have a lattice background that adds to the beauty of this etching. Harvester is most often found on Ebony or Amber, but there are pieces of Cheriglo and green. Most pieces are etched on a #210 blank, but a few #701 and #191 pieces have been found. The Amber batter set can be found with either an Ebony lid or an Amber one. That set could have been made in crystal or all Ebony, but I've never seen or heard of one. I like this etching, but the prices haven't risen much above middle ground. Of course, there are rare pieces, like those of the batter sets, that are so hard to find that most collectors are willing to part with a little more money to own them. The Amber is a rich shade that is perfect for the etching. Harvester is a great pattern to start with when collecting Paden City.

Amber #210 flat candy. $75.00 – 95.00.

Amber #210 high-footed comport. $65.00 – 85.00.

Description	Line	Size	Amber	Ebony	Cheriglo/Green
batter jug	11	8"	$125-150		
bowl, ftd. (comport)		9¾"x3½"	$75-95	$100-120	$125-150
bowl, handled	210	9"	$65-85	$75-95	
cake plate	210	7½"x2½"	$85-100	$100-130	$125-150
candlestick	210	2¼"x4½"	$45-55 ea.	$55-65 ea.	$65-75 ea.
candy, flat	210	4⅞"x6⅜"	$75-95	$85-115	$120-150
candy, ftd.	210	6¼"	$100-125	$125-150	$145-165
comport	210	5½"x7"	$65-85	$70-80	$75-95
creamer	210		$35-45	$40-50	$50-60
creamer	701		$40-45	$45-50	
mayonnaise	210	6¾"x3½"	$65-85	$75-100	$100-135
mayonnaise liner	210	7½"	$25-30	$35-50	$45-55
pitcher, milk	11	7"	$120-130		
plate, handled		12"	$45-65	$65-85	$75-100
rose bowl		4½"		$65-85	
sugar	210		$25-35	$35-45	$40-50
sugar	701		$30-40	$40-50	
syrup	11	5¼"	$75-100		
tray, loop handled	210	10½"	$65-85	$70-90	$90-110
tray, tall handled	210	10½"	$65-85	$70-90	$90-110
vase	210	6"	$75-95	$100-110	$100-135
vase	210	10"	$100-120	$120-150	$150-175
vase	191½	4½"	$250-300	$300-325	$325-350
vase, genie		8¼"		$175-200	$200-250
vase, smoke stack	210	5½"	$225-275	$250-295	$275-325

Amber #701 wide optic cream and sugar.
$70.00 – 85.00.

Amber #210 mayonnaise comport and liner. $90.00 – 115.00.

Amber #210 10½" center-handled server. $65.00 – 85.00.

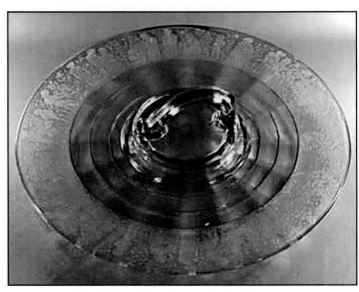

Amber #210 10½" loop-handled server. $65.00 – 85.00.

Amber #210 mushroom candlestick. $45.00 – 55.00.

Amber #210 handled bowl. $65.00 – 85.00.

Amber #11 7" milk pitcher. $120.00 – 130.00.

Amber #210 11¼" low-footed cake plate.
$85.00 – 100.00.

Amber #210 sugar and creamer. $60.00 – 80.00.

Close-up of pattern.

Amber #11 8" batter jug. $125.00 – 150.00.

Ebony #191½ 4½" vase. $300.00 – 325.00.

Ebony #210 mushroom candlestick. $55.00 – 65.00.

Ebony #210 6¼" vase. $100.00 – 110.00.

Ebony #210 base of footed candy. $65.00 – 75.00 base, $125.00 – 150.00 complete with lid.

Ebony #210 10" vase. $120.00 – 150.00.

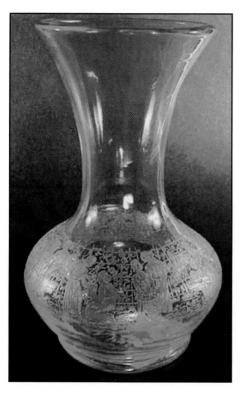

Green 7½" genie vase. $200.00 – 250.00.

Cheriglo #210 6" vase. $100.00 – 135.00.

Hillsboro

This is a dainty little etching that is very attractive. I don't have much of a list for this pattern, so please e-mail me with information about pieces you own or have seen.

Description	Line	Size	Crystal
candlestick	900	3"	$25-35 ea.
candy	777 top, 215 base	7"x3¾"	$75-100
creamer	777		$18-20
sugar	777		$15-18
tray, center handled	777	11"	$65-85

Crystal/Ruby flat candy, with #777 Comet lid and #215 Glades 3-part base.

Different view of candy dish in preceding photo. $75.00 – 100.00.

129

Irwin

Irwin is commonly found on the #881 Gadroon line and exists in most of the colors used for that line. The wide band of decoration works well with the wide expanse of smooth surface found on the Gadroon pieces. All the pieces listed here are #881 Gadroon. The 12" console bowl comes flared, rolled edge, or flattened edge, all of which measure differ-ently. The price applies for all of these shapes. The mayo liner is also used for the cream soup. Gadroon was also made in Mulberry, so it is possible that there may be Mulberry-colored pieces with the Irwin etching. If so, the price would fall in the Ruby/blue price range.

Amber #881 11½" bowl and 11⅞" underplate. $80.00 – 110.00.

Close-up of pattern.

Description	Size	Amber/Crystal	Ruby/Blue	Cheriglo/Green/Yellow
bowl, center handled	10"	$40-60	$100-120	$75-100
bowl, ftd. (comport)	10"x5¼"	$55-75	$100-125	$75-100
bowl, handled	12"	$45-65	$120-150	$100-120
bowl, handled	9"	$40-60	$100-120	$75-100
bowl, oval, vegetable	10"x7⅝"	$55-75	$100-125	$75-95
cake plate	10½"	$45-65	$125-150	$100-125
candlestick	6"	$35-45 ea.	$75-95 ea.	$65-85 ea.
candy, flat, 3-part	7"	$65-85	$100-150	$75-95
comport	6¾"x7"	$35-50	$65-95	$45-60
creamer		$20-25	$35-50	$25-30
cream soup		$20-25	$25-40	$25-30
cup		$18-20	$35-55	$25-40
mayonnaise	5"x3"	$18-20	$35-55	$25-40
mayonnaise liner	6½"	$8-12	$15-20	$12-15
plate, bread & butter, rd.	6½"	$10-12	$18-20	$12-15
plate, dinner	9⅝"	$25-45	$45-65	$35-45
plate, handled	13"	$20-30	$75-95	$60-80
plate, luncheon, rd.	8½"	$18-22	$40-50	$25-35
plate, square	8¼"	$18-22	$40-50	$25-35
saucer, rd.	5¼"	$8-12	$15-20	$12-15
sugar		$15-18	$25-45	$20-25
tray, center handled	10½"	$35-55	$65-85	$45-65

Amber #881 11" center-handled server.
$35.00 – 55.00.

Amber #881 9¼" x 5¼" large footed bowl.
$55.00 – 75.00.

Amber #881 7" flat 3-part candy. $65.00 – 85.00.

Amber #881 creamer. $20.00 – 25.00.

Amber #881 sugar bowl. $15.00 – 18.00.

Amber #881 8¼" square luncheon plate. $18.00 – 22.00.

Amber #881 cup and saucer. $26.00 – 32.00.

Crystal/Ruby #881 flat candy. $100.00 – 120.00.

Crystal/Ruby #881 mayonnaise set. $18.00 bowl,
$15.00 – 20.00 plate.

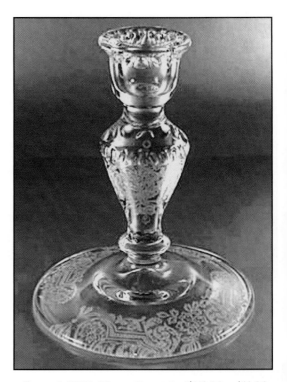

Crystal #881 6" candlestick. $35.00 – 45.00.

Ruby #881 sugar and creamer. $60.00 – 95.00.

Ruby #881 mayonnaise set. $50.00 – 75.00.

Ruby #881 8½" round luncheon plate. $45.00 – 50.00.

Ruby #881 6½" round plate. $18.00 – 20.00.

Ruby #881 high-footed comport. $65.00 – 95.00.

Ruby #881 12½" handled bowl. $120.00 – 150.00.

Ruby #881 9" handled bowl. $100.00 – 125.00.

Leeuwen (Loo-when, Dutch for "Lion")

Leeuwen is a beautiful, delicate-looking etching that depicts stylized lions and birds and has a flowering urn in the center. Crow's Foot Round (#890) is the primary blank used for this design, but a few pieces of #412 Crow's Foot Square have been found. Leeuwen is especially beautiful on Ruby. I'm certain there are more pieces than those on my list, so please let me know what you have. The #300 comport listed here shares a number with the Archaic line, but instead of having the curved edge associated with Archaic, the top is angled.

Description	Line	Size	Crystal/Amber	Ruby/Blue
bowl, center handled	890	9¾"	$75-100	$175-250
bowl, ftd., console	890	11½"	$75-90	$150-200
bowl, handled, veg.	890	11½"	$80-120	$175-250
cake plate, low ftd.	890	12"	$150-175	$250-300
candlestick, triple	890	6½"	$75-90 ea.	$125-150 ea.
cheese & cracker	890	10½"	$125-150	$200-250
comport	300		$50-75	
mayonnaise, 2-pc.	890		$65-85	$125-175
plate, cracker	890	10½"	$75-90	$150-200
plate, luncheon	411	8¼"	$20-40	
relish	890	11½"	$35-55	
server, center handled	890	10½"	$75-100	$175-250
vase	412	12"	$150-200	$300-350

Crystal #412 12" vase. $150.00 – 200.00.

Crystal #890 10" footed, flared console bowl. $75.00 – 90.00.

Crystal #890 6¼" x 7¾" triple candlestick. $75.00 – 90.00.

Ruby #890 10½" plate. $150.00 – 200.00.

Close-up of pattern.

Ruby #890 9¾" center-handled bowl. $175.00 – 250.00.

Lela Bird

This is one of the most elaborate etchings done by Paden City. There is a castle, a rearing horse, trees, flowers, water, mountains, clouds, and of course, the bird that gives it the Lela Bird name. It's hard to imagine how Paden City fit all that detail into one etching, but it did exactly that on the vases. The design did have to be scaled back for the small-er pieces, and the #300 candlesticks have only the bird and a few flowers. The batter sets were sold with Ebony lids, but there may be a few crystal ones out there. Most of the pieces can be found with color inlaid. Add 20% to the crystal price for gold or silver, and 25% for red or other colors.

Ebony #184 10" vase. $200.00 – 250.00.

Ebony #182 8" gold-encrusted elliptical vase.
$200.00 – 250.00.

Description	Line	Size	Crystal	Ebony	Cheriglo/Green
batter jug	11	8"	$100-150		
bowl, console	210	12"		$75-90	$75-100
bowl, console	300	13½"	$50-65		$75-100
bowl, console	300	10⅝"	$50-65		$75-100
bowl, ftd.	300	9½"x4"	$100-125		$175-200
cake salver	210	11"		$150-175	$200-225
cake salver	300	11½"			$200-225
candlestick	300	5¼"	$25-30 ea.		$40-50 ea.
candy & lid, flat	210			$150-175	$200-225
candy & lid, flat	300		$50-125		$200-250

Description	Line	Size	Crystal	Ebony	Cheriglo/Green
comport	300	6"x8"			$100-125
creamer	701				$45-55
ice bucket	902	6"		$150-200	$175-225
mayonnaise	210	6¾"x3⅛"		$75-95	$100-125
mayonnaise liner	210	7¼"		$20-25	$25-35
mayonnaise set	300		$75-125		
pitcher, milk	11	7"	$100-125		
sugar	701				$40-50
syrup, w/lid	11	5¼	$100-125		
vase	184	10"		$200-250	$225-275
vase	184	12"		$250-300	$275-300
vase	210	10"		$225-275	$250-300
vase, elliptical	181½	5"	$125-150	$175-225	$200-225
vase, elliptical	182	8"	$150-175	$200-250	$225-275

Ebony #182 8" silver-encrusted elliptical vase.
$200.00 – 250.00.

Ebony #182 5½" elliptical vase. $175.00 – 225.00.

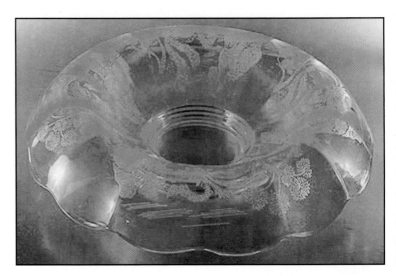

Green #300 12" rolled-edge console bowl. $75.00 – 100.00.

Ebony #184 12" vase. $250.00 – 300.00.

Green #300 mushroom candlestick. $40.00 – 50.00.

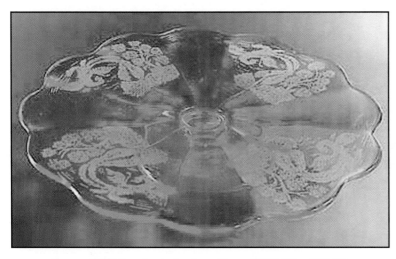

Green #300 low-footed cake salver. $200.00 – 225.00.

Green #300 9½" x 4" low-footed bowl.
$175.00 – 200.00.

Green #210 mayonnaise set. $125.00 – 155.00.

Green #210 11" low-footed cake salver. $200.00 – 225.00.

Green #210 flat candy. $200.00 – 225.00.

Green #210 10" vase. $250.00 – 300.00.

Green #701 ribbed creamer. $45.00 – 55.00.

Cheriglo #300 11" rolled-edge console bowl. $75.00 – 100.00.

Cheriglo #210 10" vase. $250.00 – 300.00.

Cheriglo #300 8" high-footed comport. $100.00 – 125.00.

Cheriglo #300 mushroom candlestick. $40.00 – 50.00.

Cheriglo #184 12" vase. $250.00 – 300.00.

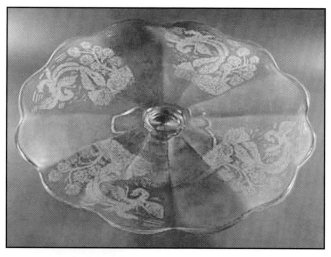

Cheriglo #300 low-footed cake salver. $200.00 – 225.00.

Loopie

I really don't like the name of this etching. *Loopie* just doesn't do justice to this beautiful etching, but unfortunately, we are stuck with it. Loopie has been found on #220 Largo, #881 Gadroon, #211 Spire, and #221 Maya. I've only seen it in Copen Blue, Ruby, and crystal. Ruby pieces are absolutely beautiful and command the highest prices, but blue isn't far behind. I don't have a large list, so please let me know if you have other pieces.

Description	Line	Size	Blue	Crystal	Ruby
bowl, console	220	12"		$125-150	$300-350
bowl, console	881	12"		$125-150	$300-350
candlestick, duo				$75-95 ea.	
candlestick, duo	220			$50-75 ea.	$125-150 ea.
plate, handled	221	13"	$100-120		

Ruby #220 12" console bowl. $300.00 – 350.00.

Close-up of pattern.

Crystal #881 12" console bowl. $125.00 – 150.00.

Crystal double candlestick. $75.00 – 95.00.

Louise

This is a very ornate etching done by the Lotus Decorating Company. It combines a very attractive etching in the corners and a gold border etching that connects those corners. I've only seen it on #412 Crow's Foot Square blanks. You must remember that not every piece with this pattern was made by Paden City. Lotus bought blanks from many companies, and occasionally it used a pitcher from one company and tumblers from another to complete a set. Play close attention to the blanks. I've only seen this pattern on Ruby, but there may be other colors.

Ruby #412 6¼" x 3¼" low-footed comport. $65.00 – 85.00.

Close-up of pattern.

Description	Line	Size	Ruby
bowl, centerpiece	412	12"	$100-125
bowl, handled	412	11½"x9½"	$125-150
candlestick, keyhole	412	5"	$55-75 ea.
candy, flat	412	6⅞"	$125-175
cheese & cracker	412	10"	$150-175
comport, high ftd.	412	7"	$75-95
comport, low ftd.	412	6¼"x3¼"	$65-85
creamer	412		$25-30
mayonnaise, 2-pc.	412		$145-165
sugar	412		$22-28
tray, handled	412	11½"x14"	$65-95
tray, center handled, sandwich	412	10½"	$125-150

Ruby #412 5" keyhole candlestick.
$55.00 – 75.00.

Ruby #412 7" high-footed comport.
$75.00 – 95.00.

Ruby #412 cheese and cracker set.
$150.00 – 175.00.

Magic Garden #546

Magic Garden, design #546, is a pleasing design than combines butterflies, birds, and flowers. Pieces with this etching appear to have been sold by a firm named John L. Pasmantier & Sons, which may have been a jobber or sales agent. An advertisement for this included many pieces of Spring Orchard, design #545. Both designs can be found on #220 Largo and #215 Glades. I've only seen Magic Garden on #220 Largo blanks in crystal or Copen Blue, but other lines and colors may have been used. Spring Orchard is so similar to Magic Garden that you will need to look closely at the close-ups of each.

This listing may not be complete. I believe that dinnerware may have also been etched, so please let me know if you own a cup and saucer or any of the plates.

Description	Line	Size	Copen Blue	Crystal
bowl, ftd., console	220	12"	$60-70	$45-55
bowl, handled	220	11"	$60-70	$45-55
bowl, center handled, nut tray	220	10½"	$65-85	$50-60
cake salver, low ftd.	220	11¾"	$125-175	$100-150
candlestick	220	5¼"	$50-55 ea.	$40-45 ea.
candlestick, duo	220	5¼"	$45-65 ea.	$35-55 ea.
candy, covered, flat	220	7¼"	$175-200	$125-150
cheese & cracker, covered	220		$225-300	$150-175
cheese & cracker set	220		$95-120	$75-90
comport, low ftd.	220	10"	$75-100	$70-90
creamer	220		$25-35	$20-30
mayonnaise set, 3-pc.			$60-85	$50-75
plate, cracker	220	10"	$75-85	$60-80
plate, handled	220	13"	$45-65	$35-55
plate, ftd.	220	14"	$60-70	$45-55
sugar	220		$20-30	$18-28
tray, sandwich	220	11"	$60-70	$45-60

Copen Blue #220 12" cake salver. $125.00 – 175.00.

Close-up of pattern.

Meadow Bloom

Meadow Bloom, with its grassy meadow and blooming flowers, looks exactly the way the name sounds. Bill Walker, one of the authors of *Paden City Glass Company,* reports that this etching has been found on #412 Crow's Foot Square, #411 Mrs. B., #1504 Chaucer, and #444 Vale. I searched newsletters and every other Paden City source I have, and only found four items to list. Please help me make this listing more complete.

Description	Line	Size	Crystal	Ruby	Ruby Flashed
candy, ftd.	444	9⅝"	$45-65	$75-100	$65-95
creamer	444		$20-22		
sugar	444		$18-22		
vase, Vimmer		8½"	$100-150		

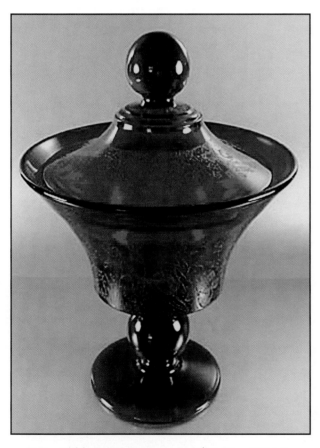

Ruby #444 9⅝" footed candy. $75.00 – 100.00.

Ruby-flashed #444 9⅝" footed candy. $65.00 – 95.00.

Nell

This is another Lotus etching done on Paden City blanks. As with the Lotus designs, not all Nell pieces will be on Paden City blanks. I've only seen this etching on #412 blanks in either crystal or Topaz (light yellow).

Description	Line	Size	Crystal	Yellow
bowl, centerpiece	412	12"	$65-75	$75-85
bowl, handled	412	11½"x9½"	$65-75	$75-85
candlestick, keyhole	412	5"	$25-35 ea.	$35-45 ea.
candy, flat	412	7"	$55-75	$65-85
cheese and cracker	412	10"	$95-115	$100-145
comport, high ftd.	412	7"	$55-65	$65-75
comport, low ftd.	412	6¼"x3¼"	$35-55	$45-65
creamer	412		$18-22	$20-24
mayonnaise, 2-pc.	412		$45-65	$55-75
sugar	412		$15-18	$18-22
tray, handled	412	11¼"x14"	$45-65	$55-75
tray, center handled, sandwich	412	10½"	$45-65	$55-75

Yellow #412 12" console bowl. $75.00 – 85.00.

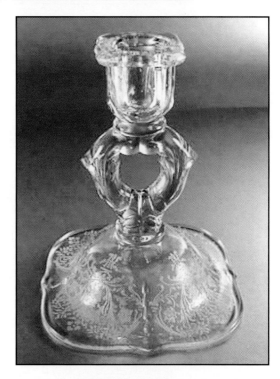

Yellow #412 5" keyhole candlestick. $35.00 – 45.00.

Yellow #412 handled bowl. $75.00 – 85.00.

Close-up of pattern.

Yellow #412 center-handled server. $55.00 – 75.00.

Orchid

Paden City's Orchid etching is absolutely beautiful on any color, but on Ruby or Cobalt, it is exquisite. Introduced in 1929, it was and still is a very popular design coveted by collectors, especially when on Ruby, Cobalt Blue, or Ebony. Be prepared to spend money if you decide this pattern is your favorite, but if you like the lighter colors, bargains can still be found. There are several variations of Orchid, because the size of the piece being decorated dictated the size of the etching. I'm including all those plate-etched variations in this listing. The sand-carved pieces are listed under Baby Orchid.

There are some very exciting pieces on these pages. On the #300 variant bowl, there is a row of indents on every other lobe. The Ruby #412 center-piece bowl has several colors inlaid into the design, which makes it one of the most spectacular pieces here. Paden City did a lot of that type of decorating, and it's always beautiful. The #888 vase is so rare that I couldn't find one to photograph, but it looks similar to the #215 Glades whiskey shown on page 264. An Ebony pitcher, made by adding a handle to the genie vase, has been found with the Orchid etching. The Ruby vase without an etching is shown on page 157, because a ruby vase has been found with the Orchid etching.

Ebony #184 10" vase. $300.00 – 375.00.

147

Description	Line#	Size	Ebony	Blue/Ruby	Crystal	Cheriglo/Green	Yellow
bowl	411	10″	$250-325				
bowl, console	300	14″				$200-250	
bowl, console	300 variant	12″				$250-300	$200-250
bowl, console	412	12″	$250-300	$325-400	$60-80	$250-300	
bowl, console	895	12″				$125-150	$100-125
bowl, console, decorated	412	12″		$550-600			
bowl, ftd.	412	4½″x9½″		$450-500	$75-85		$225-300
bowl, ftd., rolled edges	411			$400-475			
bowl, handled	412	10″		$375-425			
bowl, square	412	8″		$275-350		$50-65	
bowl, square	412	10″	$225-300	$350-450			
cake salver	412	9½″x2″		$275-325	$65-75	$175-225	$150-200
candlestick, keyhole	412	5″	$100-125 ea.	$150-175 ea.	$65-85	$100-125 ea.	$100-125 ea.
candlestick, mushroom	412	2½″	$75-100 ea.	$125-150 ea.	$55-75 ea.	$75-100 ea.	
candy, cloverleaf	412	6¾″		$200-275	$55-75	$150-200	
candy, flat	411	6½″				$250-325	
candy, flat	412	6⅞″		$250-350	$55-75	$150-200	
candy, flat	701	6½″				$375-425	
candy, flat, round base	411	6½″				$275-325	
candy jar	701	8″				$250-300	
cheese & cracker	412	10¼″		$300-350	$100-150	$275-325	
comport	300 variant	8″					$225-300
comport, high ftd.	412	7″		$175-225	$60-80	$75-100	$75-95
comport, low ftd.	412	6½″x3½″		$150-200	$35-55	$150-200	$125-175
creamer	412			$75-100	$25-30	$65-85	
gravy, ftd.	412			$175-200			
mayonnaise set, 2-pc.	412	6½″x4″		$250-300	$65-85		
pitcher	154	8″					$425-550
pitcher, genie			$1200				$250-350
plate, handled	412	14″x11¾″		$150-200	$75-85		$85-100
rose bowl, any top	412			$150-200			
server, center handled	411	10½″		$250-300	$40-50	$150-200	
sugar	412			$65-95	$20-25	$50-75	
tray, center-handled	412	10¼″		$250-300	$40-50	$150-200	$125-175
tray, plain	210	10⅞″x4⅜″		$35-50		$30-45	
vase	184	10″	$300-375	$450-600		$325-375	
vase	184	12″	$325-400	$475-550	$75-90	$350-395	
vase	184	8″	$225-275	$400-500		$275-325	
vase	191½					$375-550	
vase	210	10″	$300-375		$150-225	$350-450	
vase	411	10″	$425-525			$475-550	
vase	412	10″		$550-700	$200-250		
vase	888	9″		$650-800			
vase, any top	412	12″	$350-400	$600-750			
vase, collared		7½″	$400-475	$500-575			
vase, elliptical	182	5½″	$350-400				
vase, elliptical	182	8″	$450-600		$150-200	$375-550	
vase, genie		8″	$300-400	$350-450			

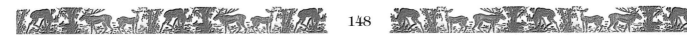

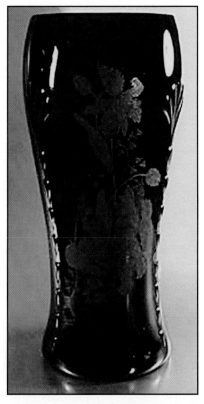

Ebony #412 12" vase. $325.00 – 400.00.

Ebony #182 8" elliptical vase. $450.00 – 600.00.

Ebony #182 5½" elliptical vase. $350.00 – 400.00.

Royal Blue #412 10¼" center-handled tray. $250.00 – 300.00.

Royal Blue #412 10" cupped-top vase. $550.00 – 700.00.

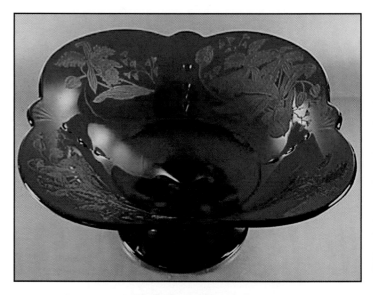

Royal Blue #412 9¼" x 4" low-footed bowl. $450.00 – 500.00.

Royal Blue #412 flat candy. $250.00 – 350.00.

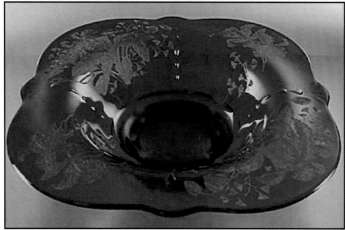

Royal Blue #412 12" console bowl. $325.00 – 400.00.

Royal Blue #412 handled plate. $150.00 – 200.00.

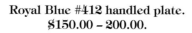

Crystal #412 7" high-footed comport.
$35.00 – 45.00.

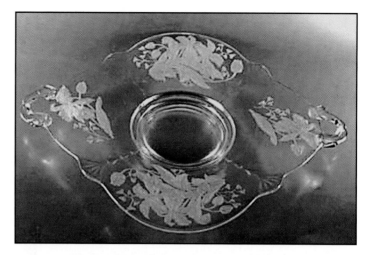

Crystal #412 14⅜" x 11¾" handled plate. $75.00 – 85.00.

Crystal #412 flat candy. $55.00 – 75.00.

Crystal #412 5" keyhole candlestick. $65.00 – 85.00.

Crystal #411 6½" x 3½" comport.
$35.00 – 55.00.

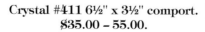

Crystal #412 mayonnaise set. $65.00 – 85.00.
Spoon, $15.00 – 18.00.

Crystal #412 9¼" x 4" low-footed bowl $75.00 – 85.00.

Green #412 center-handled server. $150.00 – 200.00.

Green #412 mushroom candlestick. $75.00 – 85.00.

Green #411 9½" x 4" low-footed
bowl with deep-rolled edge.
$275.00 – 325.00.

Green #300 14" rolled-edge console bowl. $200.00 – 250.00.

Green #411 footed rose bowl. $150.00 – 200.00.

Green #184 10" vase. $325.00 – 375.00.

Green #411 6" x 3¾" comport.
$150.00 – 200.00.

Cheriglo #412 flat candy.
$150.00 – 200.00.

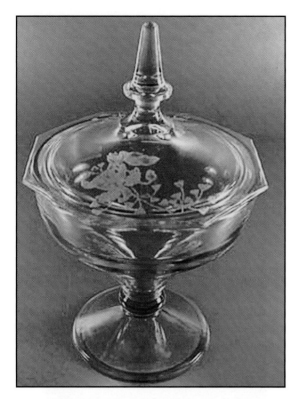

Cheriglo #701 8" candy. $250.00 – 300.00.

Ruby #412 cream and sugar, with tray. $160.00 – 225.00.

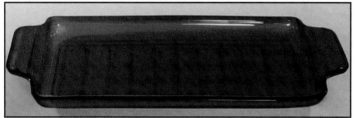

Ruby 10⅞" cream and sugar tray, not etched. $35.00 – 50.00.

Ruby #412 cloverleaf candy. $200.00 – 275.00.

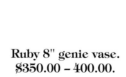

Ruby 8" genie vase.
$350.00 – 400.00.

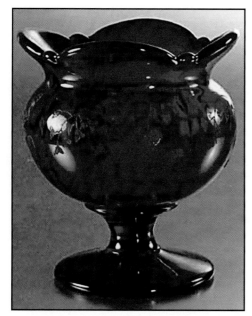

Ruby #412 footed rose bowl. $150.00 – 200.00.

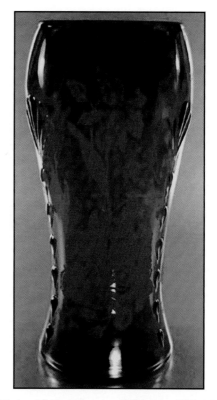

Ruby #412 10" vase. $550.00 – 700.00.

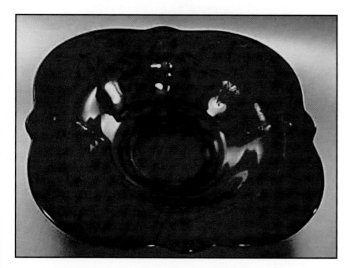

Ruby #412 12" console bowl. $325.00 – 400.00.

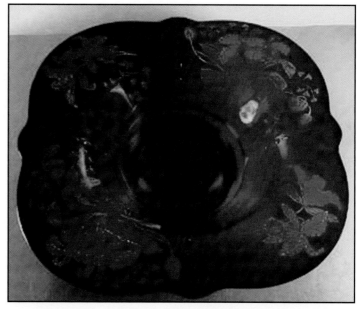

Ruby #412 12" console bowl, inlaid with Ruby, green, and yellow. $550.00 – 600.00.

Ruby #412 5" keyhole candlestick.
$150.00 – 175.00.

Ruby #412 mayonnaise set. $250.00 – 300.00.

Ruby #412 6½" x 3½" low-footed comport. $150.00 – 200.00.

Ruby #412 10" handled bowl. $375.00 – 425.00.

Ruby #412 7" high-footed comport. $175.00 – 225.00.

Ruby #412 low-footed cake salver. $275.00 – 325.00.

Ruby #184 12" vase. $600.00 – 750.00.

Ruby #412 center-handled tray. $250.00 – 300.00.

Ruby #412 cloverleaf candy with a metal frame.
$225.00 – 300.00.

Ruby #412 flat candy. $250.00 – 350.00.

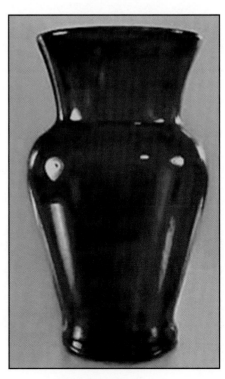

Ruby vase. This shape has been found with
the Orchid etching. $500.00 – 575.00 with
etching, $50.00 – 75.00 plain.

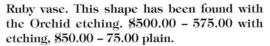

Yellow #412 10" x 4" low-footed bowl. $225.00 – 300.00.

Yellow #300 12" console bowl with circles on every other panel. $200.00 – 225.00.

Yellow #412 7" comport.
$75.00 – 95.00.

Oriental Garden

As beautiful as this pattern is, I'm puzzled by the lack of pieces available. It appears that the line was developed as a companion pattern for the many Blue Willow dinnerware sets. Crystal is the most common color for Oriental Garden, but even that is very hard to find. All other colors are rare. The Ruby bowl is crying out for matching candlesticks. Please e-mail me if you have other pieces with this etching, so that I can add those to the price list.

Description	Line	Size	Amber	Crystal	Pink	Ruby
bowl, console	895	11½"	$100-125	$75-95	$125-150	$175-200
candlestick, double	185	5"	$65-85 ea.	$45-65 ea.	$60-80 ea.	$100-125 ea.
candlestick, single	890		$65-85 ea.			
cheese & cracker	895	10½"		$65-85	$100-125	
creamer	503			$25-35		
ice bucket	893			$50-75		

Description	Line	Size	Amber	Crystal	Pink	Ruby
plate, handled	895	11½"			$65-85	
relish	895			$45-55		
server, center handled	895	10½"		$45-65		
sugar	530			$20-30		
tumbler	175	2 oz.		$65-85		
vase, elliptical	182	5½"		$75-100		

Crystal #182 5½" elliptical vase. $75.00 – 100.00.

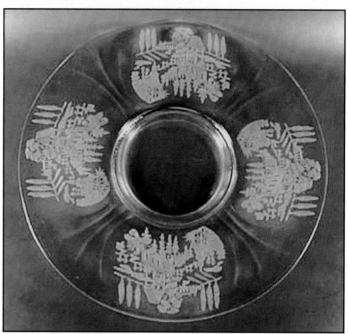

Crystal #895 10½" cracker plate. $55.00 – 75.00.

Crystal #895 12" console bowl. $75.00 – 95.00.

Crystal #895 10½" center-handled plate. $45.00 – 65.00.

Crystal #895 cheese and cracker set. $65.00 – 85.00.

Crystal #503 sugar bowl, no panels.
$20.00 – 30.00.

Amber #895 double candlestick. $65.00 – 85.00.

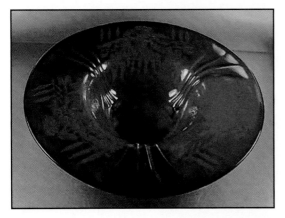

Ruby #895 12" console bowl. $175.00 – 200.00.

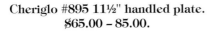

Cheriglo #895 11½" handled plate.
$65.00 – 85.00.

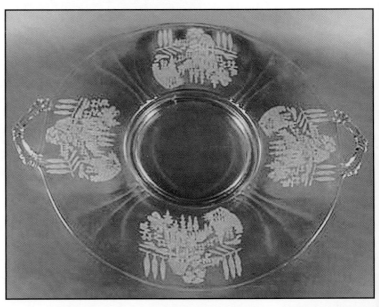

Pam's Foral, a.k.a. Heather & Primrose

This etching is beautiful and versatile. The S-shaped design fits easily on small or large pieces. It is usually found on #555 Nerva, #221 Maya, and #220 Largo blanks. A Largo #220 cigarette box has been found in Ruby, but it is rare, and I was unable to locate one for a photo. I'm certain that more blanks were used for Pam's Floral, so please help me add listings.

Description	Line	Size	Crystal	Ruby
bowl, oval, Nerva		12"x7½"	$65-85	
bowl, ftd., console	221	12"	$65-75	
box, cigarette	220		$125-175	$250-300
box, heart shaped	555	7½"x7⅛"	$75-100	
creamer	555		$20-22	
cup, punch	555		$15-18	
cheese & cracker	555	12"	$100-125	
platter	555	15"	$45-50	
punch bowl	555	10½"	$100-125	
punch bowl liner	555	15"	$45-60	
server, center-handled	221	11"	$45-60	
sugar	555		$18–20	

Crystal #555 punch cup; this may also be used as a coffee cup. $15.00 – 18.00.

Crystal #555 punch bowl and liner. $100.00 – 125.00.

Crystal Nerva 12" oval, handled bowl.
$65.00 – 85.00.

Crystal #555 heart-shaped candy, etched on the underside of lid. $75.00 – 100.00.

Crystal #555 cream and sugar. $38.00 – 42.00.

Peacock & Rose/Nora Bird

The Peacock and Rose etching was named twice by Hazel Marie Weatherman in her *Colored Glass of the Depression Era, Book 2,* published in 1974. Without realizing that it was part of the same pattern, she named a variation of this design Nora Bird. It was an easy mistake to make, because one design shows a flying bird that looks like a cross between a pheasant and a peacock, and the other pictures a beautiful standing peacock. Until Gene and Cathy Florence noticed the similarities between the two etchings, no one questioned the two names. This has been the subject of many debates between collectors and authors, but the answer lies right in the pages of Weatherman's *Book 2,* on page 304. In the lower left hand corner, there is an advertisement for Peacock and Rose that shows and lists many pieces. Illustrated in that 1928 advertisement are candlesticks, a footed candy, and a piece called a 3-part covered relish by Paden City but a 3-part covered candy by most collectors. All three of those pieces are easily recognized as the pieces we have called Nora Bird. The lists of pieces made, but not illustrated in that ad, included a mayonnaise set and a cream and sugar set. None of these illustrated pieces and neither of these listed sets exist in the full Peacock and Rose pattern.

This advertisement also makes it obvious that the pieces we have called Nora Bird and Peacock and Rose were introduced together as one pattern, not a year apart as several authors have stated. There are no small pieces of Peacock and Rose, no large pieces of Nora Bird. If we are to believe that these two etchings are separate and equal, we must also believe that Paden City made console bowls without candlesticks, candlesticks with no matching bowl, pitchers without tumblers, and tumblers with no pitcher. That both of these etchings are part of the same pattern becomes even more clear when you look at the 2-piece covered night set. The base is Peacock and Rose, but the top is Nora Bird. I know that separate etching plates exist for this pattern, but there will always be modified plates to be used for specific shapes. Paden City used many etchings that were redrawn to fit smaller pieces. Lela Bird is a great example of this.

When an etching is assigned a name by someone other than the glass company, understandable mistakes may be made, but those mistakes should be corrected as soon as possible. I am adding Nora Bird pieces to the Peacock and Rose listings, to honor Paden City's original intent. To avoid confusion, I'm marking the pieces previously called Nora Bird with an asterisk. This should help the collectors who have been mystified by the lack of plates, cups and saucers, cream and sugars, tumblers, or mayonnaise sets to match their sets. Please note that the #701 flat candy, only, has been found with both versions. I listed and priced the two vesions separately.

I was able to photograph some very rare pieces, but some items might not be as noticeable as others.

162

The #300 pitcher, the matching stem, and the night set easily qualify as rare. There is an Amber #191 Party Line 11" bowl that has been done in a reverse etching. The background is satinized, leaving the pattern shiny. Paden City rarely used this technique. There are several pieces that have a modified etching. The green-handled #701 plate has an insect in the etching, and the pink #300 cake plate has a larger design than is usual. Amber and crystal are hard to find, but Ruby and blue (light aqua) are very rare. Until I noticed the aforementoned 1928 advertise-ment, I only knew of two pieces in the blue color, the console bowl and the elliptical vase. I have listed all the pieces mentioned in that ad as having been made in blue, but that color has to be considered exceptionally rare. The prices are only a guess of what an advanced collector might be willing to pay. If you see a piece in blue, buy it; you may never have another chance. There are also pieces in a deep green that Paden City called Teal. Pieces in that color sell for about 50% higher than those in traditional green.

Amber #300 14" console bowl. $125.00 – 150.00.

Amber #300 mushroom candlestick. $35.00 – 50.00.

Description	Line	Size	Amber	Blue (Lt. Aqua)	Ebony	Pink/Green	Crystal
bowl, console	300	12"	$125-150	$350-450	$175-200	$150-175	$75-100
bowl, console	300	14""	$125-150		$175-200	$150-175	$75-100
bowl, console	701	12"	$120-150			$175-200	
bowl, fruit	701	11½"	$120-150			$175-200	
bowl, ftd. (comport)	300	10"		$600-650		$150-175	$75-100
bowl, handled	701	9"	$125-150			$150-225	
bowl, oval	300	8½"				$125-175	$45-65
bowl, salad	191	11"	$225-250				
bowl,* salad	191	11"	$250-275				
cake plate	300	9"		$500-550		$200-225	$65-95
candlestick,* mushroom	701		$65-85 ea.			$65-95 ea.	
candlestick,* mushroom	300	3"	$35-50 ea.	$100-125 ea.	$50-65 ea.	$45-65 ea.	$20-25 ea.
candy,* w/lid, high ftd.	300	7"		$500-600		$165-200	$65-95
candy,* flat	701	7"	$175-200			$225-325	
candy, flat	701	7"	$175-200			$225-325	
candy, flat	300	6½"		$450-550		$175-225	$55-75
cheese & cracker	300	10½"				$200-225	$65-95
cheese & cracker	701	11"	$175-200			$200-225	

Description	Line	Size	Amber	Blue (Lt. Aqua)	Ebony	Pink/Green	Crystal
comport,* high ftd.	412	6½"x7"				$125-150	
comport, high ftd.	300	8"		$450-550		$125-150	$45-65
comport,* low ftd.	215	7"x3½"				$75-100	$40-60
creamer*	300			$150-175		$30-35	$18-22
creamer*	701		$45-55			$30-35	
guest set	499	7⅜"				$1000-1200	
ice bucket	191	6¼"	$125-150			$175-250	
ice bucket	210	4"	$75-95		$125-150	$100-125	
ice bucket	300	4⅝"x6"		$500-600	$125-150	$100-125	$45-65
ice bucket	902	6"				$125-150	
mayonnaise*	300	6⅛"x3¼"				$75-100	$45-55
mayonnaise liner*	300	8¼"				$20-22	$18-20
mayonnaise set*	300			$350-550		$100-125	$65-75
pitcher	300	8½"				$1000-1500	
plate, cracker, w/o ridges	701	10"	$75-90			$100-125	
plate, cracker, w/ridges	701	10"	$75-90			$120-140	
plate, handled	701	11"	$100-125			$120-140	
plate,* luncheon	300	8½"				$45-65	$20-30
plate,* luncheon	701	8"	$65-85			$75-100	
rose bowl*	412	4½"					$45-60
sugar*	300			$125-150		$25-30	$15-18
sugar*	701		$40-50			$25-30	
syrup	11	5½" w/lid				$150-175	$100-125
tray*	210	10⅞"x4⅜"				$150-200	
tray, candy, loop handled	300	11"		$475-525		$125-150	$35-55
tray, loop handle	300	10½"		$450-500		$125-150	$35-55
tray, oval	300	10½"x7⅝"				$75-95	$25-35
tray, oval, center handled	700	12½"x9⅜"	$75-100				
tumbler *	2102	4"				$150-200	
tumbler*	2102	5⅜"				$100-150	
tumbler,* whiskey	2102	2¾"				$175-225	
vase	184	12"			$175-200		
vase	210	10"			$175-225	$150-200	
vase	210	6½"			$125-150		
vase *	184	10"			$150-200		
vase, cylinder	180	12"				$300-375	
vase, elliptical	182	5"			$175-225		
vase, elliptical	182	8"		400-450	$300-350	$275-325	
vase, fan	300	8½"				$550-750	
vase, fan	503	8½"				$550-750	

Colors, continued							
Description	Line	Size	Cobalt Blue	Ruby	Yellow	Red Inlay	
cheese & cracker	300	10"		$350-425			
cracker plate	300	10"		$300-375			
vase	184		$450-550		$425-500	$325-375	

Amber #701 mushroom candlestick. $65.00 – 85.00.

Amber #191 salad bowl. $225.00 – 250.00.

Amber #300 8" high-footed comport. $150.00 – 175.00.

Amber #191 6¼" ice bucket. $125.00 – 150.00.

Amber #701 12" console bowl.
$120.00 – 150.00.

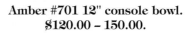

Amber #701 11" x 12¾" handled plate. $100.00 – 125.00.

Ebony #210 ice bucket. $125.00 – 150.00.

Ebony #182 8" elliptical vase. $300.00 – 350.00.

Ebony #184 10" vase with rare red-encrusted etching. $325.00 – 375.00.

Ebony #182 5½" elliptical vase. $175.00 – 225.00.

Ebony #210 6½" vase. $135.00 –150.00.

Green #300 tab-handled ice bucket.
$100.00 – 125.00.

Ebony #184 10" vase. $150.00 – 200.00.

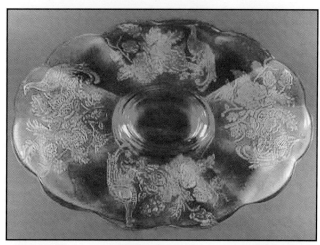

Green #300 10½" x 7⅝" oval tray.
$75.00 – 95.00.

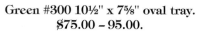

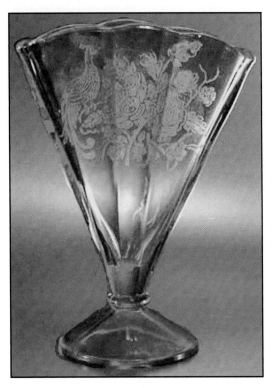

Green #300 8⅝" fan vase. $550.00 – 750.00.

Green #300 flat candy. $175.00 – 225.00.

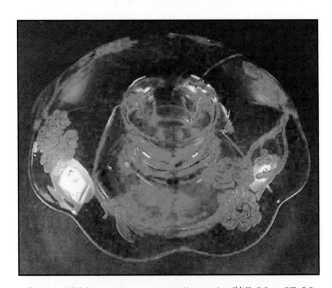

Green #300 mushroom candlestick. $45.00 – 65.00.

Green #300 12" console bowl. $150.00 – 175.00.

Green #300 mayonnaise set.
$100.00 – 125.00. Ladle, $35.00.

Green #184 10" vase. $150.00 – 200.00.

Green #701 sugar and creamer. $55.00 – 65.00.

Green #300 7" footed candy. $165.00 – 200.00.

Green #412 7" comport. $125.00 – 150.00.

Green #701 flat candy.
$225.00 – 325.00.

Green #184 12" vase. $175.00 – 225.00.

Green #300 oval bowl. $125.00 – 175.00.

Green #300 footed, flared bowl. $175.00 – 200.00.

Green #300 10" cracker plate. $100.00 – 125.00.

Green #300 14" salad bowl.
$150.00 – 175.00.

Green #300 11¼" low-footed cake plate. $200.00 – 225.00.

Green #300 cream and sugar. $55.00 – 65.00.

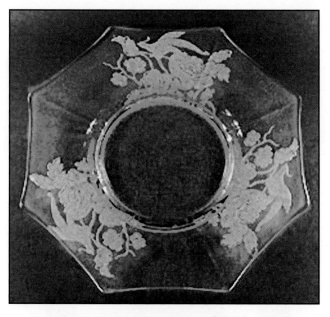

Green #701 8" luncheon plate. $50.00 – 75.00.

Green #300 8" comport. $125.00 – 150.00.

Green #701 handled plate, with full version of this etching. $120.00 – 140.00.

Close-up of pattern on green #701 plate.

Green #300 comport; comparison of height differences in mold.

Green #300 cheese and cracker. $200.00 – 225.00.

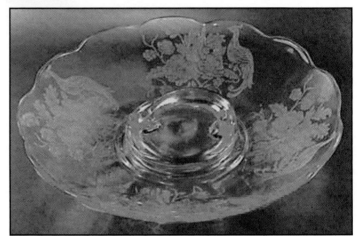

Green #300 loop-handled tray. $120.00 – 150.00.

Green #300 12" flared bowl. $150.00 – 175.00.

Teal #182 8" elliptical vase (rare). $400.00 – 450.00.

Green #2102 5⅜" tumbler.
$100.00 – 125.00.

Green #2102 2¾" whiskey.
$175.00 – 225.00.

Green #2102 2¾" whiskey, opposite side.
$175.00 – 225.00.

Cheriglo #182 8" elliptical vase. $275.00 – 325.00.

Cheriglo #300 footed candy. $165.00 – 200.00.

Cheriglo #300 8½" pitcher.
$1,000.00 – 1,500.00.

Cheriglo #300 6" stem, 6 oz.
$125.00 – 150.00.

Cheriglo #300 6" stem, different view.

Cheriglo #2102 5¼" tumbler.
$100.00 – 125.00.

Cheriglo #191 4" tumbler.
$100.00 – 125.00.

Cheriglo #191 4⅞" footed
soda, 6 oz. $75.00 – 100.00.

Cheriglo #300 oval bowl. $125.00 – 175.00.

Cheriglo #300 cheese and cracker. $200.00 – 225.00.

Cheriglo #300 10" cracker plate. $150.00 – 175.00.

Cheriglo #300 low-footed bowl. $175.00 – 200.00.

Cheriglo #300 12" console bowl.
$150.00 – 175.00.

Cheriglo #300 mushroom candlestick. $45.00 – 65.00.

Cheriglo #300 mayonnaise set. $100.00 – 125.00.

Cheriglo #300 tab-handled ice bucket. $100.00 – 125.00.

Cheriglo #300 10½" loop-handled server. $125.00 – 150.00.

Cheriglo #184 12" vase.
$175.00 – 225.00.

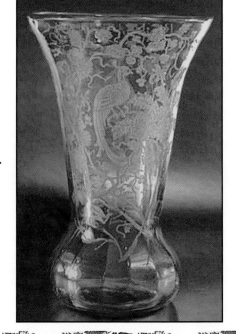

Cheriglo #70 12" bowl. $175.00 – 200.00.

Cheriglo #300 sugar and creamer. $55.00 – 65.00.

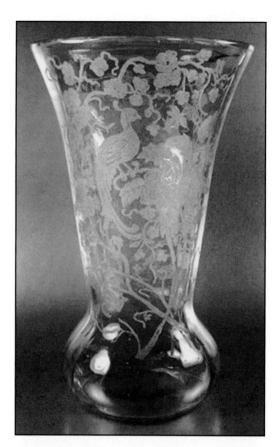

Cheriglo #184 10" vase. $150.00 – 200.00.

Cheriglo #300 rolled-edge footed bowl. $175.00 – 200.00.

Cheriglo #902 6" ice bucket.
$125.00 – 150.00.

Cheriglo #210 10" vase. $150.00 – 200.00.

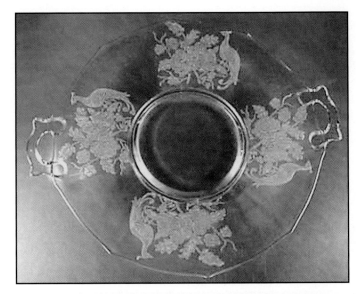

Cheriglo #701 11" handled plate. $120.00 – 140.00.

Cheriglo #701 cream and sugar. $55.00 – 65.00.

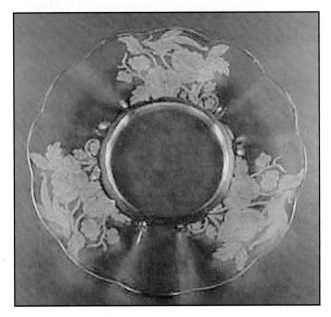

Cheriglo #300 8½" luncheon plate. $45.00 – 65.00.

Cheriglo #11 5" syrup.
$150.00 – 175.00 with
lid, $120.00 – 150.00
without lid.

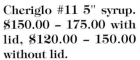

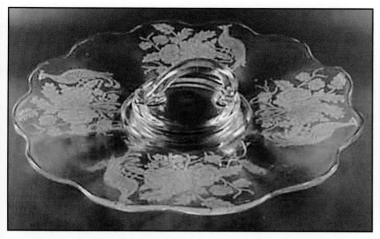

Pale Salmon #300 10½" loop-handled server (rare color).
$125.00 – 150.00.

Cheriglo #300 loop-handled bowl. $125.00 – 150.00.

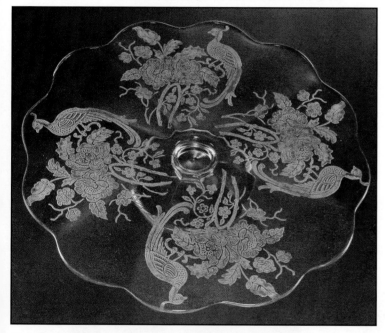

Cheriglo #300 low-footed cake plate with larger etching than
normal. $225.00 – 275.00.

Close-up of etching on #300 cake salver.

Cheriglo #499 guest set. $1,000.00 – 1,200.00.

Crystal #300 oval bowl. $45.00 – 65.00.

Crystal #300 14" rolled-edge console bowl. $75.00 – 100.00.

Crystal #300 mushroom candlestick. $20.00 – 25.00.

Crystal #300 8" high-footed comport. $65.00 – 85.00.

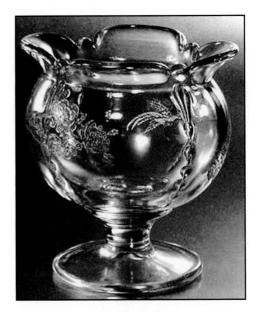

Crystal #412 4½" gold-encrusted rose bowl.
$45.00 – 60.00.

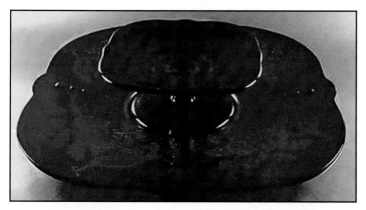

Ruby #300 cheese and cracker. $350.00 – 425.00.

Ruby #300 10" cracker. $325.00 – 400.00.

Ice Blue #182 8" elliptical vase.
$475.00 – 550.00.

Rose Bouquet

This etching consists of several long-stemmed open roses that are too large to appear on anything but a vase. The perfect Valentine's day gift would be one of the various Rose Bouquet vases filled with a dozen roses.

Paden City used its #184, #412 Crow's Foot, and #180 blanks for this large and showy etching. I've only seen crystal, green, Cheriglo, and Ebony pieces, but more colors probably exist.

Description	Line	Size	Crystal	Ebony	Cheriglo	Green
vase	180	10"			$600-650	
vase	184	10"		$300-400	$300-375	$350-400
vase	184	12"		$350-450	$350-450	
vase	412	12"	$300-350	$400-450	$425-525	
vase	2121	14"	$350-400			

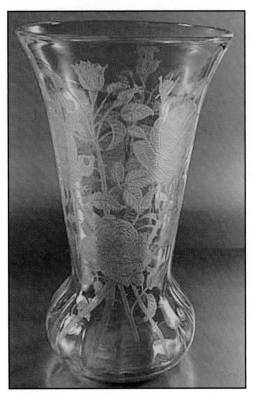

Green #184 10" vase. $300.00 – 375.00.

Cheriglo #184 10" vase. $300.00 – 375.00.

Rose with Jasmine

Paden City often used roses for the primary flower in its etchings. This pattern adds a flower that appears to be jasmine to the roses. It's a very simple pattern without many frills. It's been found on #191 Party Line, #330 Cavendish, #220 Largo, the very simple #118 candlestick, and has been reported in #412 Crow's Foot Square.

Description	Line	Size	Crystal
candlestick	118	2"	$18-25 ea.
candlestick	220	5⅛"	$40-55 ea.
candy, covered	330	7"	$125-150
vase, fan	191	7"	$50-75

Crystal #118 2" candlestick.
$18.00 – 25.00.

Crystal #191 7" fan vase. $50.00 – 75.00.

Sasha Bird

Paden City did love birds, and this is one of its best bird etchings. It's very similar to Delilah Bird, but it has an all-over pattern that leaves very little blank space. This etching is quite rare, and when a piece is offered for sale it is usually priced high.

Sasha Bird is found in crystal and yellow on #412 Crow's Foot Square blanks. Because there is a console bowl, I'm sure there are candlesticks, but without knowing for certain, I'm not yet listing them. Please let me know if you have seen or own a pair.

Description	Line	Size	Crystal	Yellow
bowl, console		12"	$175-200	$200-250
bowl, handled	412	10"	$125-150	$150-200
candy	412	6⅞"	$275-325	$350-450
comport, high ftd.	412	7"	$150-200	$175-225
creamer	412			
sugar	412			
tray, center handled	412	10¼"	$150-175	$175-225
tray, 2 handles	412	10½"	$150-175	$175-225

Primrose #412 high-footed comport. $175.00 – 225.00.

Primrose #412 10" handled bowl. $150.00 – 200.00.

Crystal #412 center-handled server with no fans on the edges.
$150.00 – 175.00.

Primrose #412 flat candy. $350.00 – 450.00.

Primrose #412 handled
plate. $175.00 – 225.00.

Sherry's Rose

As I said in the dedication, I am calling this rare and beautiful etching Sherry's Rose, in memory of Sherryl Ponti, a rare and beautiful person. Sherry's Rose is very similar to Rose Bouquet, but in this one there are rosebuds; in the other, the roses are open. Not only is the etching rare, the Ruby vase is one of only a few Gadroon vases that have been found. This vase was listed on eBay recently and brought a whopping $2,600. It is too soon to know if others will surface, but my guess is that they will and won't bring that price again for some time to come. I do think that the vase would sell for $1,200+, even if several surfaced.

Description	Line	Size	Ebony	Ruby
vase	184	10"	$600+	
vase	881	12"		$1200+

Ruby #881 12" vase. $1,200.00+.

Spring Orchard

This reverse etching is a busy pattern that includes daisies and swallows. It was used extensively on blanks from the #215 Glades pattern piece with this etching, but can be found on #890 Crow's Foot Round, #991 Penny Line, #211 Spire, #220 Largo, and a #184 vase. There are so many decanters in this pattern that I'm sure I missed a few. Most of the decanters are in the Glades pattern, but most of the stems sold with those decanters are Penny Line. Spring Orchard must have been very popular when it was introduced, because there is so much of it available. That is not to say that all pieces can be found easily. There are many pieces, like the Glades straight-sided vase, that must be considered rare. I've only seen one Popeye and Olive #994 piece with this etching, and I wasn't able to photograph it. As far as I've seen, almost every piece is crystal, but a very rare cigarette holder and matching ashtrays have been found in Ruby. Add 15% for pieces with gold inlay or for decanters with lettering such as "rye," "scotch," etc. Add 50% if found in ormolu.

Crystal #215 11" cocktail shaker.
$95.00.

Crystal #215 cocktail shaker with #991 cordials.
$175.00 – 195.00.

Description	Line	Size	Crystal	Ruby
ashtray			$45-60	
bowl, ftd. (comport)	890	5" x10"	$65-95	
bowl, handled	215	11"	$45-60	
candlestick	211	5"	$30-45 ea.	
candlestick, duo	215		$45-65 ea.	
candlestick, duo	220		$45-65 ea.	
candlestick, open center	895		$85 ea.	
candy box	215	7½"	$125-150	

Description	Line	Size	Crystal	Ruby
cheese & cracker, w/lid	215		$200-225	
cheese cracker, w/o lid	215		$125-150	
cigarette holder			$200-250	
cocktail, corset shaped	215	3⅜", 3 oz.	$50-70	
cocktail, ftd.	215	3½"	$45-55	
cocktail, high ftd.	215	4½"	$35-50	
cocktail shaker	215	11⅛"	$95	
comport, high ftd.	215	5⅝"	$75-95	
cordial	991	3¼", 1 oz.	$20-25	
creamer	895		$18-22	
decanter	215½	12 oz.	$25-30	
decanter	555	11¾"	$175-200	
decanter	994	10½"	$175-200	
decanter(etched on flat side)	215	9"	$60-75	
decanter, 4 lobes	211	10¼"	$85-100	
decanter, colonnade	215		$125-150	
decanter, horseshoe	211	9"	$45-55	
decanter, horseshoe, handled	211		$75-95	
ice tub	215	6½"x4"	$45-50	
plate	220	6½"	$20-25	
plate, handled	215	13"	$55-75	
relish, 2-part	215	7"	$65-85	
relish, 4-part	215	11¼"x9½"	$45-55	
sugar	895		$15-18	
tray, center handled	215	11½"	$120-135	
vase	184	10"	$150-175	
vase, straight sides	215	9"	$100-125	
vase, straight sides	215	12"	$125-150	
whiskey	215	1¾ oz.	$65-85	

Crystal #991 4" cordial, 2 oz.
$20.00 – 25.00.

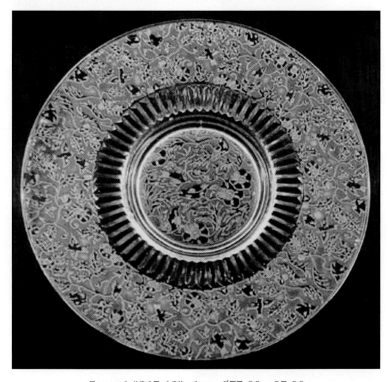

Crystal #215 12" plate. $75.00 – 95.00.

Crystal #215 9" decanter with flat sides.
$60.00 – 75.00.

Crystal #215 10¾" gold-encrusted decanter with matching cordials. $225.00 – 270.00.

Crystal #215 7¼" flat candy. $125.00 – 150.00.

Crystal #555 11¾" gold-encrusted decanter.
$250.00 – 300.00.

Crystal #215 11⅝" center-handled server.
$120.00 – 135.00.

Crystal #890 10" x 5" footed bowl with six medallions.
$65.00 – 95.00.

Crystal #220 6¾" plate. $20.00 – 25.00.

Crystal #184 10" vase. $150.00 – 175.00.

Crystal #215 flat tumber. $60.00 – 85.00.

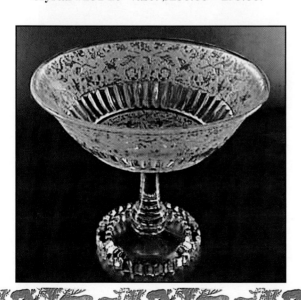

Crystal #215 high-footed comport.
$75.00 – 95.00.

Crystal #215 ice bucket. $45.00 – 50.00.

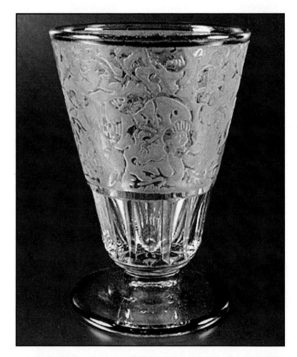

Crystal #215 double candlestick. $45.00 – 65.00.

Crystal #211 decanter set. $125.00 – 155.00.

Crystal #215 3½" whiskey, 4 oz. $45.00 – 55.00.

Crystal #215 3⅜" trumpet
cocktail, 3 oz. $50.00 – 75.00.

Crystal #215 cheese and cracker. $125.00 – 150.00.

Crystal #215 1¾ oz. whiskey. $60.00 – 85.00.

Crystal #215 covered cheese and cracker. $200.00 – 225.00.

Crystal #215 center-handled server with heavy gold encrusting. $150.00 – 165.00.

Crystal #215 4-part relish. $45.00 – 55.00.

Crystal 4½" stem. $35.00 – 50.00.

Spring Rose

Spring Rose is a delicate border etching that resembles Cosmos and was used in the same way, as a secondary as well as a primary pattern. It was not previously named, so I am giving it a name that is appropriate to its beauty. I'm only listing pieces I've seen, but I will welcome any additions you may have.

Description	Line	Size	Amber	Blue	Cheriglo
candy, high ftd.	503	9"	$45-55		
candy, low ftd.	503	7"			$45-55
candy, low ftd.	555	7"		$45-65	
comport, low ftd.	191	4"x8"			$22-35
vase, fan	502	8½"			$40-50

Cheriglo #191 8" comport, 4" tall. $22.00 – 35.00.

Close-up of pattern.

Cheriglo #503 7" footed candy. $45.00 – 55.00.

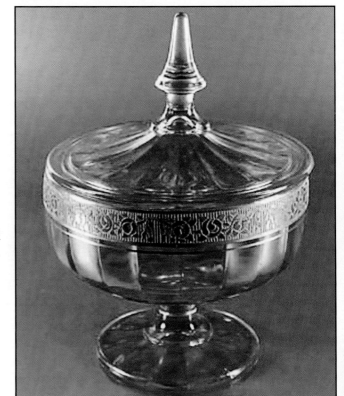

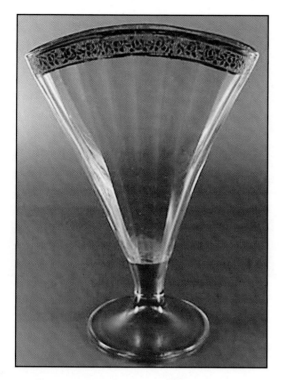

Cheriglo 8½" fan vase. $40.00 – 50.00.

Amber #503 9" footed candy. $45.00 – 55.00.

Tassel

Both Tassel and Art Nouveau Tassel are very simple but striking etchings. Tassel is usually found on #211 Spire pieces. Tassel is a plate etching that isn't heavily collected and is seldom recognized as Paden City, which is why it's not an expensive line. Pieces are found with or without a gold edge, but the price difference is insignificant.

Description	Line	Size	Crystal
bowl, console	211	12"	$35-45
candlestick	211	5"	$20-30 ea.
cream	211		$12-15
plate, center handled	211	11"	$35-45
plate, ftd.		12"	$35-45
sugar			$10-12

Crystal #211 sugar and creamer with Cosmos border. $22.00 – 27.00.

Crystal #211 12" footed plate. $35.00 – 45.00.

Crystal #211 11" center-handled server. $35.00 – 45.00.

Tassel, Art Nouveau

This is a great example of needle etching. This is probably the last pattern that would have been identified as Paden City. This etching is done on crystal, not colored glass, and is unlike any other done by Paden City.

Description	Size	Crystal
plate, bread & butter	6½"	$8–10
tumbler, thin, blown	3½"	$12-15

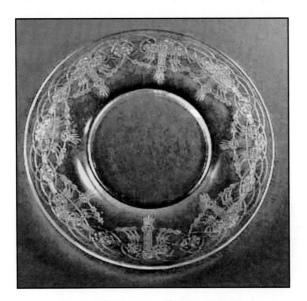

Crystal 6¼" plate. $8.00 – 10.00.

Crystal 3¾" 5 oz. thin, blown tumbler. $12.00 – 15.00.

Trumpet Flower/Trumpet Flower Bouquet

The Trumpet Flower etching is one of the most elusive and coveted designs. On the smaller pieces, the etching is a grouping of three trumpet-shaped flowers; on the large Gadroon vase, a whole bouquet of these flowers is used. Because of that difference, many use the name Trumpet Flower Bouquet to differentiate the two versions. Often, we tend to forget that Paden City was in the business of selling glass and had no reason to believe that people would someday be collecting that glass and would be confused by etchings that change according to the size of the piece. While we accept the differences in Lela Bird without changing the name of the etching, there has been a natural urge to give every other variation its own name. I'm going to resist that urge and list both versions as one etching. Trumpet Flower reaches the pinnacle of beauty when it's used on Ruby or Cobalt Blue. Those are also the most expensive pieces.

Take note of the Radiance decanter made by New Martinsville/Viking. It is most likely to have been made by Viking after Paden City closed its doors. This etching plate was bought by L. G. Wright, a sales agency that bought molds and etching plates so that it could have glass factories produce glassware to be sold under its company name. The Black Forest goblets are a good example of this company's work. Even though I'm certain that the decanter is a later non–Paden City product, I'm listing and pricing it here for information value. Add 25% for color inlay. Add 15% for pieces in ormolu. An Ebony Gadroon vase recently sold for $2,800, but that is unlikely to happen again if more vases surface.

Crystal #182 8" elliptical vase in ormolu holder.
$225.00 – 250.00.

Crystal #182 8" elliptical vase. $150.00 – 175.00.

Description	Line	Size	Crystal	Ebony	Pink/Yellow/ Green	Ruby/Blue
bowl, console	211	10"	$50-65			
bowl, ftd.	412	10"x4"	$100-150		$225-375	$350-450
cake salver, low ftd.	412	9½"x2"	$125-150		$175-250	$250-350
candy, flat	412		$75-100		$225-250	$250-300
celery dish	890	11½"	$75-90			
cheese & cracker set			$125-150		$200-300	$300-450
comport	211	6"	$60-80			
comport	412	7"	$65-75			$175-225
decanter, Radience		9"	$100-150			
hat, large		8½"x5"	$250-300			
jug, batter	11	8"	$125-150			
mayonnaise, 2-pc.	412				$175-200	$250-300
pitcher, milk	11	7"	$100-125			
plate, cracker	412	10"	$65-85		$75-100	$125-150
syrup	11	5¼"	$75-100			
vase	182	8"	$150-175			
vase	184	12"		$500-700+	$500-700+	$650-850+
vase	881	12"		$900-1200+		$900-1200+
vase, genie		8"		$150-200+	$175-225+	

Crystal 5" tall hat (large) with 8¼" brim. $250.00 – 300.00.

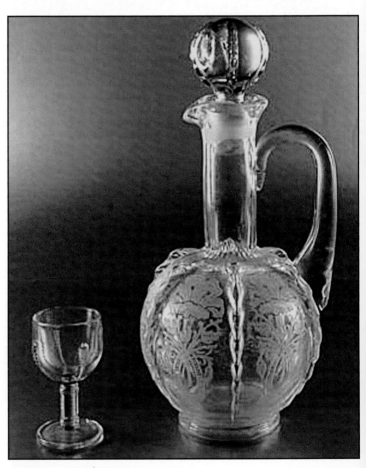

Crystal New Martinsville Radience decanter and cordial. These were probably made for L. G. Wright after Paden City closed. $100.00 – 150.00.

Crystal #11 7" milk pitcher. $100.00 – 125.00 with lid, $75.00 – 100.00 without lid.

Ruby #412 flat candy. $250.00 – 300.00.

Ruby #184 12" vase. $650.00 – 850.00.

Ruby #881 12" Gadroon vase. $900.00 – 1,200.00+.

Yellow #412 low-footed cake salver. $175.00 – 250.00.

Ruby #412 9¼" footed bowl. $350.00 – 450.00.

Royal Blue #184 12" vase. $650.00 – 850.00.

Ebony 8" genie vase. $150.00 – 200.00.

Royal Blue #184 12" vase with gold-encrusted design.
$850.00 – 1,100.00+.

Cheriglo #184 12" vase. $500.00 – 700.00+.

Utopia

Utopia and Gazebo are easily confused, because they are so alike that they may have been meant to be the same pattern. It's another case in which pieces with large, plain areas have the larger (Utopia) etching and pieces with less space have the smaller (Gazebo) etching. I doubt that Paden City gave much thought to the way it changed etchings to fit the glassware being made. With the absence of proof that they are one and the same, I'm listing these etchings the way most collectors have accepted as correct, but keep in mind that these two patterns combine beautifully. If you collect Gazebo and want a vase, you will find a good match in Utopia.

Utopia features a gazebo with a wreath of flowers surrounding it. It is always found on larger pieces or pieces that have a wide expanse of blank space, such as the large heart-shaped candy box. Most Utopia pieces are in crystal or Ebony; the other colors are very hard to find.

Add 15% for gold or other color inlays. Add 50% for ormolu holders. There are three shades of blue: Copen Blue, Light Cobalt, and Dark Cobalt. The Dark Cobolt shade is very rare.

Ebony 10¼"
Swanson vase.
$250.00 – 325.00.

Description	Line	Size	Crystal	Ebony	Cheriglo/Green	Copen Blue/ Lt. Cobalt Blue
candy, heart shaped	555	7½"x8½"	$120-150			$175-225
decanter, 3-part		12"	$150-175			
decanter, w/rooster		13⅛"	$225-250			
relish	555	10"	$100-125			
tray,* 5-part		12"	$100-150			
vase	182	8"	$125-150	$200-275	$600-800	
vase	184	10"	$75-125	$200-225	$300-350	$400-550
vase	184	12"	$100-150	$225-275	$350-450	$450-600
vase	411	9"	$175-275	$250-325		
vase, Swanson		10"	$175-275	$250-325		

*210 tray without the ridges, $400-500

Colors, continued					
Description	Line	Size	Yellow	Dark Cobalt Blue	Ruby
vase	184	10"	$350-400		
vase	184	12"	$400-500		$450-650
vase	411	9"		$800-1000	

Ebony #182 8¼" elliptical vase. $200.00 – 275.00.

Ebony #411 9" vase. $250.00 – 325.00.

Crystal 10¼" Swanson vase.
$175.00 – 275.00.

Crystal #411 9" vase. $175.00 – 275.00.

Crystal 3-part cocktail shaker.
$150.00 – 175.00.

Crystal #555 3-part relish. $100.00 – 125.00.

Crystal #184 10" vase with gold and Ebony
applied to etching. $95.00 – 150.00.

Crystal #555 heart-shaped candy. $120.00 – 150.00.

Crystal 10¼" Swanson vase in ormolu holder.
$250.00 – 350.00.

Light Cobalt #184 10" vase. $400.00 – 550.00.

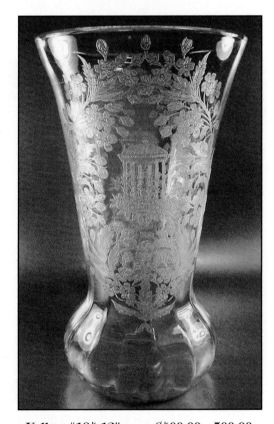

Yellow #184 12" vase. $400.00 – 500.00.

Zinnia & Butterfly

This is a very attractive design that features beautiful large zinnia and butterflies. I suspect that this may not be a Paden City etching. There have been a few pieces found that are on blanks not usually associated with Paden City. Of course, new discoveries are the rule and not the exception with this company. Still, without confirmation that those pieces were made by Paden City, I'm only listing those items that we know were.

Description	Line	Size	Cheriglo/Green
vase	184	12"	$175-225
vase	300	8"	$125-150
vase, cylinder	180	12"	$225-250

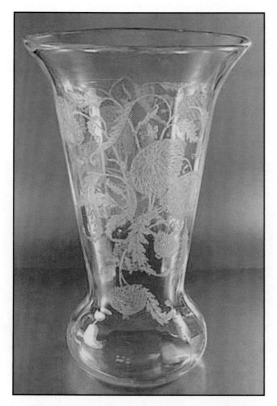

Green #184 12" vase. $125.00 – 150.00.

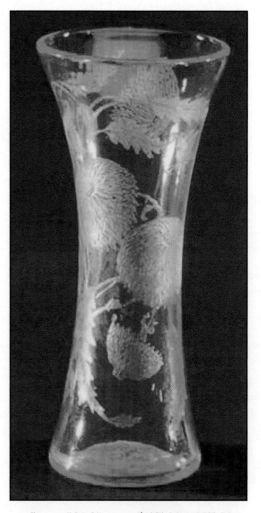

Green #61 8" vase. $175.00 – 225.00.

Miscellaneous Etchings

Wheeling Decorating Co. Doves, Roses, and Daisies

This etching is an all-over brocade that resembles Spring Orchard. It has been found on the #412 candy box, the only piece with this etching I have seen, but there are probably other pieces with this pattern.

Royal Blue #412 gold-encrusted flat candy. $250.00 – 300.00.

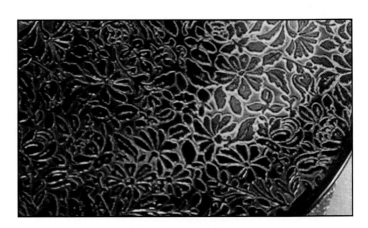

Close-up of etching.

Description	Line	Size	Cobalt Blue	Ebony
candy, flat	412	6"	$125-150	$125-150

Pinwheel Flower

I'm taking the liberty of naming this etching Pinwheel flower.

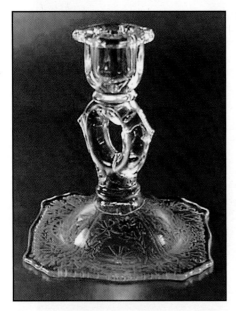

Crystal #411 5" keyhole candlestick. $50.00 – 75.00.

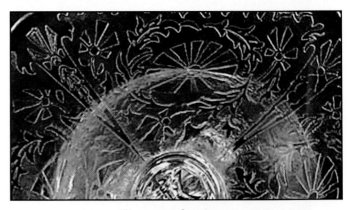

Close-up of etching.

Description	Line	Size	Crystal
candlestick, keyhole	411	5"	$45-50 ea.
candy, cloverleaf	412		$75-100

Daffodil

This is one of Paden City's etchings that is not well known, because only a few pieces have surfaced. The design is so shallow that it looks more like a silk screen than an etching.

Description	Line	Size	Crystal
candlestick, duo	220	5¼"	$35-45 ea.
candy, heart shaped	555	7½"x8½"	$75-85
platter, handled	555	12"	$50-65
relish	1504	11½"x7"	$50-65

Crystal #555 heart-shaped candy.
$75.00 – 95.00.

Banks Retriever

I have no information about this etching except that it is signed "Banks" and is found on several Paden City blanks.

Description	Line	Size	Crystal
cocktail shaker,			
w/rooster top	903		$500-600
tumbler, whiskey	2003	2 oz.	$100-150

Crystal 2 oz. shot glass. $75.00 – 95.00.

Banks signature on crystal shot glass.

Flamingo Sun

Flamingo Sun is another etching done by the Lotus Decorating Company. It's a very flamboyant etching, especially when Ebony glass is used. This design is seen on #210 Regina pieces, but is so scarce that I am sure there are pieces with it I am not aware of.

Ebony #210 creamer, front view. $35.00 – 40.00.

Ebony #210 creamer, side view.

Description	Line	Size	Ebony	Cheriglo
candlestick, mushroom	210	2½"	$45-65 ea.	$35-55 ea.
creamer	210		$40-45	$35-40
sugar	210		$38-42	$33-38

Golden Fruit

The gold inlay makes this a very attractive etching, but there is no attribution for it. It seems to be a later design.

Crystal #555 (fill in) candlestick.
$25.00 – 35.00.

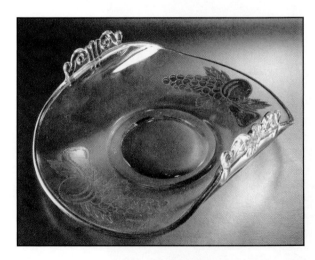

#1503½ 5½" plate with turned-up sides. $18.00 – 22.00.

Rambler Rose

Crystal #700 12" service plate. $50.00 – 65.00.

Cheriglo #701 candy jar. $65.00 – 85.00.

Description	Line	Size	Crystal
candlestick (fill in)	555	5"	$25-30 ea.
plate, lemon	1503	5½"	$18-22
server, goose handled	1504		$100-125

Close-up of Rambler Rose etching.

Archaic #300

Archaic is one of the blanks that Paden City used for almost every one of its etchings. The soft and curving lines add a touch of elegance to etchings like Peacock & Rose, Cupid, Orchid, Ardith, and Lela Bird. Several #300 pieces were modified by adding a series of indented circles to every other scallop. Add 20% for decorated pieces. A few items have been found in Ebony, but they are rare. Add 50% to the price of Aqua if you find an Ebony item.

Green 14" console bowl. $80.00 – 100.00.

Cheriglo covered butter dish. $80.00 – 100.00.

Aqua 14" console bowl. $100.00 – 115.00.

Aqua mushroom candlestick. $25.00 – 28.00.

Description	Size	Crystal	Amber/Yellow	Cheriglo/Green	Aqua
bowl, center handled	11"	$40-65	$60-80	$80-100	$100-120
bowl, console	12"	$35-45	$40-55	$65-85	$75-95
bowl, console	14"	$45-65	$60-80	$80-100	$100-115
bowl, melon	8½	$45-65	$60-80	$80-100	$100-115
bowl, oval salad	9"	$35-50	$40-55	$65-85	$75-95
butter tub	5"	$50-65	$65-95	$80-100	$100-125
cake plate, high ftd.	9"	$40-55	$65-85	$80-100	$100-125
cake plate, low ftd.	10"	$40-55	$65-85	$80-100	$100-125
candlestick, mushroom	3"	$15-18 ea.	$20-22 ea.	$22-25 ea.	$25-28 ea.
candy, flat	6½"	$25-40	$40-60	$55-85	$100-120
candy, low ftd.	6"	$30-45	$50-65	$65-95	$100-120
cheese & cracker	10½"	$50-75	$60-85	$75-100	$120-140
comport, high ftd.	8"	$35-50	$50-65	$65-75	$75-95
comport, low ftd.	10"	$50-75	$60-80	$70-90	$100-125
creamer	5 oz.	$10-12	$12-15	$15-18	$18-20
creamer	7 oz.	$12-14	$15-18	$18-22	$22-25
cup		$25-30	$30-40	$40-60	$50-75
goblet	8 oz.	$25-30	$30-40	$40-60	$50-75
ice tub	6"	$35-50	$50-65	$65-85	$75-95
lemon dish, handled	6"x7"	$12-15	$15-25	$20-40	$30-45
mayonnaise (flared sugar)	3"	$20-24	$24-28	$30-40	$40-60
mayonnaise set		$50-65	$65-85	$80-95	$75-100
plate	8½"	$15-20	$20-25	$25-30	$30-40
plate	11"	$35-45	$45-65	$65-85	$100-115
plate, oyster	10½"	$65-85	$75-100	$100-125	$120-140
saucer		$8-10	$10-14	$14-16	$15-18
server, loop handle	11"	$40-65	$60-75	$75-95	$100-115
sherbet, low ftd.	5 oz.	$10-12	$12-15	$15-18	$18-22
sugar	5 oz.	$10-12	$12-15	$15-18	$18-20
sugar	7 oz.	$12-14	$15-18	$18-22	$22-25
vase, bud	9"	$25-40	$35-50	$45-55	$50-60
vase, fan	8½"	$35-45	$50-75	$65-85	$75-95
vase	8"	$20-22	$25-30	$30-40	$40-50

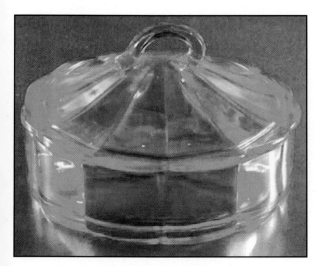

Green flat candy dish. $55.00 – 85.00.

Amber 14" console bowl. $60.00 – 80.00.

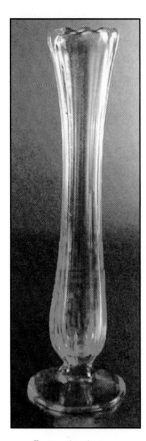

Cheriglo mushroom candlestick. $22.00 – 25.00.

Yellow footed candy base. $35.00 – 40.00.

Green bud vase.
$45.00 – 55.00.

Cheriglo handled mayonnaise from sugar bowl mold. $30.00 – 40.00.

Cheriglo 12" console bowl. $65.00 – 85.00.

Green handled mayonnaise from sugar bowl mold.
$30.00 – 40.00.

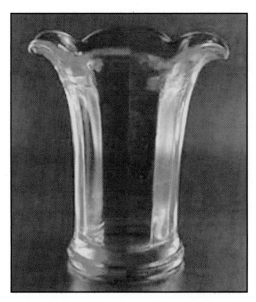

Green 8" vase. $30.00 – 40.00.

Green 3-piece mayonnaise. $80.00 – 95.00.

Green 8" comport. $65.00 – 75.00.

Green 6" x 7" lemon dish.
$20.00 – 35.00.

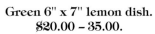

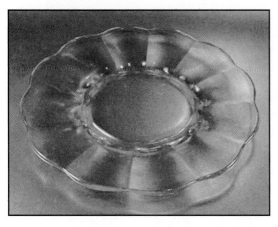

Green 8½" luncheon plate. $25.00 – 30.00.

Green 8½" melon bowl. $80.00 – 100.00.

Yellow 8" comport with circle in alternating panels.
$75.00 – 100.00.

Top view of yellow 8" comport. $75.00 – 100.00.

Cheriglo loop-handled server
with cutting. $90.00 – 115.00.

Cavendish #330

This is one of the few patterns that has a documented original name. Cavendish is a simple design that has a certain understated beauty that fits with almost any decor. Unfortunately, it isn't one of the more common patterns, possibly because it was a late pattern made shortly before Paden City closed its doors. It was made in a very good crystal, Ruby, and Mulberry. The single candlestick with a heart shape to the stem has been reproduced in Ruby, but the color is very poor, nothing like Paden City's Ruby. The tidbit bowls were used for the Emerald Glo line sold to the Rubel Company. Add 40% to pieces found with ormolu frames.

Ruby covered cheese and cracker. $100.00 – 125.00.

Ruby cup and saucer. $30.00 – 40.00.

Ruby 7" covered candy in ormolu holder. $100.00 – 125.00.

Ruby 7" covered candy. $60.00 – 80.00.

Ruby double candlestick. $75.00 – 90.00.

Mulberry 9¼" plate. $30.00 – 45.00.

Description	Size	Crystal	Mulberry/ Dark Green	Ruby
bowl	6"	$8-10	$18-20	$20-24
bowl, berry	9½"	$10-12	$20-24	$24-28
bowl, console	12"	$24-28	$30-35	$35-40
bowl, ftd., console	11"	$24-28	$30-35	$35-40
bowl, flared	12"	$24-28	$30-35	$35-40
bowl, handled	6"	$8-10	$18-20	$20-24
bowl, handled	9"	$10-12	$20-22	$24-28
bowl, handled, divided	6"	$10-14	$22-26	$25-30
bowl, 2 handles	11"	$18-24	$30-35	$35-40
bowl, salad	10½"	$18-24	$30-35	$35-40
bowl, shallow	10"	$18-24	$30-35	$35-40
cake plate	12"	$40-45	$65-85	$75-125
candlestick	6½"	$20-25 ea.	$45-65 ea.	$50-65 ea.
candlestick, duo		$35-45 ea.	$50-65 ea.	$75-90 ea.
candy, covered	7½"	$35-40	$50-65	$60-80
cheese & cracker, covered	10½"	$40-45	$75-100	$100-125
comport, cheese	5½"	$10-12	$15-18	$18-20
comport, high ftd.	7"	$12-15	$20-24	$24-28
cup		$8-10	$12-16	$15-20
ice tub		$20-25	$35-50	$50-70
mayonnaise bowl	4"	$10-12	$15-20	$20-25
plate, cupped edge	12"	$15-22	$35-50	$45-60
plate, dinner	9¼"	$15-22	$30-45	$35-40
plate, flat or crimped	6"	$8-10	$10-14	$14-18
plate, flat or crimped	8"	$12-15	$14-18	$18-22
plate, flat or crimped	12"	$15-22	$35-50	$45-60
plate, ftd.	13½"	$18-22	$40-45	$50-75
plate, handled	13"	$18-22	$40-45	$50-75
relish, 3-part	7"	$18-24	$45-50	$50-75
saucer		$8-10	$12-15	$15-20
server, center handled	10"	$20-25	$45-65	$65-95
tidbit bowl, center hole	6"	$8-10	$12-15	$15-18
tidbit bowl, center hole	8¼"	$12-15	$15-18	$18-24
tidbit bowl, center hole	9"	$15-18	$18-24	$24-35
tray, 2 handles	11"	$20-22	$25-35	$35-45

Chevalier #90

Chevalier is a beautiful pattern, but I was unable to find it in any piece other than a sherbet. That piece will help you identify this pattern, and I will list items I know were made. The colors Chevalier was made in are crystal, Amber, and Copen Blue.

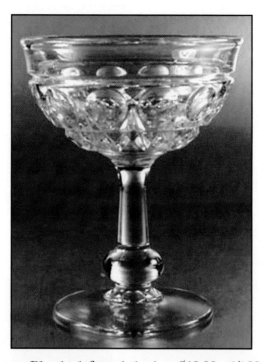

Copen Blue high-footed sherbet. $12.00 – 14.00.

Description	Size	Crystal	Amber	Blue
bowl	4½"x8"	$12-15	$18-20	$22-25
champagne	3½ oz.	$10-12	$12-14	$14-16
claret	3½ oz.	$10-12	$12-14	$14-16
cocktail	3 oz.	$10-12	$12-14	$14-16
cordial	1¾ oz.	$18-22	$22-26	$25-30
cream	6 oz.	$8-10	$10-12	$12-14
decanter, cordial	4¾"	$30-40	$35-50	$45-60
decanter, sq.	24 oz.	$25-30	$30-45	$40-55
decanter, rd.	24 oz.	$25-30	$30-45	$40-55
goblet	6¼", 10 oz.	$12-15	$14-16	$14-18
ice tea	5⅝", 12 oz.	$12-14	$13-15	$15-18
jug, ice lip	44 oz.	$45-65	$65-75	$75-90
plate	6"	$6-8	$8-10	$10-12
plate	8"	$9-10	$10-12	$12-15
plate	11"	$15-18	$18-20	$25-35
sherbet	3", 4 oz.	$8-10	$10-12	$12-14
sugar	6 oz.	$8-10	$10-12	$12-14
tumbler	3⅜", 5 oz.	$8-10	$12-16	$15-18
tumbler	3⅞", 9 oz.	$10-12	$14-16	$16-20
tumbler	4¹³⁄₁₆", 12 oz.	$12-14	$15-17	$18-22
whiskey	2 oz.	$18-20	$20-22	$24-28
wine	2½ oz.	$12-14	$15-17	$18-22

Comet

Comet is a later pattern that is very attractive. It looks a little like a comet with a tail or like a comma. It was made in Ruby, Light Ice Blue, and crystal. The #900 candlestick also appears to have been used for the Comet line. It wasn't unusual for a glass factory to make a double-duty candlestick.

Aqua creamer. $20.00 – 24.00.

Aqua 11" center-handled server. $65.00 – 85.00.

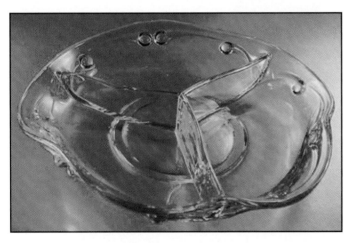

Aqua 8⅛" crimped 3-part relish. $28.00 – 32.00.

Aqua 7" 3-part candy. $50.00 – 75.00.

Crystal/Ruby 7" 3-part candy. $50.00 – 75.00.

Description	Size	Aqua	Crystal	Ruby
bowl	4¾"	$20-24	$10-15	$24-28
bowl	5"	$20-24	$10-15	$24-28
bowl, flared	5½"	$20-24	$10-15	$24-28
bowl, shallow	6"	$20-24	$10-15	$24-28
candy, flat	7"	$50-75	$25-45	$65-85
creamer		$20-24	$12-18	$22-26
relish, 3-part	8⅛"	$28-32	$14-18	$30-34
server, center handle	11"	$65-85	$35-45	$75-95
sugar		$20-24	$12-18	$22-26

Crow's Foot Round #890 and Square #412

Although both Crow's Foot Square #412 and Crow's Foot Round #890 are usually listed as one patten, they are distinctly different; one is round and one is square. Because Paden City obviously meant them to be different patterns, I decided to list them that way. Most collections include examples of both styles, however, and I don't want to discourage that practice.

While it would seem easy to tell the square and the round patterns apart, it is more complicated than that. The general rule is that #412, Crow's Foot Square, always has four fans, with darts under each of them. Crow's Foot Round, #890, always has six fans, three of which have the darts below them. There are also exceptions to those rules. The cloverleaf candy only has three fans with three darts, but it belongs to the #412 pattern. If you look closely, you will see that the finial on the lid is in the same style as the handles on the #412 cups and bowls. The cups are also difficult to identify, because of course, they are all round. Both cups have four fans with darts, but on the #412 cups, the handle is spaced evenly between two of the fans. On the #890 cup, the handle is directly over one of the fans. The #890 cream and sugar are very difficult to recognize. They have four lobes, each with an upside down fan at the base of that lobe. The creamer has a fan for its spout.

To make it even more confusing, both #412 and #890 patterns have variants within each pattern. Instead of the usual 5-part fans, some pieces only have a 3-part fan. To see more differences, look at the fans. In the round version, the fans extend to the edge of the piece and actually add to the shape of the piece. The fans on the square version come close to the edge but don't touch, leaving the shape the same as it would be without them. Vases have traditionally been listed as #890, but because they have all the characteristics of the #412 line, I'm listing them as such. I don't think we will ever be certain which numbers Paden City used for these pieces.

Lucy #895 is a variant of #890, and the two patterns are sometimes combined in one piece. The #895 comport has a 3-part fan on the stem, and several #890 candy lids have been found on #895 bases. I've listed this comport under Lucy #895. Because I don't believe that the base would make a difference to a Crow's Foot collector, the value of the candy found with the Lucy base remains the same as it would be with the #890 base.

While these patterns came in most of Paden City's colors, I've never seen them in Neptune Blue (dark aqua), Copen Blue (light blue), or Ice Blue (light aqua). Both patterns were decorated by Paden City and by other decorating firms who bought these blanks. Opal pieces have been found in both square and round patterns, and in the case of the 2-tier server shown here, the two were combined. When decorated, the Opal pieces are as beautiful as the Ruby or the Cobalt Blue and sell for very high prices.

Pattern detail of Crow's Foot Round #890.

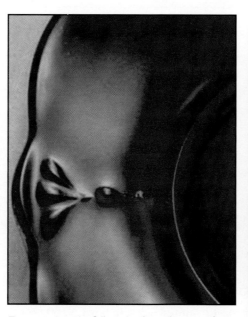

Pattern detail of Crow's Foot Square #412.

Pattern detail of Crow's Foot Square #412.

Crow's Foot Round #890

Description	Size	Amber	Amethyst	Cheriglo/Green	Crystal	Ebony	Royal Blue/Ruby
bowl	2½"x6½"	$20-35	$35-45	$30-40	$20-25	$75-85	$75-85
bowl, ftd.	7 ¼" x2½"	$20-35	$35-45	$30-40	$20-25	$75-85	$75-85
bowl, ftd., flared	12"	$75-125	$125-150	$100-125	$50-75	$150-200	$175-200
bowl, handled	11½"x9½"x3"	$40-50	$60-80	$50-70	$30-40	$75-95	$75-95
bowl, nasturtium	8"x6"	$125-150	$175-200	$150-175	$75-95	$225-275	$250-275
cake plate	12¼"x2½"	$125-150	$175-200	$150-175	$75-95	$225-275	$250-275
candlestick	6¾"	$45-55 ea.	$75-95 ea.	$65-85 ea.	$35-45 ea.		$100-125 ea.
candlestick, 3-light	8¼"x6"	$45-55 ea.	$75-95 ea.	$65-85 ea.	$35-45 ea.		$100-125 ea.
candy, covered	5¾"x5¾"	$65-85	$150-175	$125-175	$50-75		$175-225
celery tray	11¾"x5"	$35-$50	$65-85	$50-65	$25-40		$75-95
comport, cheese	2⅞"x5⅛"	$18-22	$25-35	$22-30	$15-$20		$40-60
comport, high ftd.	6¾"x7"	$30-45	$50-75	$50-75	$40-50		$75-95
comport, low ftd.		$25-40	$45-65	$40-55	$30-40		$65-75
creamer		$18-22	$25-35	$22-30	$15-$20		$40-60
cup		$20-25	$55-65	$25-40	$18-22		$40-50
cup, punch (roly poly)		$10-12					$15-20
eggcup		$35-45	$45-65	$45-60	$25-35		$60-75
gravy, flat		$25-35	$45-55	$40-55	$24-32		$55-75
mayonnaise, ftd.	4"x3⅝"	$60-75	$100-125	$75-90	$50-65		$125-150
plate, bread & butter	6"	$8-10	$16-22	$12-16	$8-10		$20-25
plate, cracker	11"	$45-65	$75-100	$55-75	$30-45		$100-120
plate, dinner	9¼"	$35-45	$50-65	$40-55	$25-35		$60-75
plate, handled	13"x11½"	$35-45	$75-100	$65-85	$25-35		$100-120
plate, luncheon	8"	$30-40	$40-50	$35-50	$18-22		$40-45
punch bowl	8¾"						$700-950
saucer	6"	$8-$10	$12-15	$10-12	$6-8		
sugar		$18-22	$25-35	$22-30	$15-20		$40-60
tumbler	4¼"	$50-65	$65-85	$60-80	$45-50		$75-100

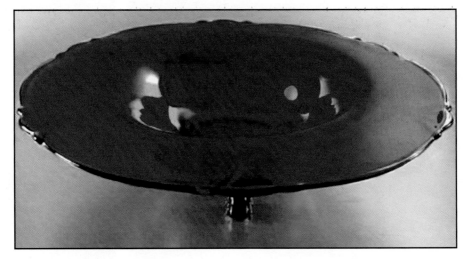

Royal Blue 12" footed console bowl. $150.00 – 200.00.

Royal Blue 7¼" x 2⅝" rolled-edge bowl. $75.00 – 85.00.

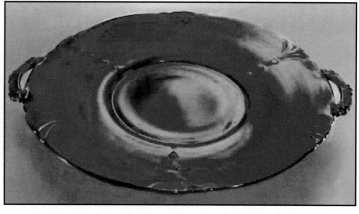

Royal Blue 12" x 11½" handled plate. $100.00 – 120.00.

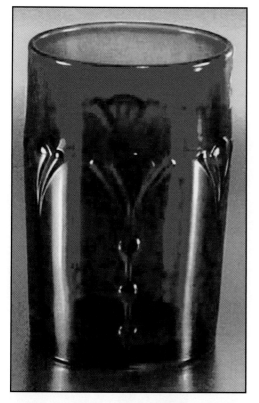

Royal Blue 4¼" tumbler. $75.00 – 100.00.

Royal Blue 8¾" punch bowl, $700.00 – 950.00, and 2¼" roly poly punch cup, $15.00 – 20.00.

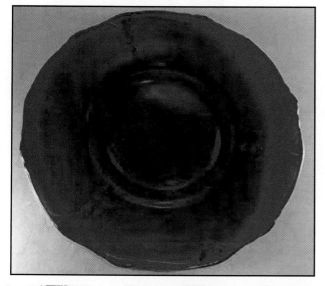

Royal Blue 9¼" dinner plate.
$60.00 – 75.00.

Green 11¾" x 5" celery tray. $50.00 – 65.00.

Crystal cheese comport with a silver edge.
$15.00 – 20.00.

Crystal 3-part covered candy. $50.00 – 75.00.

Crystal triple candlestick. $35.00 – 45.00.

Detail on crystal triple candlestick.

Ruby 12¼" x 2½" low-footed cake salver. $250.00 – 275.00.

Ruby 7" high-footed comport. $75.00 – 95.00.

Ruby 9¼" dinner plate. $60.00 – 75.00.

Ruby footed candy dish.
$175.00 – 225.00.

Ruby 6" plate. $20.00 – 25.00.

Ruby 6½" bowl. $75.00 – 85.00.

Ruby 6¾" footed, flared bowl. $75.00 – 85.00.

Ruby 7" bowl. $75.00 – 85.00.

Ruby 12" console bowl, $150.00 – 200.00, and triple candlesticks, $200.00 – 250.00 (set).

Ruby 11½" x 9½" handled bowl. $75.00 – 95.00.

Ruby 4¼" tumbler. $75.00 – 100.00.

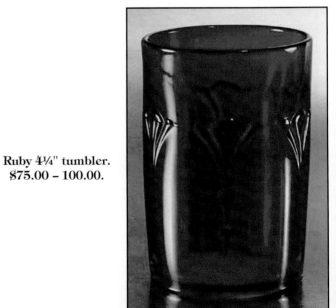

Ruby cup and saucer. $52.00 – 65.00.

Ruby cheese comport. $40.00 – 60.00.

Ruby mayonnaise set. $125.00 – 150.00.

Ruby 7" low-footed comport. $65.00 – 75.00.

Ruby low-footed oval comport/gravy. $65.00 – 75.00.

Ruby center-handled server. $150.00 – 175.00.

Ruby punch set. $700.00 – 950.00. Cups, $15.00 – 20.00 each.

Ruby triple candlestick. $100.00 – 125.00.

Mulberry cup and saucer. $55.00 – 65.00.

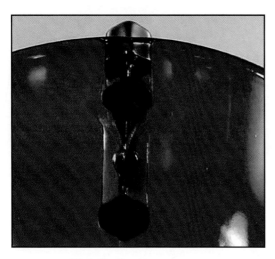

Detail of pattern on cup.

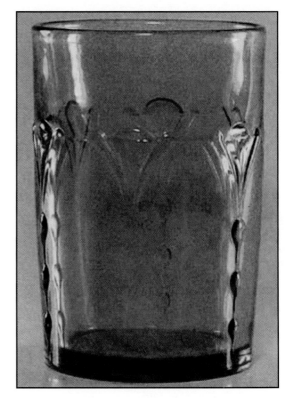

Amber 4¼" tumbler. $50.00 – 65.00.

Amber footed mayonnaise and spoon. $45.00 – 60.00. Spoon, $10.00 – 15.00.

Amber 7¾" x 5½" nasturtium bowl. $125.00 – 150.00.

Cheriglo candy with a #503 base. $125.00 – 175.00.

Crow's Foot Square #412

Royal Blue 10" flared vase. $200.00 – 225.00.

Royal Blue 9½" low-footed cake salver. $125.00 – 150.00.

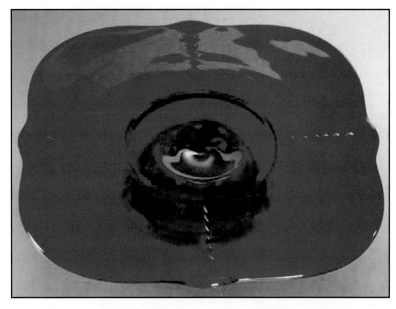

Top view of Royal Blue cake salver. $125.00 – 150.00.

Royal Blue sugar and creamer. $50.00 – 75.00.

Description	Size	Amber/ Yellow	Mulberry/ Dark Green	Cheriglo/ Green	Crystal	Royal Blue/ Ruby	Ebony	Opal
bowl	6¾"x2¼"	$25-35	$35-45	$30-40	$22-26	$40-55	$40-50	$40-50
bowl, dessert	5"	$15-18	$25-30	$18-22	$12-15	$25-30	$25-28	$25-28
bowl, divided oval	7¼"x9¼"	$35-50	$50-65	$45-55	$25-35	$75-100	$65-90	
bowl, flared or rolled edge	12"	$45-55	$75-95	$65-85	$35-45	$100-120	$125-159	$125-150
bowl, ftd. (lg. comport)	10"x4"	$125-150	$175-200	$150-175	$65-85	$200-250		
bowl, ftd., oval (comport)	10¾"	$125-150	$175-200	$150-175	$65-85	$200-250		
bowl, handled	11½" x 9½"x3¾"	$100-120	$145-165	$125-150	$65-95	$150-175	$135-165	
bowl, vegetable, oval	9½"	$30-45	$50-65	$45-55	$25-35	$75-100		
cake plate	8½"x4½"	$75-100	$100-125	$95-115	$50-75	$125-150		$125-150
cake plate	9½"x2"	$75-100	$100-125	$95-115	$50-75	$125-150		$125-150
candlestick, keyhole	5"	$25-40 ea.	$65-85 ea.	$50-70 ea.	$18-22ea.	$65-85 ea.	$45-65 ea.	$34-$50 ea.
candlestick, mushroom	4½"x2½"	$20-22 ea.	$40-45 ea.	$30-35 ea.	$18-20ea.	$18-22 ea.		
candlestick, rolled-up edge		$25-28 ea.	$42-48 ea.	$32-38 ea.	$20-25ea.	$20-25 ea.		
candy, #412½	6¾"	$65-85	$100-125	$75-90	$50-65	$120-140	$125-150	$125-145
candy, sq., flat	6⅞"x2"	$65-85	$100-125	$75-90	$50-65	$120-140	$125-150	$125-145
comport, cheese	5"x2"	$18-22	$22-25	$20-22	$8-12	$35-50		$30-40
comport, cupped	7" x6½"	$25-35	$50-65	$30-40	$20-24	$45-65		$65-$80
comport, low ftd.	6½"x3¾"	$25-35	$50-65	$30-40	$20-24	$75-95		$45-$60
comport, low, oval	7½"x4¼"	$25-35	$50-65	$30-40	$20-24	$75-95		$45-$60
comport, tall	7"x6½"	$35-50	$75-100	$65-85	$30-35	$85-115		
cracker plate	10"	$35-50	$75-100	$65-85	$30-35	$85-115		$45-$60
cream		$12-16	$20-30	$18-24	$10-12	$25-35		$20-$22
cream soup	6¼"x2¼" .	$18-24	$25-32	$24-28	$15-18	$45-65		
cream soup liner	6"	$8-10	$10-15	$8-12	$6-8	$12-18		
cup		$20-25	$25-35	$24-26	$18-20	$35-40		
gravy boat	7½"x5"x2½"	$50-75	$100-120	$75-100	$20-30	$125-150		
gravy boat, ftd.	7½"x5¼"x4⅜"	$50-75	$100-120	$75-100	$20-30	$125-150		
mayonnaise set, 2-pc.		$50-75	$100-120	$75-100	$20-30	$125-150		$75-$95
plate	6"	$12-15	$15-18	$12-15	$10-12	$20-30		
plate, handled	14"x11¼"	$45-50	$75-95	$60-75	$25-35	$80-100		$45-$60
plate, luncheon	8¾"	$15-18	$18-22	$15-18	$12-15	$20-25		
platter, oval	11"x8½"	$25-35	$45-65	$35-50	$20-25	$50-75		
sandwich server, center handled	10¼"	$50-75	$75-95	$60-75	$40-50	$150-175		$75-100
saucer	6"	$12-15	$15-18	$12-15	$10-12	$20-25		
sugar		$12-16	$30	$18-24	$10-12	$25-35	$25-45	$18-$22
tidbit,* 2-part	8¼" top, 11" base	$45-65	$75-100	$65-85	$35-50	$75-100		$100-125
vase	8"	$75-100		$150-175	$65-85	$175-200	$200-225	
vase	10"	$100-125		$175-200	$75-95	$200-225	$225-275	
vase	12"	$150-175	$250-300	$200-250	$75-100	$300-350	$350-400	

* base is #890

Royal Blue keyhole candlestick. $65.00 – 85.00.

Royal Blue 6¾" x 2¼" bowl. $40.00 – 55.00.

Royal Blue 7½" low-footed comport/gravy. $125.00 – 150.00.

Royal Blue flat, oval gravy. $125.00 – 150.00.

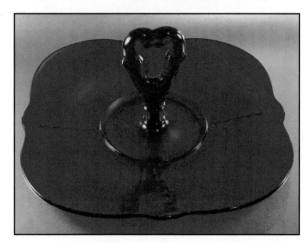

Royal Blue 10¼" center-handled server. $150.00 – 175.00.

Royal Blue mushroom candlestick. $18.00 – 22.00.

Royal Blue square-handled vegetable bowl.
$150.00 – 175.00.

Cheriglo wheel-cut cloverleaf candy. $80.00 – 100.00.

Royal Blue 8" flared vase. $175.00 – 200.00.

Ebony cloverleaf candy. $125.00 – 150.00.

Cheriglo 10¼" wheel-cut center-handled server.
$75.00 – 85.00.

Ebony 10¼" center-handled server.
$150.00 – 175.00.

Green cup and saucer. $36.00 – 40.00.

Ebony 12" flared vase.
$350.00 – 400.00.

Ebony 10" cupped vase.
$225.00 – 275.00.

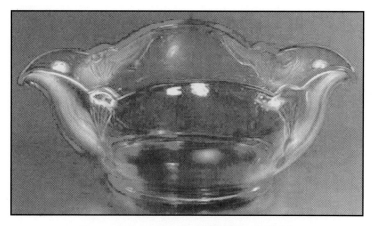

Green flat, oval gravy. $75.00 – 100.00.

Green 8" flared vase.
$150.00 – 175.00.

Green handled vegetable bowl. $45.00 – 55.00.

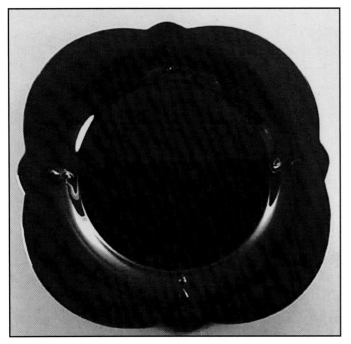

Mulberry cup and saucer. $40.00 – 50.00.

Mulberry 8¾" plate. $18.00 – 22.00.

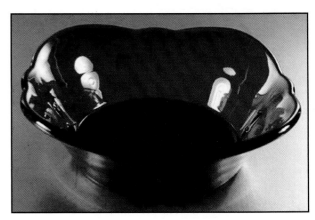

Mulberry 5" dessert dish. $25.00 – 30.00.

Mulberry sugar and creamer. $40.00 – 60.00.

Mulberry 6½" low-footed comport. $50.00 – 65.00.

Mulberry 11" oval platter, $45.00 – 65.00, and 9½" oval vegetable bowl, $50.00 – 65.00.

Ruby cream soup, $45.00 – 65.00, and liner, $12.00 – 18.00.

Mulberry keyhole candlestick. $60.00 – 85.00.

Ruby 6" cream soup liner. $12.00 – 18.00.

Ruby 2-part candy. $120.00 – 140.00.

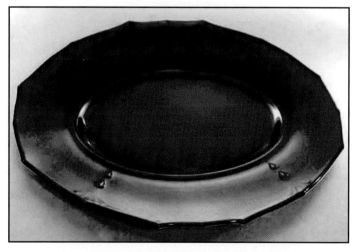

Ruby 11" x 8½" oval platter. $50.00 – 75.00.

Ruby 9½" x 7" oval bowl. $75.00 – 100.00.

Ruby cup and saucer. $55.00 – 70.00.

Ruby 6¼" saucer. $18.00 – 20.00.

Ruby 6" bread and butter plate. $18.00 – 20.00.

Ruby 7" low-footed comport. $55.00 – 75.00.

Ruby sugar and creamer on tray. $85.00 – 120.00.

Ruby 7½" x 5¼" low-footed oval comport/gravy, 4⅝" tall. $125.00 – 150.00.

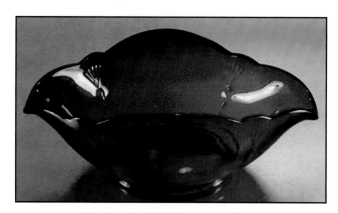

Ruby 7¾" x 5⅛" flat gravy. $125.00 – 150.00.

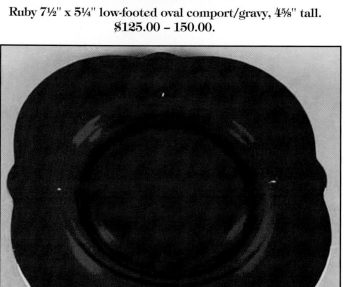

Ruby 9½" dinner plate. $25.00 – 40.00.

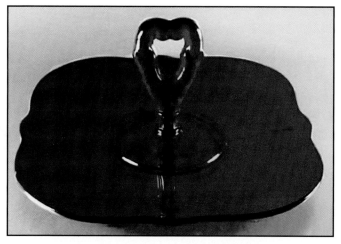

Ruby 10½" center-handled server. $150.00 – 175.00.

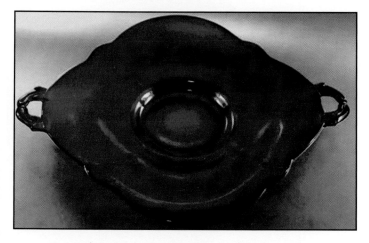

Ruby 14" x 11½" handled plate. $80.00 – 100.00.

Ruby 8⅝" luncheon plate. $20.00 – 25.00.

Ruby 10" x 12" handled vegetable bowl. $75.00 – 100.00.

Ruby 12" rolled-edge console bowl. $100.00 – 120.00.

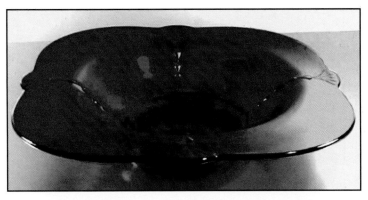

Ruby 12" flared console bowl. $100.00 – 120.00.

Ruby 5" keyhole candlestick. $65.00 – 85.00.

Ruby 7" high-footed comport. $85.00 – 115.00.

Ruby 7" oval, high-footed comport. $85.00 – 115.00.

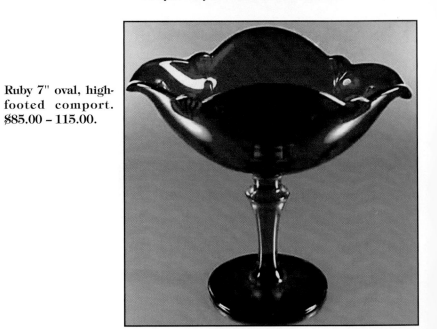

Ruby 3-part cloverleaf candy. $125.00 – 150.00.

Ruby 5" dessert bowl. $25.00 – 30.00.

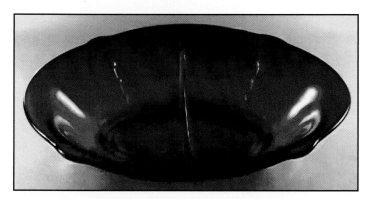

Ruby 7¼" x 9¼" oval divided vegetable bowl. $75.00 – 100.00.

Ruby 8" cupped vase.
$175.00 – 200.00.

Ruby 10" flared vase.
$200.00 – 225.00.

Ruby 12" flared vase.
$300.00 – 350.00.

Ruby 12" cupped vase. $300.00 – 350.00.

Ruby 8" flared vase. $175.00 – 200.00.

Ruby square ruffled bowl. $100.00 – 120.00.

Ruby cloverleaf candy base with metal top. $50.00 – 65.00.

Ruby 10" low-footed bowl. $200.00 – 250.00.

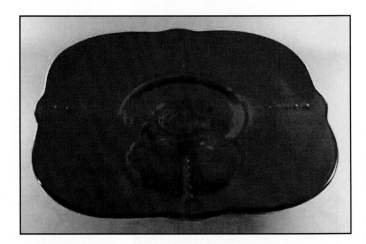

Ruby 9½" low-footed cake salver. $125.00 – 150.00.

Ruby mushroom candlestick. $18.00 – 22.00.

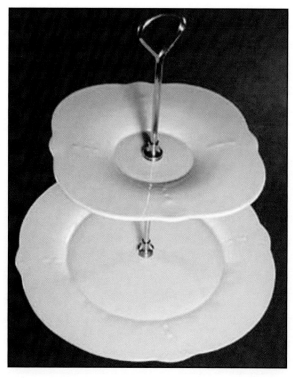

Opal (milk glass) 2-tier server; top is #412 square, base is #890 round. $100.00 – 125.00.

Opal handled vegetable bowl. $135.00 – 165.00.

Opal cloverleaf candy. $125.00 – 145.00.

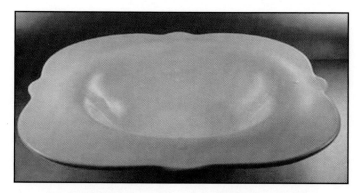

Opal 12" flared console bowl. $125.00 – 150.00.

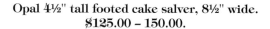

Opal 4½" tall footed cake salver, 8½" wide.
$125.00 – 150.00.

Opal cloverleaf candy with rare Art Deco decoration.
$150.00 – 175.00.

Opal 7" comport with rare Art Deco decoration.
$125.00 – 150.00.

Opal cream and sugar with rare foxglove decoration. $100.00 – 125.00.

Crystal wheel-cut center-handled server. $40.00 – 50.00.

Crystal cloverleaf candy with floral cutting. $50.00 – 65.00.

Crystal wheel-cut square candy. $50.00 – 65.00.

Crystal wheel-cut mushroom candlestick.
$18.00 – 20.00.

Crystal wheel-cut cloverleaf candy. $50.00 – 65.00.

Crystal 4" mushroom candlestick. $18.00 – 20.00.

Crystal mush-
room candle-
stick with
rolled-up edges.
$20.00 – 25.00.

Crystal satin cloverleaf candy in metal frame.
$65.00 – 85.00.

Crystal cloverleaf candy in an Art Deco nude ormolu (rare).
$100.00 – 125.00.

Yellow 6¾" x 9½" oval vegetable bowl. $30.00 – 45.00.

Yellow wheel-cut square candy.
$65.00 – 85.00.

Emerald Glo

Emerald Glo was a product line made by Paden City but sold by the Rubel Company, a sales organization similar to L. G. Wright. Rubel used many existing Paden City molds, but letters from Kurt Rubel indicate that the Rubel Company was also active in the design of many of its products and paid for the production of the molds used to made them. The agreement between the two companies was that Paden City would produce glass for Rubel, combine it with holders furnished by Rubel, store the inventory, and ship orders directly to Rubel's customers. It was a great deal for Rubel, which never touched the merchandise it sold and so had no need for a warehouse or a workforce to handle an inventory.

When Paden City closed its doors, Rubel went to the Fenton Art Glass Company and made the same arrangement with that company. Frank Fenton remembers that Rubel already had molds, some of which belonged to Rubel, but many that had been lent to them by Sam Fisher, president of Paden City Glass. Frank also remembers using the same gold metal that was used by Paden City.

The first delivery of the molds for the Rubel pieces was in November of 1951. All of the leftover Paden City inventory of Emerald Glo was also shipped to Fenton. In a letter to Kurt Rubel, Frank Fenton said that Fenton had so much Paden City inventory that they had not shipped any of their own stock, making it impossible for Fenton to make any profit from the arrangement. By June of 1952, Rubel was using iron stands. If you consider the amount of glass made by Paden City that was later shipped to Fenton and used to fill orders, I doubt that Fenton produced many pieces with the gold metal. If you want to be certain you are buying Paden City pieces, you should feel fairly safe buying the pieces in the traditional gold metal. I think this overload of inventory may explain why some of the Emerald Glo pieces are found with Cavalier Glass labels. Cavalier Glass was similar to Rubel in that it sold glass pro-

duced by glass factories and put its own labels on it. It's a logical guess that Rubel arranged to sell the Paden City inventory to them in order to keep its agreement with the Fenton Art Glass Company.

It was always assumed that only Paden City used the star cuttings that are found on many Emerald Glo pieces, but I was able to photograph a bowl with a Fenton production label that has the same star cutting. Fenton's Emerald Green is a little darker than Paden City's, as you can tell by the color comparison of the cruets made by both companies. As far as I have found, no molds for Glades #215 or Cavendish #330 were brought to Fenton. The hurricane lamp shown in this section was also only made by Paden City, but the beverage server with the ice bladder was probably made by both companies.

While I was at the Fenton factory researching my book *Fenton, Made for Other Companies*, I found a Rubel catalog in one of Frank Fenton's filing cabinets. It appears to be the last catalog issued that was shipped fom Paden City. The photos from that catalog give us an exciting view into Rubel's product line. The hor d'oeuvres server and the cheese server were both sold with bases that could turn those pieces into lazy Susans. The Crystal Daisy lazy Susan is not something I would have identified as either Paden City or Fenton. I also didn't know that the lazy Susan cruet set and the Plume epergne and candlesticks (shown on page 312) were part of the Emerald Glo items. I'm listing all items in crystal as well as green because the correspondence I have read indicated everything was made in both colors. The Crystal Daisy lazy Susan is always crystal, but the base can be either crystal or green. It is important to remember that every piece shown in the catalog was also made by Fenton.

When Rubel discontinued the line of glass it had been selling, it sold its molds to Fenton for $650. Sam Fisher contacted Frank and offered him the molds that he had lent to Rubel. Those molds sold for $400. Although these would seem to be very low prices for those molds, Fenton has only used the swirl ashtray molds, so the molds were expensive in that respect. You will find a list of the Paden City molds sold by Mr. Fisher after the listing of prices in this section. The epergne and candlesticks are not on the list of molds sold by Mr. Fisher, but they do appear on Rubel's list of molds. That fact indicates that those molds were commissioned and owned by Rubel, not Paden City. They would not have been a part of Paden City's line and would have only been sold as a Rubel product.

Description	Line	Size	Crystal	Emerald Green
ashtray, swirl		5½"	$8-12	$12-15
ashtray, swirl		8½"	$12-15	$15-18
beverage server	900	8½"	$65-85	$100-125
bowl, dressing		12"	$50-65	$75-100
bowl, dressing, divided	900	5"	$18-22	$28-35
bowl, salad	900	9"	$30-45	$45-55
bowl, salad		11½"	$45-55	$60-75
candlestick, heart shaped	888		$20-22	$25-35 ea.
candy, metal lid	900	7"	$20-25	$35-45
cheese & cracker, metal lid	900	12"	$35-55	$55-70
cheese server/lazy Susan		14¼"	$75-95	$100-125
cocktail shaker	215	11"	$45-65	$75-100
condiment set	900	3"	$45-55	$60-70
cream & sugar set, individual	900		$18-22	$22-26
cruet, oil, small	900		$18-25	$25-35
cruet set, lazy Susan base			$65-95	$100-125
Crystal Daisy lazy Susan			$45-$65	$50-70
epergne	888		$175-200	$200-250
hor d'oeuvres server/lazy Susan		12"	$75-100	$100-125
hurricane lamp		7"	$50-65	$100-125
ice bowl, w/tongs	900		$45-55	$65-85
jam set, 1-pc., w/metal jams	900	3¼"	$18-22	$25-35
jam set, 2-pc.	900	3¼"	$18-22	$25-35
jam set, 3-pc.	900	2½", 3¼"	$30-45	$45-55
marmalade	900	5½"	$15-18	$22-26
nappy, handled, divided	1503		$12-15	$20-24

Description	Line	Size	Crystal	Emerald Green
nappy, divided, cheese	702		$12-15	$18-22
oil & vinegar set	900		$45-55	$65-75
plate, handled	1503	5½"	$12-18	$20-22
plate, handled	1503	7⅜"	$12-18	$24-26
platter		14½"	$18-22	$24-30
relish, 5-section	900	12"	$35-50	$45-55
relish, 5-section, wide metal rim	900		$20-22	$35-42
relish, 5-section, w/lid	900	12"	$40-55	$55-65
salt & pepper	900	3"	$15-20	$22-25
sugar, covered, w/liner	900		$12-15	$18-22
syrup	900		$22-35	$35-45
tidbit, 1-plate	900		$15-18	$20-24
tidbit, 2-bowl	330		$24-30	$40-50
tidbit, 2-plate	900	lg. 14", sm. 7"	$20-25	$30-40

Paten City Molds sold to Fenton by Sam Fisher

Description	Line	Size
base	700	
beer mug	399	30 oz.
bowl, salad	215	10½"
bowl,* shallow	1503	12"
cheese cover	220	
communion glass	2101	¼ oz.
comport	215	4"
decanter & stopper	211	
decanter & stopper, sq.	444	
jug	203	
jug, ice lip	186	70 oz.
ladle		9½"
mayonnaise, optic	1187	5¼"
mustard and cover	400	3½ oz.
nappy, ball, 2 handled		6½"
nappy, ball, 2 handled		7½"
nappy, heart shape	900	
oil and vinegar bottle	829	
oil bottle & stopper	407	
punch bowl	9500	
punch bowl & cup	303	
punch cup	211	
punch ladle	9500	
roly poly**	2123	5 oz.
shaker	132	
shaker	144	
spoon	12	
stopper	829	
sugar, handled	400	3½ oz.
sugar and creamer	702	
tray	902	7½"
tumbler	203	5 oz.
tumbler	994	12 oz.
tumbler	994	17 oz.
tumbler	994	

*This mold was also used to make a 14" plate.
**This is the same one PC used for its Crow's Foot punch bowls.

244

Emerald Green #900 dressing bowl.
$58.00 – 65.00.

Side view of Emerald Green #900 dressing bowl.
$28.00 – 35.00.

Emerald Green #330 two-bowl server.
$40.00 – 50.00.

Emerald Green #1503 divided nappy. $20.00 – 24.00.

Emerald Green star-cut syrup. $35.00 – 45.00.

Emerald Green star-cut center-
handled server. $30.00 – 40.00.

Emerald Green #900 star-cut marmalade.
$20.00 – 26.00.

Emerald Green center-handled plate. $20.00 – 24.00.

Emerald Green 3" salt and pepper.
$22.00 – 25.00.

Emerald Green 8½" star-cut pitcher with
ice bladder. $100.00 – 125.00.

Emerald Green #900 triple jam or condiment set.
$60.00 – 70.00.

Cavalier label on the bottom of one of the jams.

Emerald Green #900 12" cheese plate with metal lid.
$55.00 – 70.00.

Emerald Green #900 9" salad bowl with spoons. $45.00 –
55.00 bowl, $20.00 – 25.00 spoons.

Green 7" hurricane candlelamp. $100.00 – 125.00.

Emerald Green #900 12" lazy Susan. $55.00 – 70.00.

Emerald Green #215 cocktail
shaker. $75.00 – 100.00.

Emerald Green #900 condiment with two brass condiments and brass tray. $20.00 – 25.00.

Emerald Green #702 divided cheese nappy.
$18.00 – 22.00.

Green large Fenton spoon, and Emerald Green small Paden City spoon. $18.00 – 20.00 large, $10.00 – 15.00 small.

Emerald Green #900 jams in metal holder.
$25.00 – 30.00.

Milk glass double condiment set (rare).
$75.00 – 100.00.

Emerald Green double condiment
set. $50.00 – 60.00.

Emerald Green condiment out of holder.
$18.00 – 20.00.

Emerald Green cream and sugar. $20.00 – 26.00.

Green #900 relish set with pierced metal top for toothpicks. $55.00 – 65.00.

Tray $10.00 – 15.00, and spoons $20.00 – 25.00.

Crumb pans. $10.00 – 15.00.

Emerald Green star-cut cruet. $20.00 – 25.00.

Emerald Green 12" plate with metal rim. $20.00 – 30.00.

Emerald Green 12" divided plate with metal rim.
$35.00 – 42.00.

Emerald Green #1503 salad server. $100.00 – 125.00.

Emerald Green Fenton oils in black metal.
$75.00 – 95.00.

Left: Fenton's Emerald Green oil. Right:
Paden City oil. $20.00 – 25.00 each.

Crystal cruet set. $65.00 – 95.00.

Crystal/Emerald Green shrimp server. $75.00 – 100.00.

Crystal lazy Susan. $75.00 – 100.00.

Can be found in Emerald Green, Amber, and crystal.
$12.00 – 15.00.

Crystal/Emerald Green server. $75.00 – 100.00.

Crystal lazy Susan cheese server. $75.00 – 95.00.

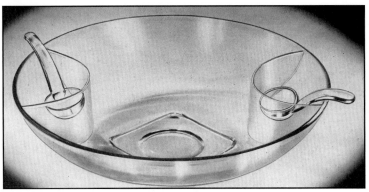

Crystal salad server. $75.00 – 95.00.

Emerald Green 11½" salad bowl, $60.00 – 75.00, on 14½" crystal platter, $18.00 – 22.00.

Gadroon #881

This pattern was introduced in 1932, and is the first of the rope-edged patterns. An early ad lists the colors made as crystal, green, Ebony, Cheriglo, Amber, Amethyst, Royal Blue, Topaz (yellow), and Ruby. There are two flat candy boxes; one is 6" and one is 7". I have listed the cake plate twice, because the catalog says it is 10½" but I photographed a 12" one. Gadroon is often found with Paden City's Irwin etching, but other etchings were also used. A center-handled server of Royal Blue was found with the Orchid etching. Those pieces are listed in their respective etching sections. Add 15% for cuttings.

Description	Size	Crystal/ Amber/ Topaz	Cheriglo/ Green	Ruby/ Royal Blue	Ebony/ Amethyst
bowl, console	12"	$35-55	$45-65	$65- 95	$75-100
bowl, ftd. (comport)	10"	$50-65	$65-85	$100-125	$125-150
bowl, handled	13"	$40-55	$55-65	$75-100	$75-100
bowl, oval	10"x7⅝"	$40-60	$50-75	$65- 80	$65- 80
bowl, salad	8"	$35-45	$45-60	$50-95	$50- 65
cake plate, low ftd.	10½"	$65-75	$75-95	$100-125	$100-125
cake plate, low ftd.	12"	$65-75	$75-95	$100-125	$100-125
candlestick	6"	$35-40	$50-65	$75-95	$75-95
candy, 3-part	6"	$35-55	$75-100	$100-150	$100-150
candy, 3-part	7"	$35-55	$75-100	$100-150	$100-150
comport, high ftd.	7"	$35-45	$50-65	$75-100	$75-100
creamer		$20-22	$25-35	$30-40	$30-45
cream soup	4½"	$20-22	$35-40	$45-55	$45-55
cup		$18-22	$30-40	$35-45	$40-45
mayonnaise, 3-pc.	3"x4⅝"	$25-40	$40-55	$55-70	$55-70
mayonnaise liner	6⅜"	$12-15	$14-16	$16-18	$16-18
plate, rd.	9½ "	$18-22	$25-40	$35-50	$40-50
plate, rd.	12"	$25-40	$35-55	$50-70	$65-75
plate, sq.	8½"	$20-35	$30-45	$45-65	$50-65
plate, handled	14"	$35-60	$45-70	$65-85	$70-85
relish, 3-part, handled	7¼x10"	$65-75	$60-80	$70-95	$75-95
saucer, rd.	5½"	$8-10	$10-12	$12-15	$14-16
sherbet, high ftd.	4½"	$15-20	$22-30	$25-35	$25-35
sugar		$22-30	$25-35	$30-40	$30-40

Description	Size	Crystal/ Amber/ Topaz	Cheriglo/ Green	Ruby/ Royal Blue	Ebony/ Amethyst
tray, center handled	10"	$65-85	$75-95	$100-135	$100-150
tray, nut, center handled	10½"	$75-100	$100-125	$125-155	$125-175
tray, rectangular	10"x7¼	$60-85	$95-120	$120-135	$120-135
vase	12"	$150-175	$175-200	$200-300	$200-300

Royal Blue 8¼" square luncheon plate. $45.00 – 65.00.

Royal Blue sugar and creamer. $60.00 – 80.00.

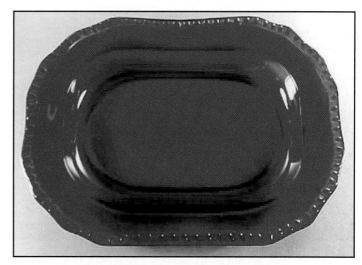

Royal Blue 10" x 7¼" rectangular tray. $65.00 – 80.00.

Royal Blue mayonnaise bowl. $65.00 – 80.00.

Royal Blue 10" x 7⅝" rectangular bowl. $65.00 – 85.00.

Royal Blue 9½" round dinner plate. $35.00 – 50.00.

Royal Blue 8½" round luncheon plate. $30.00 – 40.00.

Royal Blue cream soup and 6⅜" liner. $60.00 – 75.00.

Ruby 12" footed cake salver. $100.00.

Ruby cup and saucer. $45.00 – 60.00.

Ruby high-footed sherbet. $20.00 – 35.00.

Ruby cream soup. $60.00 – 75.00.

Ruby 6⅜" cream soup liner. $16.00 – 18.00.

Ruby mayonnaise set. $55.00 – 70.00.

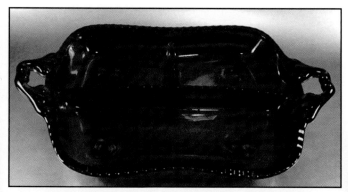

Ruby 14" handled plate. $65.00 – 85.00.

Ruby 12" handled 3-part relish. $70.00 – 90.00.

Ruby 10" x 7¼" rectangular bowl. $65.00 – 85.00.

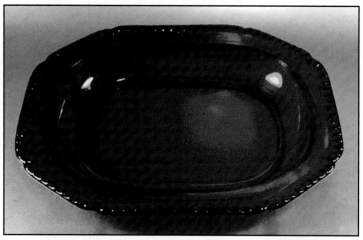

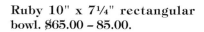

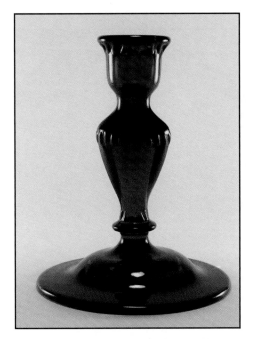

Ruby 6" candlestick. $75.00 – 95.00.

Mulberry cup and saucer. $55.00 – 60.00.

Mulberry tray. $65.00 – 80.00.

Mulberry cream soup and liner. $60.00 – 75.00.

Mulberry cream and sugar. $60.00 – 80.00.

Mulberry 9½" round dinner plate. $40.00 – 50.00.

Amber 9½" dinner plate. $18.00 – 22.00.

Ruby 23 oz. bar bottle.
$100.00 – 125.00.

Crystal 12" plate with satin etching. $25.00 – 40.00.

Close up of unidentified satin etching.

Georgian #69

Georgian is the most difficult Paden City pattern to identify. This pattern was also made by Fenton, Cambridge, Viking, Duncan, Canton, Central, and Beaumont. As a rule, the honeycomb on the Paden City pieces is slightly elongated, but that is not always true of the smaller pieces. The cocktail shaker and the decanter/bar bottle are distinctive and easy to identify, and there are several blown pieces that were not made by any other company. Luckily, a Paden City catalog exists that has very detailed measurements of all the pieces. I have included Paden City's information so that it will be easier for you to discern the differences between Paden City items and those made by other companies.

Description	Size	Amber/Crystal	Cheriglo/Green	Royal Blue/Ruby
ashtray	4½"	$8-10	$10-12	$15-18
banana split		$18-20	$20-24	$25-30
bar bottle	23 oz.	$50-60	$75-95	$100-125
bowl, finger	h. 2⅜", td. 4⅛", bd. 2³⁄₁₆"; 4"	$6-8	$8-10	$12-15
bowl, nappy	6"	$8-12	$12-15	$15-18
bowl, nappy	7"	$8-12	$12-15	$15-18
bowl, oval	7½"x10½"	$15-18	$18-22	$22-30
cocktail shaker	30 oz.	$50-60	$75-95	$100-125
cocktail, low ftd., #69½	h. 3½", td. 2⁹⁄₁₆", bd. 2⅝"; 3½ oz.	$6-8	$7-9	$10-12
cocktail, Old Fashioned #69½	h. 3⁵⁄₁₆", td. 2⅞", bd. 2¼"; 6 oz.	$8-10	$10-12	$15-18
goblet	4¼", 5 oz.	$8-10	$10-12	$15-18
goblet	6", 8 oz.	$8-10	$10-12	$15-18
goblet, high ftd.	h. 5¹³⁄₁₆", td. 3½", bd. 2¹⁵⁄₁₆"; 9 oz.	$8-10	$10-12	$12-15
goblet, low ftd., #69½	h. 5³⁄₁₆", td.3³⁄₁₆", bd. 3³⁄₁₆"; 10 oz.	$8-10	$10-12	$12-15
jug, w/o lid	60 oz.	$65-75	$80-100	$125-175
jug, covered, #69½	60 oz.	$75-95	$100-125	$175-200
marmalade, covered	12 oz.	$12-15	$18-20	$20-25
oil	3½"; 3 oz.	$15-20	$35-40	$75-95
oil, GS, #69½	h. 6⅜", td 1³⁄₁₆", bd. 3⅝"; 6 oz.	$25-30	$40-50	$65-75
parfait, #69½	h.5½", td. 2⅝", bd. 2¾"; 5 oz.	$10-12	$12-15	$18-20
peach melba	h. 5¹³⁄₁₆", td. 3⁷⁄₁₆", bd. 2⅞"; 9 oz.	$8-10	$10-12	$12-15
plate	6½"	$8-12	$12-15	$15-18
plate	8½"	$8-12	$12-15	$18-22
plate, finger bowl liner	td. 6"	$4-5	$7-9	$10-12
plate, oval	8½"x12"	$12-15	$15-18	$18-22
shaker, #69½	h. 3⁷⁄₁₆", td. 1", bd. 1¹¹⁄₁₆"; 1½ oz.	$10-12	$15-18	$25-30
sherbet, #69½	h. 3⅞", td. 3¾", bd. 3; 5 oz.	$6-8	$8-10	$12-15
sherbet, low ftd., cupped, #69½	h. 3³⁄₁₆", td. 3⅜", bd. 2½"; 3½ oz.	$6-8	$8-10	$12-15
sherbet, low ftd., flared, #69½	h. 3¼", td. 3½", bd. 2⁷⁄₁₆"; 3½ oz.	$6-8	$8-10	$12-15
sherbet, reg.	h. 2¹⁵⁄₁₆", td. 3³⁄₁₆", bd. 2⁷⁄₁₆"; 4 oz.	$6-8	$8-10	$12-15
side water, #69½	h. 3⅜", td. 2⅝", bd. 2³⁄₁₆"; 5 oz.	$8-10	$10-12	$15-18
soda, ftd.	h. 5¼", td. 3¾"; 8 oz.	$8-10	$10-12	$15-18
sundae, tulip	h. 5¼", td. 4⅜"; 5½ oz.	$10-12	$14-16	$18-22
syrup, covered	12 oz.	$18-20	$35-40	$50-60
tumbler	h. 2⁹⁄₁₆", td. 2", bd. 1¹⁵⁄₁₆"; 2½ oz.	$12-15	$15-18	$18-22
tumbler	h. 3¹⁵⁄₁₆", td. 2½", bd. 2¹⁄₁₆"; 5 oz.	$8-10	$10-12	$12-15
tumbler	h. 4¹⁄₁₆", td. 2¹⁄₁₆", bd. 2¾"; 9 oz.	$8-10	$10-12	$12-15
tumbler	h. 5", td. 3⅛", bd 3"; 12 oz.	$8-10	$10-12	$12-15
tumbler, #69½	3¹⁵⁄₁₆", 5 oz.	$8-10	$10-12	$12-15
tumbler, #69½	h. 4", td. 2⅜", bd. 2⅜"; 7 oz.	$8-10	$10-12	$12-15
tumbler, #69½	h. 4", td. 2¹³⁄₁₆", bd. 2⅜; 9 oz.	$8-10	$10-12	$12-15
tumbler, high ball	5", 8 oz.	$8-10	$10-12	$12-15
tumbler, ice tea, #69½	h. 5⅝", td. 2⅝", bd. 2½"; 11 oz.	$8-10	$10-12	$12-15
tumbler, ice tea, #69½	12 oz.	$10-12	$12-15	$15-18
tumbler, soda	h. 6", td. 3⅛"; 14 oz	$10-12	$14-16	$18-22
tumbler, whiskey, #69½	3 oz.	$12-15	$15-18	$18-22
vase, ruffled top	5"	$5-18	$18-25	$35-50

Ruby peach melba. $12.00 – 15.00.

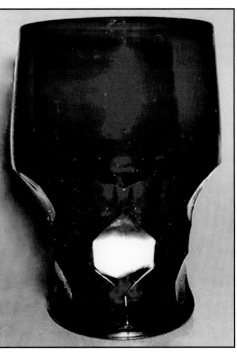

Ruby 12 oz. tumbler. $12.00 – 15.00.

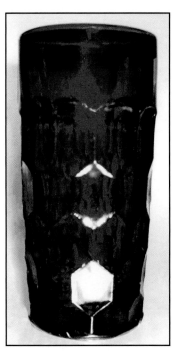

Ruby #69½ 12 oz. ice tea tumbler. $15.00 – 18.00.

Royal Blue 23 oz. bar bottle. $100.00 – 125.00.

Royal Blue 4 oz. sherbet. $12.00 – 15.00.

Light Green 4 oz. sherbet. $8.00 – 10.00.

Light green 9 oz. tumbler.
$10.00 – 12.00.

Mulberry 4 oz. sherbet. $10.00 – 12.00.

Cheriglo 12 oz. pressed tumbler.
$10.00 – 12.00.

Cheriglo 8 oz. blown tumbler.
$15.00 – 22.00.

Dark Green 4 oz. sherbet. $8.00 – 10.00.

Amber shaker. $10.00 – 12.00.

Glades #215

During the 1930s and 1940s, almost every glass company produced a vertical rib pattern. Heisey had Ridgeleigh, Fenton had Sheffield, Imperial had Empire, and Paden City had Glades. Glades is particularly beautiful in Ruby and Cobalt Blue. It was also made in crystal, Mulberry, Amber, Copen Blue, and Forest Green. The cologne bottles have been found in Ebony, so there may be other pieces in that color. Glades is often found with the Spring Orchard etching. The oval tray was used under the cream and sugar as well as with the dresser set. The cigarette holder and the ashtrays alternate flat panels with the ribbed design; the colonnade decanter has a similar look. I'm sorry I don't have a photo of this decanter, but I will try to describe it for you. It is oval, and the sides have ribs, but the front is a flat panel that is perfect for etching. It can be found with the Spring Orchard etching. Many pieces of Glades are found with Farberware holders. Add 25% for those pieces. Keep in mind that although I have priced all pieces in all colors, I haven't seen all these.

Ruby 4" x 6¼" ice bowl and tongs with silver decoration. $75.00 – 95.00.

Ruby 4½" x 6½" comport. $45.00 – 55.00.

Description	Size	Crystal/ Amber	Copen Blue/ Forest Green/ Mulberry	Ruby/Blue/ Ebony
ashtray		$6-8	$8-10	$10-12
bowl, centerpiece	12½"	$35-45	$65-85	$75-95
bowl, deep	4½"	$10-12	$12-15	$15-20
bowl, ftd. (comport)	11½"x4"	$45-55	$75-125	$100-150
bowl, handled	11"	$35-50	$50-75	$75-100
bowl, oval	9¾"x7¼"	$35-50	$65-85	$75-95
bowl, shallow	5"	$18-22	$20-25	$25-30
cake salver	12½"x2"	$50-75	$75-95	$100-125
candlestick, double	5"	$25-35 ea.	$45-65 ea.	$65-85 ea.
candy, cloverleaf, metal lid		$30-40	$50-65	$65-80
candy, rd.	7⅛"	$65-95	$75-125	$100-150
celery dish	11"	$22-26	$28-35	$32-38
cheese & cracker	12"	$65-95	$100-125	$125-150
cheese & cracker, w/cover	12"	$100-150	$125-175	$150-225
cocktail, corset shaped	3⅜"	$15-20	$20-25	$25-30
cocktail, cupped top	3", 3 oz.	$15-20	$20-25	$25-30
cocktail, ftd.	3½"	$10-13	$13-16	$15-18

Description	Size	Crystal/ Amber	Copen Blue/ Forest Green/ Mulberry	Ruby/Blue/ Ebony
cocktail shaker	11"	$65-85	$75-100	$100-125
comport, high ftd., any top	5½" x7"	$40-55	$50-75	$65-95
comport, low ftd.	7" x3½"	$25-40	$35-45	$45-55
creamer	7 oz.	$20-24	$23-25	$24-27
cream soup		$18-22	$24-26	$24-30
cup		$8-12	$12-15	$15-18
decanter, colonnade		$95-120	$115-130	$125-150
decanter, cordial, tilt	12 oz.	$22-26	$25-35	$30-40
decanter, ribbed sides	9"	$45-60	$50-75	$75-95
goblet, high ftd.		$12-15	$15-18	$18-22
gravy, flat	7¼" x5¼"	$20-40	$30-45	$45-60
ice tub	6¼" x4"	$30-45	$45-65	$65-85
pickle dish	6"	$12-16	$15-20	$20-24
plate, dinner	9¼"	$15-20	$24-28	$30-38
plate, handled	13"	$25-35	$40-60	$50-75
plate, luncheon	7"	$14-16	$20-24	$25-30
plate, tab handles	6"	$12-15	$15-20	$20-24
platter, ftd.	15"	$45-60	$55-70	$60-85
platter, oval	11"	$25-35	$40-60	$50-75
powder		$35-45	$45-60	$50-75
relish, 4-part, rd.	11¾"x9½"	$30-40	$55-75	$75-95
relish, sq.	7"	$30-45	$40-50	$50-65
saucer	6¼"	$8-10	$10-12	$12-15
server, center handled	11⅝"	$35-50	$50-75	$65-95
sherbet, low ftd.		$10-12	$14-16	$15-18
shot glass, flat	2"	$15-18	$20-25	$20-35
sugar	7 oz.	$18-20	$22-24	$23-26
tray, oval	11" x 7¼"	$45-65	$50-75	$75-95
tray, oval (cream & sugar)		$18-24	$24-28	$25-35
tray, rd.	13"	$20-35	$30-45	$40-65
tumbler	9 oz.	$30-45	$45-65	$50-80
vase, cylinder	9"	$45-65	$75-95	$100-125
vase, cylinder	12"	$50-85	$85-120	$120-150
whiskey, cupped	1¾ oz.	$50-65	$65-85	$75-95
whiskey, flared	1¾ oz.	$50-65	$65-85	$75-95

Ruby cream soup and liner. $34.00 – 42.00.

Ruby 8 oz. goblet. $18.00 – 22.00.

Close-up of stem detail on 8 oz. goblet.

Ruby 3⅜" corset cocktail, 3 oz. $25.00 – 30.00.

Ruby 2" flat whiskey. $20.00 – 35.00.

Ruby cocktail shaker. $100.00 – 125.00.

Ruby double candlestick. $65.00 – 85.00.

Ruby oval comport/gravy, top view. $45.00 – 55.00.

Ruby oval comport/gravy, side view. $45.00 – 55.00.

Ruby flat 3-part candy. $100.00 – 150.00.

Ruby 5⅝" high-footed comport. $65.00 – 95.00.

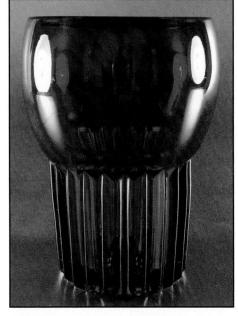

Ruby 3" whiskey, 3 oz. $75.00 – 95.00.

Ruby 9¾" x 7¼" oval vegetable bowl. $75.00 – 95.00.

Ruby basket made from 9" plate and Farberware frame.
$55.00 – 75.00.

Ruby 11¼" low-footed bowl. $100.00 – 150.00.

Ruby 5" cereal bowl. $25.00 – 30.00.

Ruby 9¼" plate. $30.00 – 38.00.

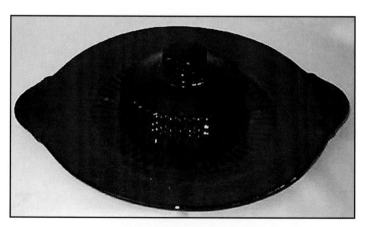

Ruby covered cheese and cracker. $150.00 – 225.00.

Ruby 4-part relish. $75.00 – 95.00.

Amber 12¼" footed console bowl, side view. $35.00 – 45.00.

Amber 3⅜" corset cocktail, 3 oz.
$15.00 – 20.00.

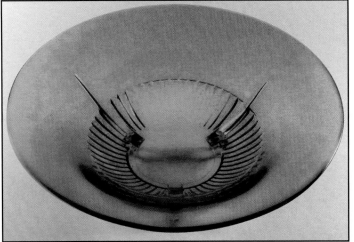

Mulberry 9⅛" plate. $24.00 – 28.00.

Amber 12¼" footed console bowl, top view.

Mulberry cup and saucer. $22.00 – 27.00.

Mulberry cup, top view. $12.00 – 15.00.

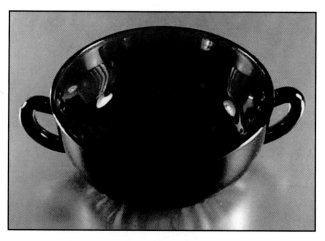

Mulberry cream soup. $24.00 – 26.00.

Mulberry oval vegetable bowl. $65.00 – 85.00.

Mulberry cloverleaf candy with a metal lid.
$50.00 – 60.00.

Royal Blue cream and sugar. $47.00 – 51.00.

Royal Blue ice tub. $65.00 – 85.00.

Forest Green 7" low-footed, crimped comport. $35.00 – 45.00.

Crystal double candlestick. $25.00 – 35.00.

Copen Blue low-footed comport/gravy. $35.00 – 85.00.

Largo #220

Introduced in the 1930s, Largo is a favorite pattern of many collectors. It can be found in crystal, Copen Blue, Amber, Mulberry, and Forest Green, and can of course be found in those most popular colors of Ruby and Royal Blue. This blank was used for the etchings Loopie, Magic Garden, Black Forest, Eleanor, Frost, and Spring Orchard. Other combinations may exist.

Largo is a design that is often mistaken for Cambridge's Caprice, but the circles of the Largo design have a ridge; Caprice circles are rounded. On Caprice, the pattern goes all the way to the edge; on Largo, the design stops about halfway to the edge. Cambridge's Moonlight Blue is a little less intense than Paden City's Copen Blue, but for the novice collector, it is hard to tell the difference unless they are together.

Under the crystal/Amber listings, the low price is for crystal and the high for Amber. Add 15% for cuttings or other decorations. Pieces with an etching will be priced in the proper listing in the Etchings section.

Ruby 7½" x 5¾" flat gravy. $50.00 – 75.00.

Ruby 10¼" x 6½" high-footed comport.
$100.00 – 125.00.

Ruby 13" handled plate. $60.00 – 80.00.

Ruby sugar and creamer. $70.00 – 110.00.

Description	Size	Crystal/ Amber	Copen Blue/ Forest Green/ Mulberry	Ruby/ Royal Blue
ashtray		$8-10	$10-12	$14-16
bowl	7"	$25-45	$45-65	$75-85
bowl, center handled	10½"	$50-75	$85-125	$125-150
bowl, deep	7½"	$35-55	$55-75	$85-95
bowl, ftd., console	13"	$35-55	$55-75	$85-95
bowl, handled	11"	$40-60	$65-85	$85-100
bowl, handled crimped	12¾"x7¾"	$35-55	$55-75	$85-95
cake salver	11¾"	$50-75	$65-95	$100-125
candlestick	5¼"	$20-30 ea.	$40-50 ea.	$60-65 ea.
candlestick, duo	5¼"	$20-30 ea.	$40-50 ea.	$60-65 ea.
candy, ftd.	7¼"	$35-55	$75-95	$100-125
cheese & cracker	10½"	$50-65	$75-100	$110-130
cheese & cracker, covered	12½"	$60-75	$100-125	$125-150
cigarette box		$60-75	$75-95	$100-125
comport, low ftd.	6½"x10"	$40-65	$75-100	$100-125
creamer		$20-30	$30-40	$35-55
cup		$18-22	$20-30	$35-50
gravy	7½"	$30-45	$40-60	$50-75
mayonnaise set		$40-50	$50-75	$75-100
plate	9"	$18-20	$22-25	$25-30
plate	9⅜"	$20-30	$30-45	$35-55
plate, ftd., serving	14"	$40-65	$50-65	$60-80
plate, handled	13"	$40-65	$50-65	$60-80
platter	13"	$25-40	$35-55	$50-70
platter, oval	11½"x9½"	$30-50	$40-75	$65-95
relish, 5-part, oval		$35-50	$50-75	$75-100
saucer		$8-12	$12-15	$15-18
server, center handled	10½"	$50-75	$85-125	$125-150
sugar		$20-30	$30-40	$35-55
vase		$65-85	$100-125	$150-175

Ruby 12" footed console bowl. $85.00 – 95.00.

Ruby 12" low-footed cake salver. $100.00 – 125.00.

Copen Blue 13" handled plate. $50.00 – 65.00.

Copen Blue cheese comport. $25.00 – 35.00.

Copen Blue center-handled bowl. $85.00 – 125.00.

Copen Blue center-handled plate. $85.00 – 125.00.

Copen Blue double candlestick. $40.00 – 50.00.

Copen Blue 5" candlestick. $30.00 – 35.00.

Mulberry cup and saucer. $32.00 – 45.00.

Mulberry sugar and creamer. $60.00 – 80.00.

Crystal 5" candlestick. $18.00 – 22.00.

Crystal footed candy. $35.00 – 55.00.

Top view of crystal footed candy.

Royal Blue 11½" handled plate. $50.00 – 65.00.

Lucy #895

Lucy is the kissing cousin of Paden City's Crow's Foot pattern. In some cases, the two patterns are combined. The handles on the serving plate as well as on the center-handled tray are the same as the Crow's Foot Round #890 pattern, and the stem on the high-footed comport is decorated with the 3-part fans that grace many of the #890 pieces. The 3-part fans match the large fleur-de-lis design on the Lucy pieces. There is a mold drawing of the 3-part relish that shows it as part of the #895 line, but a Canton catalog places it into the #890 line. It's a good match to either one, so I doubt that collectors will hesitate to buy it, regardless of which line it belongs to. The double candle-stick is still not confirmed to be Lucy, but a press release at the time it was marketed said that the double candlestick was very attractive, so we do know that one for this pattern exists. Sooner or later, some evidence will come to light either proving or disproving that the candlestick in the photo is the candlestick mentioned in that press release.

It is possible that some of the #890 molds were modified to produce Lucy, but it is more likely that Paden City made both patterns at the same time. It is possible that the candlestick shown was meant to work with either line.

Ruby 7" high-footed comport; note that this has a Crow's Foot stem. $45.00 – 50.00.

Ruby 4" tall low-footed comport with 6¼" top. $35.00 – 40.00.

272

Description	Size	Amber	Crystal	Ruby/Royal Blue
bowl	6"	$10-12	$10-12	$18-22
bowl, center handled	9"	$45-60	$35-50	$75-100
bowl, ftd., centerpiece	11½"	$45-65	$30-45	$100-125
bowl, ftd., crimped	10	$45-65	$30-45	$100-125
cake salver	12"	$65-85	$50-65	$125-175
candlestick	5"	$45-65 ea.	$25-35 ea.	$75-90 ea.
candlestick, double	5⅛"	$50-60 ea.	$35-45 ea.	$60-80 ea.
candy	7"	$65-80	$35-40	$75-85
cheese & cracker	10½"	$65-85	$40-60	$75-100
comport, high ftd.	7"	$35-40	$20-22	$45-50
comport, low ftd.	4⅛"	$30-35	$18-20	$35-40
comport, low ftd.	5"x9⅝"	$45-50	$20-25	$65-75
gravy	5"x7¼"	$25-30	$20-25	$55-65
ice tub	5⅝"	$65-75	$45-55	$75-95
mayonnaise, ftd.	3⅝"	$20-24	$18-22	$30-45
mayonnaise liner	6¼"	$10-12	$6-8	$12-14
plate	6¼"	$12-15	$8-10	$15-18
plate	7"	$14-16	$10-12	$16-19
plate	9"	$15-17	$12-14	$20-22
plate, handled	13¾"	$45-55	$25-35	$55-75
relish, 3-part		$65-75	$45-55	$75-100
server, center handled	10⅝"	$45-55	$35-45	$65-85

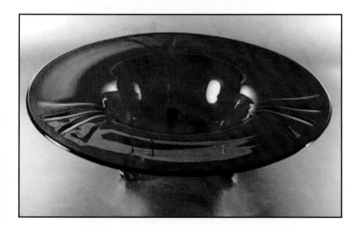

Ruby 12" centerpiece bowl. $100.00 – 125.00.

Ruby 5" x 7¼" flat gravy. $55.00 – 65.00.

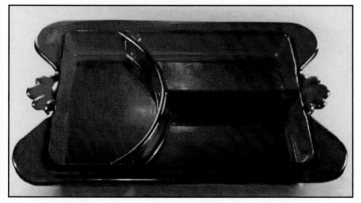

Ruby 10¼" x 7⁵⁄₁₆" 3-part relish. $75.00 – 100.00.

Ruby 6" plate. $15.00 – 18.00.

Crystal double candlestick. $35.00 – 45.00.

Crystal 5" candlestick. $25.00 – 35.00.

Royal Blue cheese comport. $18.00 – 22.00.

Royal Blue handled plate with silver overlay.
$75.00 – 100.00.

Royal Blue 9½" footed bowl. $100.00 – 125.00.

Maya #221

Maya is often confused with Largo, but although the range of items made closely resembles that of Largo, the two patterns are actually very different. The Largo design consists of four sets of radiating half circles alternating with fans. The Maya design looks similar to a thistle or an onion with open layers.

The single and the double candlesticks in this line have been the subject of some controversy. Some collectors believe that both styles were meant as fill-in candlesticks that would work with any other pattern. Although I agree with that, I'm listing both here, because these are the candlesticks found with the Maya console bowl. Maya is found in three colors: crystal, Copen Blue, and Ruby. Ruby may not be any more difficult to find, but this pattern is so spectacular in Ruby that the prices for Ruby pieces are always considerably higher. Buy what you see, because you may be waiting a long time for another piece.

Copen Blue double candlestick (also a fill-in for other patterns). $45.00 – 70.00.

Copen Blue 8¼" x 12½" oval bowl. $65.00 – 75.00.

Copen Blue 12" footed console bowl. $65.00 – 85.00.

Copen Blue center-handled server. $100.00 – 125.00.

Description	Size	Crystal	Blue	Ruby
bowl, center handled	10½"	$75-95	$100-125	$150-175
bowl, console, footed	12"	$50-65	$65-80	$75-100
bowl, handled	10½"	$50-65	$65-75	$75-100
bowl, ruffled, sq.	7½"	$45-60	$50-70	$60-85
cake salver	12"	$75-95	$100-125	$150-175
candlestick	5"	$35-40 ea.	$40-60 ea.	$50-75 ea.
candlestick, duo	5¾"	$40-45 ea.	$45-70 ea.	$65-85 ea.
candy	7⅛"	$45-65	$125-150	$150-165
cheese & cracker, covered	12½"	$50-75	$140-165	$150-175
comport	6¼"x10¼"	$35-50	$65-95	$75-100
creamer		$15-18	$20-24	$25-28
mayonnaise set		$35-50	$60-90	$75-100
plate, ftd.	14"	$50-65	$65-80	$75-100
server, center handled	11"	$50-75	$100-125	$150-175
sugar		$12-15	$20-24	$25-28

Copen Blue 10¼" footed bowl. $65.00 – 85.00.

Ruby sugar bowl. $25.00 – 28.00.

Ruby flat candy. $150.00 – 165.00.

Ruby 7½" square bowl, $65.00 – 85.00; 7" high-footed comport, $75.00 – 100.00, and 12" low-footed cake salver, $150.00 – 175.00.

Crystal 12" console bowl. $50.00 – 65.00.

Crystal double candlesticks. $55.00 – 65.00.

Mr. B./Vermilion #555

Pattern #555 is known by both Mr. B., a name bestowed in honor of Jerry Barnett, and Vermilion, the name given by Hazel Marie Weatherman. To avoid confusion, I have used the pattern number 555 in most line listings.

This pattern is remarkably close to Imperial Candlewick and is often mistaken for it. In the *Paden City Glass Society Newsletter* of December 2001, Nancy Stender reprints a note obtained from the O. O. Brown collection that refers to #555. The note was written by J. R. Price and states: "#555 line was originated by George Daner, Sr., about 1940 – 41. Originally this line had a full beaded edge. When the new mold was put into operation, I called Mr. Daner's attention to the similarity of the #555 line to Imperial's Candlewick, and after some discussion it was decided to add the tail to each bead, making a sort of teardrop edge."

The wide, unpatterned areas on these blanks made this a perfect line for etching and Paden City made good use of that feature with Baby Orchid, Gazebo, Utopia, Ardith, Basket Flower, and Pam's Floral. This pattern can be found in crystal or blue, and some pieces may be found in Ruby. A few pieces may found in Opal, and it is possible this pattern was made in other colors as well.

Copen Blue 9¾" footed candy. $35.00 – 45.00.

Copen Blue (darker shade) 9¾" footed candy. $45.00 – 55.00.

Description	Size	Crystal	Blue	Ruby
bowl	9"	$20-25	$38-42	$42-45
bowl, centerpiece	12"	$25-28	$40-45	$45-50
bowl, handled	11"	$25-28	$40-45	$45-50
candlestick		$25-30 ea.	$30-45 ea.	$65-75 ea.
candlestick, double		$28-35 ea.	$35-48 ea.	$65-85 ea.
candy, flat		$25-34	$40-50	$65-75
candy, ftd.	9¾"	$25-30	$35-45	$60-65
candy, heart shaped	7"	$65-75	$75-85	
cheese & cracker, w/lid	12"	$50-65	$75-125	$125-150
comport, flared	7½"x10"	$30-35	$40-45	$50-60
cream		$18-20	$22-25	
mayonnaise liner	6"	$6-8	$8-10	
mayonnaise set	3"	$20-22	$40-45	
plate	8"	$10-12	$18-22	
plate	11"	$15-18	$30-45	
plate	15"	$20-25	$45-65	
plate, handled	13"	$20-25	$45-65	
punch bowl		$75-125		
relish, 2-part, ruffled	6½"	$18-20	$20-22	
relish, 3-part, oval	10"	$20-24	$28-35	
relish, 3-part, sq.	10"	$22-28	$30-40	
relish, 5-part, rd.	10"	$30-38		
sugar		$15-16	$20-23	
tray, center handled	11"	$45-65	$50-75	

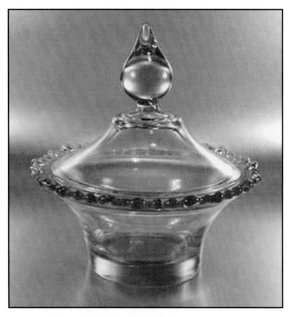

Copen Blue flat candy. $40.00 – 50.00.

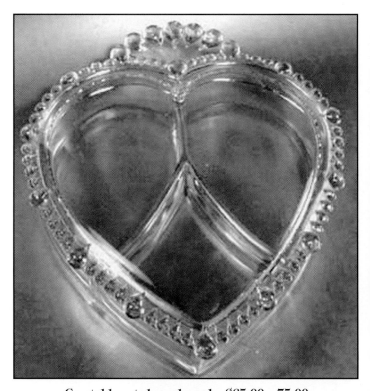

Crystal heart-shaped candy. $65.00 – 75.00.

Crystal 15" plate. $35.00 – 45.00.

Crystal/Ruby-stained heart-shaped candy, with enameled roses. $75.00 – 100.00.

Opal (milk glass) footed candy base. $60.00 – 85.00.

Crystal/Cranberry-stained 9¾" footed candy with #444 lid. $45.00 – 55.00.

Ruby 9¾" footed candy. $60.00 – 65.00.

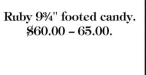

Crystal 10" flared comport. $30.00 – 35.00.

Mrs. B. #411

Paden City used this blank for a large percentage of its etchings because of the wide areas that were unpatterned. Most of the shapes are identical to those of the Crow's Foot Square pieces. Without etchings it isn't an expensive pattern, but it is still very attractive.

Yellow 6½" square candy. $75.00 – 100.00.

Yellow 6½" square candy with deep cutting. $85.00 – 115.00.

Description	Size	Crystal/Amber	Pink/Green/ Yellow/Ebony	Ruby/CobaltBlue
bowl, center handled	10"	$60-75	$75-120	$100-125
bowl, centerpiece	10½" to 11½"	$40-45	$50-65	$75-95
bowl, footed (comport)	10"x4"	$45-50	$60-75	$100-120
bowl, handled	11¼"	$40-45	$50-65	$75-95
bowl, oval, handled	13"x8¼"	$45-50	$60-75	$100-125
bowl, sq.	8¼"	$40-45	$50-65	$75-95
bowl, sq.	10"	$40-45	$50-65	$75-95
cake plate	11"	$50-65	$65-85	$100-125
candlestick, flat	4⅛" sq.	$10-20 ea.	$20-30 ea.	$30-40 ea.
candlestick, keyhole	5"	$20-35 ea.	$35-55 ea.	$50-65 ea.
candlestick, mushroom	2½" .	$18-22 ea.	$30-40 ea.	$35-50 ea.
candy, ftd., keyhole, finial	8"	$65-85	$100-120	$150-175
candy, rd. or sq. base	6½"	$50-75	$75-100	$100-125
candy tray, ftd.	9"	$50-75	$65-90	$100-125
cheese & cracker set	10"	$50-65	$65-85	$100-125
comport, high ftd.	7"	$40-55	$55-65	$75-95
comport, low ftd.	6"	$35-45	$50-60	$70-90
cream		$15-18	$18-20	$25-40
cup		$20-25	$35-50	$45-65
gravy, ftd.	7½"x4¼"	$40-45	$60-75	$75-95
mayonnaise set	6"	$35-55	$50-75	$75-100
plate	8⅜"	$18-22	$22-28	$30-35
plate, handled	11"	$25-35	$40-50	$60-80
rose bowl	4½"	$35-50	$65-85	$75-100
saucer	5¾"	$8-10	$10-14	$15-18
server, center handled	10"	$60-75	$75-120	$100-125
sugar		$15-18	$18-20	$25-40
tray, oval, handled	14"x10"	$45-65	$65-85	$75-95
vase	9"	$50-65	$65-100	$100-150

Yellow 5" keyhole candlestick with cut base.
$35.00 – 55.00.

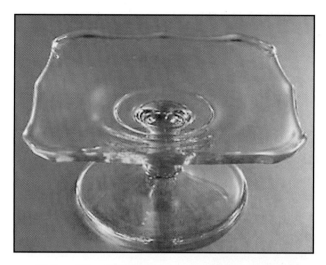

Yellow 5" x 2¼" cheese stand. $20.00 – 25.00.

Ebony 6½" square candy with silver overlay.
$95.00 – 120.00.

Ebony 4⅛" x 1¼" flat candlestick. $20.00 – 30.00.

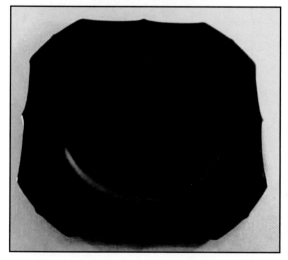

Ebony 8" luncheon plate. $22.00 – 28.00.

Amber mushroom candlestick. $18.00 – 22.00.

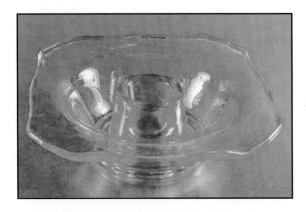

Green flat candlestick.
$20.00 – 30.00.

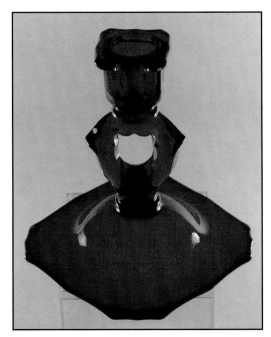

Royal Blue flat candle-
stick. $30.00 – 40.00.

Ruby 5" keyhole candlestick. $50.00 – 65.00.

Nerva

This is one of the few patterns that has an unknown number, because no catalog information has come to light. It is a series of dots, ribs, and beautiful scroll work and is spectacular, especially in Ruby.

The crystal pieces have been found with the etchings Bridal Wreath, Pam's Floral, and Nerva Flower, as well as several cuttings. The wide border is perfect for decoration.

Description	Size	Crystal	Ruby
bowl, cereal	6½"x2¼"	$18-22	$25-35
bowl, console	13"	$45-65	$75-95
bowl, fruit, handled	10"	$50-70	$75-95
bowl, oval	12"	$40-55	$65-85
cake plate	12"	$75-100	$150-175
candlestick	5¾"	$25-30 ea.	$40-60 ea.
candlestick, double	5¾"x6⅝"	$40-50 ea.	$65-85 ea.
candy, covered	6⅞"	$50-65	$100-125
cheese & cracker, w/lid	12"	$100-125	$150-200
comport	9½"	$60-80	$100-120
comport, high ftd.	6"x8"	$50-65	$75-95
creamer	3⅝"	$20-25	$35-40
cup		$20-25	$35-40
mayonnaise liner	6½"	$10-15	$20-25
mayonnaise set	3⅝"	$50-75	$75-100
relish, 3-part	6½"x11"	$45-65	$65-85
saucer	6½"	$10-15	$20-25
server, center handled	13"	$50-75	$75-100
sugar	3⅝"	$20-25	$35-40

Crystal 5¾" candlestick.
$25.00 – 30.00.

Crystal covered candy. The lid is a New Martinsville Radience pattern; this combination is either a marriage or was made later by New Martinsville. $50.00 – 65.00.

Ruby 6" tall 8" comport. $75.00 – 95.00.

Ruby footed mayonnaise. $55.00 – 75.00.

Ruby footed and cupped sugar or mayonnaise. $55.00 – 75.00.

Flat covered candy, 7". $100.00 – 125.00.

Ruby-flashed double candlestick. $50.00 – 65.00.

Ruby cup and saucer. $55.00 – 65.00.

Ruby double candlestick. $65.00 – 85.00.

Party Line #191 and #192

Party Line is one of Paden City's most prolific patterns. It was sold to restaurants, soda fountains, hotels, and cafeterias because the shapes were perfect for restaurant ware and Party Line was a sturdy pattern that could hold up under a lot of abuse. Paden City also sold a line of lighter weight dinnerware meant for the home. Party Line can be found in all of Paden City's colors, but finding Ruby, Light Aqua, Teal, or Cobalt Blue will be difficult. Like most patterns made during the depression years, green and pink seem to have been the most popular colors and are much easier to find. For a workhorse pattern, the crystal used for Party Line was of good quality and is remarkably pretty.

Party Line can be found in the more fragile blown pieces as well as the heavier and more common pressed pieces. The 74 oz. jug may not be easily recognized as Party Line, because there are four rings at the top and it has a plain base. The Amber pitcher with the Aqua handle is the only 2-color piece I've seen made by Paden City, and I'm not certain that it was. It may have been the product of a company that bought this mold after Paden City closed. Paden City included a few boudoir items in this pattern, but they are hard to find and often not recognized as Party Line. These items have a higher value because both Paden City collectors and perfume collectors are buying them, but generally this pattern is perfect for the collector who wants beautiful glass but isn't ready to buy the higher-priced etchings and patterns. Pieces of Party Line can be found with cuttings and with etchings. Cuttings add 10% to the value. Etched pieces are priced in the first half of this book.

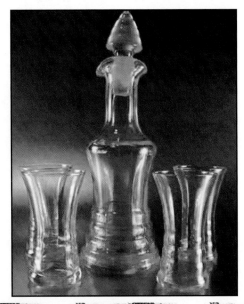

Green #191 9¼" cordial decanter, 8 oz., $125.00 – 150.00, and 3¼" whiskies, $20.00 – 22.00 each.

Green #191 12" high-footed cake salver. $65.00 – 75.00.

Green #191 10½" high-footed bowl. $65.00 – 75.00.

Description	Line	Size	Amber/ Crystal	Aqua (Lt. or Dark)	Pink/ Green	Ruby/ Blue	Mulberry/Ebony
banana split	191	8¼"	$20-24	$35-40	$25-30		
bowl, crushed fruit	191	9⁵⁄₁₆", 80 oz.	$75-95	$150-175	$100-125		
bowl, deep or flared	191	deep, 9";	$25-30	$45-50	$30-35		
		flared, 11",	$25-30	$45-50	$30-35		
bowl, high ftd.	191	10½"	$45-60	$75-95	$65-75		
bowl, indiv. berry	191	4½"	$5-10	$15-18	$10-15		
bowl, master berry	191	9"	$35-45	$65-75	$45-50		
bowl, mixing	191	7"	$15-20	$35-45	$25-35		
bowl, mixing	191	8"	$25-35	$45-65	$35-50		
bowl, mixing	191	9"	$35-45	$65-85	$50-65		
bowl, rolled edge, console	191	12"	$20-35	$65-75	$45-55		
box, fridge	191	5½"	$20-30	$65-80	$45-55		
butter box & cover	191		$35-40	$75-85	$50-75		
cake salver, high ftd.	191	6½"x12"	$45-60	$150-175	$65-85		
candlestick	192	3½"	$18-20 ea.	$30-35 ea.	$20-25 ea.		
candlestick, dome ftd.	191		$18-22 ea.	$30-35 ea.	$22-25 ea.	$40-60 ea.	$35-50 ea.
candy, blown, w/cover	191	½ lb.	$40-60	$75-95	$65-85		
candy, covered, ftd.	191½	4½"	$40-55	$75-85	$50-75		
champagne, high ftd.	191	6 oz	$10-14	$18-20	$14-16		
cheese & cracker	191	12"	$45-65	$75-95	$65-85		
cheese & cracker, covered	191	10½"	$75-95	$125-150	$100-125		
cheese dish, w/lid	191	4½"x3½"	$20-30	$40-45	$30-35		
cigarette holder & cover	191		$35-50	$65-85	$50-75		$65-85

Shape	Line	Size	Amber/ Crystal	Aqua (Lt. or Dark)	Pink/ Green	Ruby/Blue	Mulberry/Ebony
Coca-Cola	191½	4½"x2⁵⁄₁₆", 5 oz.	$10-12	$14-16	$12-14		
Coca-Cola	191½	4⁹⁄₁₆"x2⅜", 6 oz.	$10-12	$14-16	$12-14		
Coca-Cola	191½	4⅜"x2⅜", 7 oz.	$12-14	$16-18	$14-16		
Coca-Cola	191½	5"x2⁷⁄₁₆", 8 oz.	$12-14	$16-18	$14-16		
Coca-Cola	191½	5⁷⁄₁₆"x2¹⁵⁄₁₆", 10 oz.	$15-18	$22-24	$18-22		
Coca-Cola	191½	5⅜"x2⁷⁄₁₆", 12 oz.	$16-19	$25-30	$20-22		
cocktail, ftd.	191	3¾"x2⅞", 3½ oz.	$12-14	$18-20	$14-18	$20-25	
cocktail, ftd.	192	3¾"x2¹³⁄₁₆", 2½ oz.	$12-14	$18-20	$14-18	$20-25	
cocktail liner	191½	2⅜"x2⅜", 2½ oz.	$8-10	$12-14	$10-12		
cocktail liner	191½	2⁵⁄₁₆x2⅝", 3½ oz.	$8-10	$12-14	$10-12		
cocktail shaker	191	18 oz.	$100-125	$275-300	$150-200		$275-325
cocktail shaker, w/reamer top	191	18 oz.	$125-150	$300-350	$125-150		$450-500
comport, high ftd.	191	7"x7"	$30-35	$50-70	$40-50		
comport, low ft.	191	9"x3⅛"	$20-25	$45-65	$35-45		
comport, low ftd.	191	11"	$40-50	$75-100	$50-75		
creamer	191	2¾"x2⅜", 7 oz.	$10-12	$20-25	$15-18		
custard	191	6 oz.	$8-10	$14-16	$10-12		
decanter, cordial	191	9", 8 oz.	$100-125		$125-150		
decanter, wine	191	10", 22 oz.	$100-125		$125-150		
goblet	191	6³⁄₁₆"x3⅜", 9 oz.	$14-18	$24-28	$18-24	$40-50	
goblet	191½	9 oz.	$14-18	$24-28	$18-24	$40-50	
grape juice	191	5¼"	$12-16	$20-24	$15-20		
grape juice	191	4"x2⅜" dia., 4½ oz.	$15-18	$22-25	$18-22	$25-28	
ice tea	191½	5⁷⁄₁₆"x3¾", 14 oz.	$25-35	$45-50	$35-45	$50-65	
ice tea, blown	192	12 oz.	$30-35		$45-50		
ice tea, pressed	191½	5⁷⁄₁₆"x3½", 12 oz.	$25-35	$45-50	$35-45	$50-65	
ice tub, large	191	4⁵⁄₁₆"x7½"	$35-40	$50-75	$40-60		$45-70
ice tub, no. 1	191	4⅛"x6"	$35-40	$50-75	$40-60		$45-70
ice tub, no. 2, w/metal handle	191		$35-50	$75-85	$50-70		
jug, hospital	191½	5", 36 oz.	$55-75	$100-125	$75-100		$100-125
jug, w/cover, grape juice	192	32 oz.	$100-120	$155-175	$125-145		
jug, w/cover, hospital	191½	7", 36 oz.	$65-95	$125-150	$100-125		$125-150
jug, w/cover, ice tea	192	54 oz.	$120-140	$175-225	$150-175		
jug, w/cover, rings at top	191	74 oz. 10¾", 74 oz.	$120-140	$175-225	$150-175		$175-225
jug, w/cover, w/ or w/o optic	194	70 oz.	$120-140	$175-225	$150-175		
jug, w/o cover, rings at top	191	9", 74oz."	$100-120	$150-175	$125-150		$150-175
marmalade, w/glass lid	191	12 oz.	$40-45	$65-75	$45-60		
mayonnaise, low ftd. (comport)	191		$35-50	$55-70	$50-60		$65-80
mayonnaise liner	191	8"	$8-10	$12-15	$10-12		
measuring cup & reamer, #10	191		$75-125		$100-125		
measuring jug		36 oz.	$200-350	$350-450	$150-195		$500-650
measuring jug & reamer	191	36 oz.	$175-225*	$600-700	$175-225		$700-800

Description	Line	Size	Amber/ Crystal	Aqua (Lt. or Dark)	Pink/ Green	Ruby/ Blue	Mulberry/Ebony
parfait, ftd.	191	5⅝"x2¹¹⁄₁₆", 5 oz.	$15-18	$22-25	$18-22	$25-28	
perfume, w/dauber	191	5¼"	$65-80	$100-125	$75-100		$100-125
plate, bread & butter	191	6"	$8-10	$12-14	$10-12		
plate, luncheon	191	8"	$12-16	$20-24	$16-20		
plate, serving	191	10"	$18-22	$35-38	$24-28		
powder jar, ftd.	191		$35-45	$60-75	$45-60		$60-75
salt & pepper	191	3"	$18-22	$75-95	$50-65	$75-95	
server, center handled	191	11"	$35-50	$100-125	$75-95		
sherbet, high ftd.	191	4⅞"x 4⅛", 6 oz.		$8-12	$15-17	$12-15	$18-22
sherbet, low ftd.	191	3⁷⁄₁₆"x3⁷⁄₁₆", 3½ oz.	$8-12	$15-17	$12-15	$18-22	
sherbet, low ftd.	191	3 3/1"x4¹⁄₁₆", 4½ oz	$8-12	$15-17	$12-15	$18-22	
soda (new style)	191½	6⅝"x2¹⁵⁄₁₆", 12 oz	$12-15	$20-24	$15-20	$20-24	
soda, ftd.	191	4¹³⁄₁₆"x3⁷⁄₁₆", 6 oz.	$12-16	$20-24	$15-20	$20-24	
soda, ftd.	191	5¼"x3⁵⁄₁₆", 8 oz.	$12-15	$20-24	$15-20	$20-24	
soda, ftd.	191	5⅞"x3⁹⁄₁₆", 10 oz.	$15-18	$22-25	$18-22	$22-25	
soda, ftd.	191	7¹⁄₁₆"x3¹¹⁄₁₆", 12 oz.	$15-18	$24-28	$22-24	$25-30	
soda, ftd.	191	7⅜"x4" 14 oz.	$15-18	$24-28	$24-26	$30-35	
soda, ftd., cupped	191	5"x2½", 6 oz	$12-16	$20-24	$15-20	$20-24	
soda, ftd., cupped	191	5⅜"x2⅜", 8 oz.	$12-15	$20-24	$15-20	$20-24	
soda, ftd., cupped	191	5¹⁵⁄₁₆"x2⅞", 10 oz.	$15-18	$22-25	$18-22	$22-25	
soda, ftd., cupped	191	7⅛"x2⅞", 12 oz.	$15-18	$22-25	$18-22	$22-25	
soda, ftd., cupped	191	7½"x3⅛", 14 oz.	$18-20	$25-30	$22-25	$25-30	
sugar	191	2½"x3⁹⁄₁₆", 7 oz.	$10-12	$20-25	$15-18		
sugar, covered, hotel	191½	2½"x3⅝", 10 oz.	$20-25		$35-40		
sugar shaker, 6 rings	191	4½"	$125-200		$275-325		
sugar shaker, ribbed base	191	4½"	$100-175		$150-175		
sundae, crimped .	191	9 oz.	$12-15	$25-30	$15-20	$30-35	
sundae, ftd., tulip	191	5⅞"x4⅛", 4 oz.	$10-12	$20-22	$15-18	$25-30	
sundae, ftd, tulip	191	5⅞"x4½", 6 oz.	$10-12	$20-22	$15-18	$25-30	
syrup, w/glass lid	191	12 oz.	$35-50	$65-80	$65-70		
syrup, nickel plated top	191	4¾"	$35-50	$65-80	$65-70		
tumbler	191½	3¹⁵⁄₁₆"x2⅞", 7 oz.	$10-12	$20-22	$16-18	$24-28	
tumbler	191½	4³⁄₁₆"x3⅛", 9oz.	$12-14	$22-24	$18-20	$25-30	
tumbler	192	2½ oz.	$14-16	$22-24	$18-20	$28-32	
tumbler	192	5 oz.	$10-12	$20-22	$16-18	$24-28	
tumbler	192	8 oz.	$12-14	$22-24	$18-20	$25-30	
tumbler, barrel	191	4"x2⁷⁄₁₆", 9 oz.	$12-14	$22-24	$18-20	$25-30	
tumbler, blown	191	8 oz.	$14-18		$24-28		
tumbler, blown	194	10 oz. or 12 oz.	$15-20		$20-30		
tumbler, pressed	191½	7 oz. or 9 oz.	$12-14	$22-24	$18-20	$25-30	
tumbler, wine	191	3 oz.	$15-18	$23-25	$20-22	$28-30	
vase**	191		$75-100	$125-175	$100-145		$125-175
vase, crimped top	192	7"	$75-100	$125-175	$100-145		
vase, fan	191	7"	$35-40	$65-85	$50-65		
water bottle.	191	9½", 48 oz.	$50-75	$100-125	$75-100	$200-225	$200-225
wine, ftd.	191	2⁷⁄₁₆"x2⅛", 1½ oz.	$10-12	$18-20	$12-16	$20-24	
wine, ftd.	191	2⅜"x2½", 2½ oz.	$10-12	$18-20	$12-16	$20-24	

*Amber only, crystal is $500-650.

**made from 74oz. jug

287

Green #191 footed mayonnaise, $50.00 – 75.00, and spoon, $35.00.

Green #191 salt and pepper shakers. $50.00 – 65.00 (pair).

Green #191 9" low-footed comport with rolled edge. $35.00 – 45.00.

Green #192 7" crimped-top vase. $100.00 – 145.00.

Green #191 6" fan vase. $50.00 – 65.00.

Green #191 sugar and creamer. $30.00 – 36.00.

Green #191 6" plate. $10.00 – 12.00.

Green #191 36 oz. measuring jug. $150.00 – 195.00.

Green #191 ice tub, 6½" deep. $40.00 – 60.00.

Green #191 crushed fruit jar. $100.00 – 125.00.

Green #191 satinized ice tub, 6½" deep.
$40.00 – 60.00.

Green #191 cup and saucer. $125.00 – 150.00.

Green #191 74 oz. jug. $150.00 – 175.00.

Green #191 12 oz. marmalade. $45.00 – 60.00.

Green #191 12 oz. syrup and liner.
$70.00 – 75.00.

Green #191 11" low-footed comport with Gypsy
cutting. $65.00 – 85.00.

Green #191 7" high-footed comport with Gypsy cutting. $50.00 – 65.00.

Green #191 18 oz. cocktail shaker.
$150.00 – 175.00.

Green #191 3½ oz. footed cocktail.
$14.00 – 18.00.

Green #191 5 oz. parfait.
$18.00 – 22.00.

Green #191½ 12 oz. Coca-Cola.
$20.00 – 22.00.

Green #191 10 oz. soda, $15.00 – 20.00; 8 oz. soda, $18.00 – 22.00, and 6 oz. tulip sundae, $15.00 – 18.00.

Green #191 6 oz. high-footed sherbet. $12.00 – 15.00.

Green #191 4½ oz. low-footed sherbet. $12.00 – 15.00.

Green #191 10 oz. soda, $18.00 – 22.00 and 14 oz. soda, $24.00 – 26.00.

Green #191½ 12 oz. ice tea. $35.00 – 45.00.

Green #191 1½ oz. wine. $12.00 – 16.00.

Green #191 2½ oz. wine. $12.00 – 16.00.

Green #191½ 7 oz. tumbler. $16.00 – 18.00.

Amber #191 dome-footed candlestick.
$18.00 – 22.00.

Amber #191 salt and pepper shakers. $35.00 – 45.00 (pair).

Amber #191 3½ oz. cocktail
(very light yellow-Amber).
$12.00 – 14.00.

Amber #191 12 oz.
soda. $15.00 – 18.00.

Amber #191 11" low-footed comport. $40.00 – 50.00.

Amber #191 8 oz. blown tumbler, $14.00 – 18.00, and 74 oz. jug, $120.00 – 140.00.

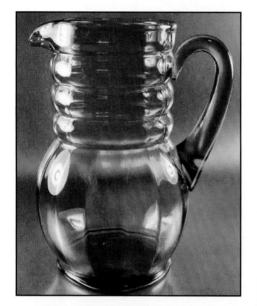

Amber/Aqua #191 74 oz. jug. $120.00 – 140.00.

Dark Aqua #191 5¼" perfume and dauber. $100.00 – 125.00.

Aqua #191 5" ruffled vase. $65.00 – 85.00.

Dark Aqua #191 dome-footed candle-stick. $30.00 – 35.00.

Dark Aqua #191 footed mayonnaise with liner,
$65.00 – 85.00, and spoon, $50.00.

Aqua #191 6½" ice tub. $50.00 – 75.00.

Dark Aqua #191 low-footed, covered candy.
$75.00 – 85.00.

Aqua #191 10 oz. soda.
$22.00 – 25.00.

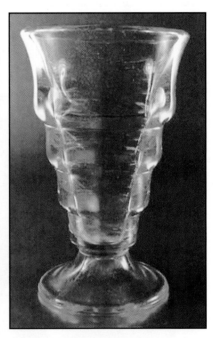

Aqua #191 5¼" grape juice, 6 oz.
$20.00 – 24.00.

Aqua #191 6 oz. soda.
$20.00 – 24.00.

Aqua #191 5 oz. parfait.
$22.00 – 25.00.

Aqua #191½ 12 oz. Coca-Cola.
$25.00 – 30.00.

Aqua #191 7" fan vase. $65.00 – 85.00.

Royal Blue #191 dome-footed candlestick (the bottom was left plain for cuttings). $40.00 – 60.00.

Crystal #191 6 oz. grape juice, $12.00 – 14.00, and 2½ oz. cocktail, $12.00 – 14.00, and #191½ 7 oz. tumbler, $12.00 – 16.00.

Crystal #191 5 oz. parfait, $15.00 – 18.00, and 4½ oz. sherbet, $8.00 – 12.00.

Cheriglo #192 3½" candlestick. $20.00 – 25.00.

Cheriglo #191 low-footed covered candy with Marie cutting. $65.00 – 95.00.

Cheriglo #191 4½" sugar shaker. $150.00 – 175.00.

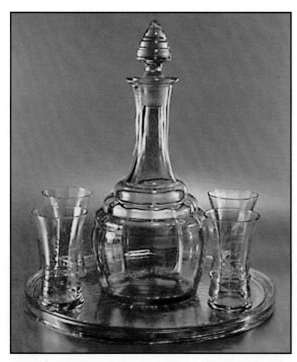

Cheriglo #191 12" flared console bowl with Gypsy cutting. $65.00 – 85.00.

Cheriglo #191 22 oz. decanter, $125.00 – 150.00; 3¼" whiskey, $20.00 – 22.00 (each), and 9¼" tray, $25.00 – 35.00.

Cheriglo #191 14 oz. footed soda. $25.00 – 26.00.

Cheriglo #191 8 oz. footed soda.
$15.00 – 20.00.

Cheriglo #191 9¼" cordial decanter, 8 oz.
$125.00 – 150.00.

Cheriglo #191 6 oz. footed soda.
$15.00 – 20.00.

Cheriglo #191 3½ oz. footed cocktail,
$14.00 – 16.00, and 2½ oz. footed wine,
$12.00 – 16.00.

Cheriglo #191 12 oz. footed soda.
$22.00 – 24.00.

Cheriglo #191 3½ oz. footed cocktail.
$14.00 – 16.00.

Cheriglo #191½ 12 oz. ice tea.
$35.00 – 45.00.

Cheriglo #194 70 oz. jug.
$150.00 – 175.00.

Cheriglo #191 6½" ice tub. $40.00 – 60.00.

Cheriglo #191 salt shaker.
$25.00 – 30.00.

Cheriglo #191 crushed-fruit jar. $100.00 – 125.00.

Cheriglo #191 dome-footed candlesticks.
$44.00 – 50.00 (pair).

Cheriglo #191 cup and saucer. $14.00 – 16.00.

Cheriglo #191 8" luncheon plate. $16.00 – 20.00.

Cheriglo #191 ½ lb. covered candy.
$65.00 – 85.00.

Cheriglo #191 dome-footed candlesticks with Gypsy cutting.
$50.00 – 56.00 (pair).

Cheriglo #191 11" low-footed comport with Gypsy
cutting. $65.00 – 85.00.

Cheriglo #191 3½" x 4¼" covered cheese dish. $30.00 – 35.00.

Cheriglo #191, 11" flared console bowl with Gypsy cutting.
$65.00 – 85.00.

Cheriglo #191 10½" high-footed bowl
with Gypsy cutting. $85.00 – 115.00.

Teal #191 8 oz. syrup. $75.00 – 85.00.

Ruby #191 salt and pepper with unusual lids.
$75.00 – 95.00 (pair).

Mulberry dome-footed candlestick.
$35.00 – 50.00.

Penny Line #991

Penny Line is one of those patterns that is readily identified as Paden City and, along with Party Line, was one of the company's most popular patterns. It remained in the line until the doors of the company were closed in 1951, 20 years after it was introduced.

Penny Line was introduced by Paden City sometime before December of 1931. There is a trade report that seems to indicate that Penny Line wasn't a brand-new product for Paden City. It says that Paden City's Penny Line was "unique in many respects. The rings are placed rather differently than they are by other factories. There seems to be a certain distinction here that is not found elsewhere, and throughout all items the placing of the rings conforms." That article goes on to name the pieces that were new to that line. It says, "The range of items has recently been extended to include stemware, tumblers, plates, candlesticks, bowls, pitcher, etc., all of which are obtainable at a popular price." I'm quoting the piece carefully, because what it says next is very important

to Paden City collectors: "They may be had in a wide selection of colors, including crystal glass. The colors include a particularly good green, a Cheriglo, which is rather akin to a pink; an Amber, a Royal Blue, a Ruby (and the Ruby is one of the most outstanding numbers in the array), AND THE PRIMROSE (my capitalization)." The reason this is important is that Amber, Cheriglo, and Primrose are all listed as colors used in Penny Line. That rules out the idea that Primrose is a shade of Amber or even an off-color Cheriglo. As you will see here, the set included a light yellow, which is the very definition of *primrose*.

In a Canton catalog page that was pictured in Hazel Marie Weatherman's *Colored Glassware of the Depression Era, Book 2*, there is a line called Futura that seems to be a new version of Penny Line.

Futura has been attributed to Paden City because of the pieces shown in the Canton catalog, but we now know for certain that Paden City never made this pattern.

Royal Blue cup and saucer. $35.00 – 40.00.

Royal Blue low-footed goblet.
$35.00 – 50.00.

Royal Blue cup and saucer, $35.00 – 45.00; low-footed goblet, $35.00 – 50.00, and 6" plate, $20.00 – 24.00; and 8" luncheon plate, $30.00 – 45.00, and low-footed sherbet, $25.00 – 30.00.

Description	Size	Crystal/Amber	Cheriglo/Green	Primrose/ Mulberry	Ruby/Blue
bowl, handled	7¾"	$25-35	$35-45	$45-65	$45-60
cocktail, high ftd.	3½ oz.	$12-16	$14-18	$16-20	$15-20
cocktail, low ftd.	3½ oz.	$12-16	$14-18	$16-20	$15-20
cocktail shaker	40 oz.	$75-100	$100-125	$150-165	$150-200
cordial	1¼ oz.	$12-18	$20-26	$22-32	$25-35
cream		$10-14	$12-16	$18-20	$20-25
decanter	22 oz.	$75-100	$100-125	$125-150	$150-175
fingerbowl		$12-15	$15-18	$20-22	$24-26
goblet, high ftd.		$18-22	$25-30	$30-40	$35-50
goblet, low ftd.		$18-22	$25-30	$30-40	$35-50
grapefruit, low ftd.		$20-24	$28-34	$34-38	$36-42
pitcher	8¼"	$100-125	$125-175	$150-200	$175-225
plate	6"	$12-14	$14-16	$16-20	$20-24
plate	8"	$15-18	$18-22	$30-35	$30-45
plate, liner	5¾"	$10-12	$12-15	$15-20	$18-24
plate, service	11"	$35-40	$40-45	$40-45	$45-50
sherbet, high ftd.		$15-18	$18-22	$22-26	$25-30
sherbet, low ftd.		$15-18	$18-22	$22-26	$25-30
sugar		$10-14	$12-16	$18-20	$20-25
tray, 2 handles		$65-95	$75-100	$125-150	$125-150
tray, center handled	10½"	$50-65	$75-85	$100-120	$125-150
tumbler, ice tea	12 oz.	$20-24	$24-30	$30-35	$30-35
tumbler, orange juice	5 oz.	$20-24	$24-30	$30-35	$30-35
tumbler, table	9 oz.	$18-20	$22-28	$28-33	$28-33
tumbler, wine	3½ oz.	$20-25	$25-30	$30-35	$30-35
wine, high ftd.	3 oz.	$12-16	$16-20	$20-25	$20-25

Original set of high-footed cocktails: Royal Blue, $15.00 – 20.00; green, $14.00 – 18.00; Primrose, $16.00 – 20.00; Cheriglo, $14.00 – 18.00; Ruby, $15.00 – 20.00; and Amber, $12.00 – 16.00.

Royal Blue high-footed cocktail.
$15.00 – 20.00.

Crystal high-footed sherbet. Penny Line
look-alike.

Green 1 oz. cordial.
$20.00 – 26.00.

Green 3 oz. wine. $16.00 – 20.00.

Mulberry 12 oz. ice tea tumbler.
$30.00 – 35.00.

Mulberry cup and saucer. $35.00 – 40.00.

Mulberry 2½ oz. wine tumbler, $20.00 – 25.00; 6 oz. low-footed sherbet, $22.00 – 26.00, and 12 oz. flat ice tea tumbler, $30.00 – 35.00.

Mulberry 11" center-handled server. $100.00 – 120.00.

Mulberry 8" x 2½" handled salad bowl. $45.00 – 65.00.

Mulberry cream and sugar. $40.00 – 50.00.

Ruby 8¼" jug. $175.00 – 225.00.

Ruby low-footed sherbet. $25.00 – 30.00.

Ruby low-footed goblet. $35.00 – 50.00.

Ruby cup and saucer. $35.00 – 40.00.

Ruby 3 oz. wine.
$20.00 – 25.00.

Ruby flat sherbet.
$25.00 – 30.00.

Ruby 11" plate. $45.00 – 50.00.

Ruby 3 oz. wine. $20.00 – 25.00.

Ruby high-footed cocktail.
$15.00 – 20.00.

Ruby high-footed goblet.
$35.00 – 50.00.

Ruby 12 oz. ice tea tumbler.
$30.00 – 35.00.

Ruby 22 oz. decanter.
$100.00 – 175.00.

Ruby high-footed cocktail.
$15.00 – 20.00.

Ruby 8" x 2½" handled salad bowl. $45.00 – 60.00.

Ruby 11" center-handled server. $125.00 – 150.00.

Ruby tumbler grouping: 5 oz. orange juice, 12 oz. ice tea, 2½ oz. wine, and 9 oz. table tumbler.

Ruby stemware grouping: low-footed goblet, high footed goblet, low-footed sherbet, high-footed sherbet, 1 oz. cordial, high-footed cocktail, and 3 oz. high-footed wine.

Ruby 2½ oz. wine. $30.00 – 35.00.

Ruby 11 oz. decanter with heavy silver overlay. $200.00 – 225.00.

Ruby sugar and creamer. $40.00 – 50.00.

Ruby 4⅝" x 2½" finger bowl. $24.00 – 26.00.

Ruby 5 oz. orange juice.
$30.00 – 35.00.

Cheriglo 3 oz. wine.
$16.00 – 20.00.

Primrose high-footed cocktail.
$16.00 – 20.00.

Amber high-footed cocktail.
$12.00 – 16.00.

Futura, Paden City or Canton Glass?

Although Futura has been accepted as a Paden City pattern by most collectors, there has always been a question as to that attribution. The only place Futura is shown is in the Canton catalog page reprinted by Hazel Marie Weatherman in her *Colored Glass of the Depression Era, Book 2* price guide. The catalog is dated 1954, after Paden City had closed its doors and Canton had purchased a large quantity of the Paden City molds. It has been assumed by many that every piece in that catalog was made using Paden City molds. Futura was incorrectly labeled Paden City, and the possibility exists that there are more patterns shown in that catalog that are original Canton pieces.

The mold drawing shown here is positive proof that Futura was being made at Canton Glass Company in 1931, twenty years before it purchased the Paden City molds. It looks as though when Canton bought those molds, it used several Penny Line molds to expand the Futura line, forever blurring the line between Penny Line and Futura. Even taking that fact into account, it is clear that Paden City did not make any items using the Futura molds, so that pattern must be dropped from this and other books written about Paden City. This situation is another good example of the reason glass research should be written in pencil.

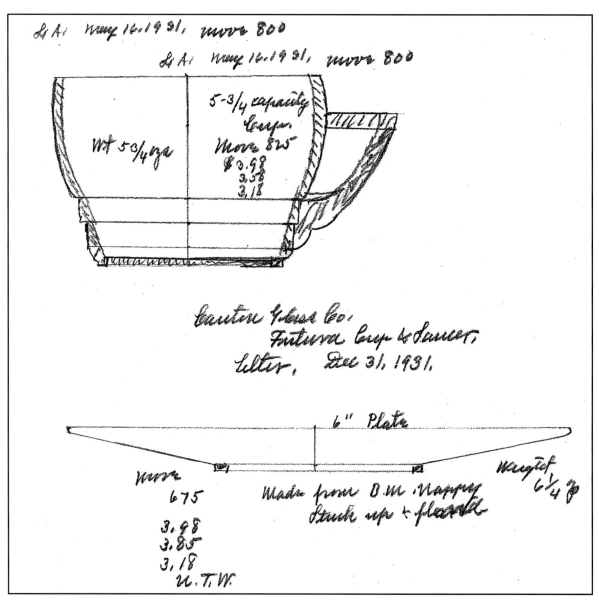

Canton Glass Company drawing of Futura cup and saucer.

Plume #888

Plume may not have been introduced until a year or two before the demise of Paden City. Some of the molds were sold to Canton Glass, but we now know that the heart-shaped candlesticks and the epergne molds were sold to the Fenton Art Glass Company. Those two pieces were made as a part of Rubel's Emerald Glo line, and appear in one of Rubel's catalogs.

According to the information I have, Rubel commissioned those molds and it owned them outright.

A letter from Sam Fisher regarding the molds he owned does not list these items. Those pieces were also produced by Fenton for Rubel in the same colors used by Paden City. This fact is unlikely to drop the value of those pieces, it will just add to the number of collectors who are looking for them. More information about the connection between Fenton, Paden City, and Rubel can be found in the Emerald Glo section.

Description	Size	Crystal	Green/Ruby
bowl, crimped	6⅜"	$18-20	$25-35
bowl, console	12"	$45-65	$65-95
bowl, ftd., console	11"	$45-65	$65-95
bowl, handled	11"	$45-65	$75-100
cake plate, ftd.	11"	$50-75	$75-125
candlestick, heart shape		$25-35 ea.	$45-55 ea.
candy, 3-part	7"	$45-75	$125-150
cheese & cracker, covered	12"	$50-75	$100-125
comport, low ftd.	10"	$50-75	$100-125
creamer	5 oz.	$18-22	$24-28
epergne	11"	$150-225	$450-600
marmalade & lid	7 oz.	$25-35	$50-65
nappy, heart shape	6¾"	$25-35	$50-65
relish, 3-part	7"	$22-28	$45-65
relish, 4-part	10"	$30-40	$50-65
server, center handled	11"	$45-55	$75-95
sugar	5½ oz.	$18-22	$24-28

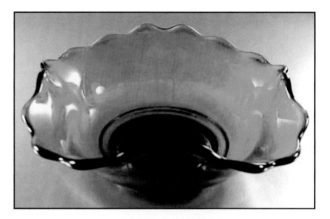

Green 6⅜" crimped bowl. $25.00 – 35.00.

Green heart-shaped nappy. $55.00 – 60.00.

Green 8½" comport, 6" tall. $100.00 – 125.00.

Green candlesticks, $15.00 – 55.00 each, and epergne, $450.00 – 600.00.

Popeye & Olive #994

This is one of the most difficult patterns to find. And because it isn't often seen, many collectors mistake Imperial's Old English pattern for Popeye and Olive. The dots on the Imperial pieces are all indented. On the Popeye and Olive pieces, there is a row of raised dots on the top side of the piece and another row of raised dots on the bottom side. None of the dots are indented.

The decanter can be found with several stoppers, but the jigger stopper is the most expensive. A han-

dled decanter has been found in blue. The tray is completely plain. It can be found in crystal, green, Ruby, Cobalt Blue, Cheriglo, Amber, Topaz (yellow), and Ebony. I've only seen this pattern in Ruby, Cobalt Blue, Cheriglo, and Ebony, but those other colors are listed in a 1932 advertisement, so they must exist. The 7" vase has been found with a shaker top, but I doubt that it was sold that way. The vase is too short to be a shaker.

Description	Size	Crystal/Amber	Ruby/Blue	Cheriglo/Green/Topaz	Ebony
bowl	8"	$35-45	$75-85	$50-75	$75-85
bowl, finger	5¼"	$20-30	$35-45	$25-35	$38-42
bowl, handled	8"	$40-50	$80-100	$60-80	$80-100
claret	3½ oz.	$10-14	$18-20	$15-18	$20-22
creamer		$20-25	$35-40	$30-35	$35-40

Description	Size	Crystal/Amber	Ruby/Blue	Cheriglo/Green/ Topaz	Ebony
cup	2½"	$10-15	$22-25	$18-22	$22-25
decanter, faceted	36 oz.	$70-90	$185-225	$150-200	$185-225
decanter, handled	36 oz.		$350-400		
decanter/jigger	36 oz.	$75-100	$200-250	$150-225	$200-250
goblet, footed	6⅛", 10 oz.	$10-15	$35-40	$30-35	$35-40
ice tea	4½", 12 oz.	$15-20	$35-40	$30-35	$35-40
ice tea	5", 17 oz.	$20-22	$38-45	$35-40	$38-45
orange juice	3"	$10-15	$22-30	$15-20	$25-30
pitcher	7½", 48 oz.	$75-100	$175-250	$150-200	$200-325
plate, bread & butter	6"	$10-12	$15-18	$12-15	$15-18
plate, handled	10"	$18-22	$35-40	$ 25-30	$35-42
plate, salad	8"	$12-15	$18-25	$15-20	$18-25
saucer	5 "	$ 8-10	$12-15	$10-12	$15-18
server, center-handled	10½"	$40-50	$75-125	$65-100	$75-125
sherbet, high ftd.	4½"	$10-15	$22-30	$15-25	$25-30
sherbet, low ftd.	3⅜"	$8-12	$20-25	$12-18	$20-25
sugar		$18-20	$30-35	$22-32	$30-35
sundae, tulip	5⅞", 7 oz.	$12-18	$35-40	$30-35	$35-40
tray, plain	9¼"	$20-25	$45-55	$35-45	$45-55
tumbler	3", 5 oz.	$18-22	$40-45	$35-45	$44-48
tumbler	4", 9 oz.	$10-15	$30-35	$20-30	$35-40
vase	7"	$50-75	$150-200	$100-125	$150-200
wine	2½", 2½ oz.	$18-20	$40-45	$30-35	$42-48

Ruby high-footed sherbet. $22.00 – 30.00.

Close-up of detail on Ruby high-footed sherbet.

Ruby 48 oz. jug. $175.00 – 250.00.

Ruby cup and saucer. $32.00 – 40.00.

Ruby 5¼" bowl. $35.00 – 45.00.

Ruby 8" luncheon plate. $18.00 – 25.00.

Ruby cream and sugar. $65.00 – 75.00.

Ruby 4½" high-footed sherbet, $22.00 – 30.00, and 3⅜" low-footed sherbet, $20.00 – 25.00.

Ruby 9 oz. tumbler, $30.00 – 35.00; 5 oz. orange juice, $22.00 – 30.00, and 2½ oz. wine, $40.00 – 45.00.

Ruby 12 oz. ice tea, $35.00 – 40.00, and 17 oz. ice tea, $38.00 – 45.00.

Ruby 9¼" decanter set tray. $45.00 – 55.00.

Ruby 7 oz. tulip sundae. $35.00 – 40.00.

Ruby 10 oz. goblet. $35.00 – 40.00.

Ruby 7" vase. $150.00 – 200.00.

Ruby 10" handled plate. $35.00 – 40.00.

Royal Blue 17 oz. ice tea. $38.00 – 45.00.

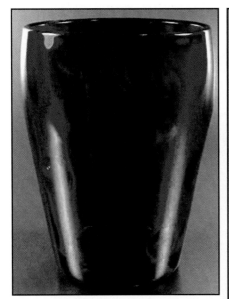

Royal Blue 12 oz. ice tea.
$35.00 – 40.00.

Royal Blue 36 oz. decanter.
$185.00 – 225.00.

Royal Blue 5 oz. wine. $40.00 – 45.00.

Royal Blue 10 oz. goblet, $35.00 – 40.00, and high-footed sherbet, $22.00 – 30.00.

Royal Blue 10½" center-handled server. $75.00 – 125.00.

Royal Blue 8" luncheon plate. $20.00 – 25.00.

Ebony 36 oz. decanter with with flat stopper. $185.00 – 225.00.

Ebony 36 oz. decanter with shot glass stopper. $200.00 – 250.00.

Ebony 2½ oz. wine. $42.00 – 48.00.

Ebony 9¼" decanter tray. $45.00 – 55.00.

Ebony 9¼" tray with 3⅞" star on base.

Close-up of pattern detail.

Cheriglo cup.
$25.00 – 35.00.

IMPERIAL OLD ENGLISH, often mistaken for Paden City's Popeye & Olive.

Regina #210

The Regina pattern is a series of layers crossed by a vertical optic that produces a block effect. Regina has a long list of pieces produced, a list almost as long as that of Party Line. Paden City was constantly adapting designs to enlarge its product line. Party Line and Regina are so similar that a Regina napkin or stationery holder has been mistakenly called Party Line for years. There are some very interesting trays that are very hard to find and a casserole that has to be called very rare. There is a photo of one of the trays in the Eden Rose section, but I have never seen a casserole, so unfortunately, I can't show one to you. The Regina cup can be found with several different handles, because of the impractical shape of the first one produced.

These blanks were used for the Ebony Forest, Harvester, Eden Rose, Ardith, Lela Bird, Delilah Bird, and Flamingo Sun etchings, as well as others. The list could go on and on, because this seemed to be one of the more popular blanks used by Paden City. Ebony Forest, on #210, was marketed by Frank L. Van Deman & Son of New York City, but that may not have been an exclusive contract.

Regina was produced for the soda fountain trade just as Party Line and Spire were. There is an incredible list of goblets and tumblers that were made, too many to list all the prices this time. The reamer sets are priced in the kitchenware section.

Cheriglo 6½" footed candy with wheel-cut design. $60.00 – 70.00.

Cheriglo 3¼" tumbler. $35.00 – 40.00.

Description	Size	Amber/Ebony	Crystal	Cheriglo/Green
banana split	8½"	$10-15*	$8-12	$15-18
bowl, closed tab handled	10"	$20-25	$18-22	$22-28
bowl, console	12"	$22-28	$20-24	$28-32
bowl, console	13"	$22-28	$20-24	$28-32
bowl, ftd. (comport)	10" x 3½"	$30-35	$25-30	$35-42
bowl, handled	10½" x 9"	$25-30	$22-25	$30-38
bowl, salad	10¼"	$22-28	$20-24	$28-32
cake plate	11"	$50-65	$40-50	$60-75
candlestick, mushroom	3"	$15-18 ea.	$12-15 ea.	$15-20 ea.
candy jar, flat	6½"	$50-65	$30-35	$50-65

Description	Size	Amber/Ebony	Crystal	Cheriglo/Green
candy jar, ftd.	6⅜"	$60-70	$35-45	$60-70
casserole, w/cover	7½"	$65-85	$45-50	$65-85
Coca-Cola	5, 6, 7, 8,10, & 12 oz.	$8-15*	$4-12	$12-18
cocktail	3½ oz.	$5-8*	$4-6	$5-8
cocktail shaker		$75-125	$50-65	$75-100
comport, bonbon	6½"	$12-15	$10-12	$15-18
comport, mayonnaise	7"x3½"	$15-18	$12-15	$18-24
creamer	3⅝"	$15-20	$10-12	$15-20
creamer, hotel		$18-22	$12-15	$15-20
cruet, oil	7 oz.	$20-25*	$18-22	$25-35
cup		$10-12	$8-10	$12-14
decanter	10"	$100-125	$75-95	$125-150
eggcup		$25-35	$18-22	$35-50
goblet, high ftd.	9 oz.	$10-12*	$8-10	$12-15
goblet, low ftd.	10 oz.	$10-12*	$8-10	$12-15
ice bucket	5½"x4"	$35-45	$20-25	$40-50
ice cream, ftd.	4"	$10-12*	$8-10	$12-15
malted milk, ftd.	6, 8,10, 12 oz.	$10-25*	$6-15	$12-28
napkin holder		$75-120	$50-75	$100-125
nappy, hotel	3½", 4", 4½"	$12-18	$8-16	$15-25
nappy, hotel	5", 6"	$20-24	$10-15	$20-35
parfait	4½ oz.	$8-12	$8-10	$10-15
pitcher, ice tea	10½"	$75-120*	$50-75	$100-150
pitcher, tankard	12 oz.	$40-55*	$20-25	$40-55
pitcher, tankard	18 oz.	$50-65*	$25-30	$50-65
pitcher, tankard	30 oz.	$65-80*	$30-35	$65-80
pitcher, tankard	47 oz.	$70-85*	$40-45	$70-85
pitcher, tankard	62 oz.	$75-100*	$45-55	$75-100
pitcher, tankard	74 oz.	$100-125*	$65-80	$100-125
pitcher, measuring	36 oz.	$150-200	$175-225	$150-200
plate, dinner	10¼"	$50-75	$20-25	$50-75
plate, handled	13⅛" x 11¼"	$50-75	$20-25	$50-75
plate, liner	7½"	$10-15	$8-10	$10-15
plate, luncheon	8¼"	$35-45	$18-22	$35-45
plate, tab handled	10"	$35-45	$18-22	$35-45
relish, 5-part, ftd.	9"x11¼"	$100-150	$75-100	$100-150
salver, candy	7"	$35-45	$18-22	$35-45
saucer		$10-15	$8-10	$10-15
shakers		$40-50	$20-30	$40-50
soda	6, 8, 10, 12 oz.	$8-20*	$6-15	$8-24
sugar	4"	$15-20	$10-12	$15-20
sugar, hotel		$18-22	$12-15	$15-20
sundae, tulip		$10-15*	$8-18	$12-18
tray (cream & sugar)	10½"	$25-35	$18-25	$30-45
tray	12½"	$35-65	$25-40	$45-75
tray, 5 compartments	12½"	$35-65	$25-40	$45-75
tumbler, blown	2½ oz.	$40-45*	$20-25	$45-60
tumbler, ice tea	12 oz.	$30-40*	$18-22	$30-40
tumble-up	8½"	$175-225	$125-175	$175-250
vase	6½"	$35-40	$20-25	$35-45
vase	10"	$40-45	$25-35	$45-55
vase, smoke stack	9"	$50-65	$30-40	$55-70
water bottle	48 oz.	$50-65*	$40-50	$65-85
wine, ftd.	3½ oz.	$14-16	$8-12	$14-16

* Amber only

Green 7 oz. oil cruet. $25.00 – 35.00.

Green 5½" x 4" small covered candy.
$50.00 – 65.00.

Cheriglo shaker. $20.00 – 25.00.

Mulberry 6½" footed candy. $60.00 – 70.00.

Mulberry 4⅜" x 6 ⅛" flared, footed mayonnaise.
$18.00 – 24.00.

Mulberry cup and saucer. $20.00 – 27.00.

Ebony cup and saucer. $20.00 – 27.00.

Ebony 10" vase. $40.00 – 45.00.

Amber shakers. $40.00 – 50.00 (pair).

Rena #154

This is another pattern that was found in *Paden City's Hotel, Restaurant, Bar and Soda Fountain Supplies Catalog, No. 3*. While restaurant ware seems to be the reason for this sturdy line, there was also a line of tableware produced for the home. A blown pitcher has been found with the Orchid etching and with the same swirl as used in the Rena pattern, but there is no catalog evidence that it is part of this line. It is priced in the Orchid listing. Rena is found in crystal, green, and Cheriglo, but other colors may exist.

Description	Size	Crystal	Cheriglo/Green
banana split	9"	$15-18	$18-22
bowl	4"	$5-7	$8-10
bowl	7"	$15-22	$22-28

Description	Size	Crystal	Cheriglo/Green
bowl	8"	$22-25	$25-30
Coca-Cola	4⁹⁄₁₆" 6 oz.	$10-12	$12-15
Coca-Cola	5 ¹⁄₁₆", 8 oz.	$12-14	$14-16
Coca-Cola	5½", 12 oz.	$15-17	$16-18
cocktail, ftd.	3⅝", 3½ oz.	$8-10	$10-12
cocktail, oyster	2⅞", 2½ oz.	$10-12	$12-15
creamer	2⁹⁄₁₆", 7 oz.	$8-10	$10-14
cruet, oil	4¾", 4 oz.	$40-50	$50-65
cruet, oil	6", 6 oz.	$42-52	$55-70
goblet, low ftd., #154½	5½", 8 oz.	$12-15	$15-18
ice tea	5", 12 oz.	$15-18	$20-24
ice tub	5½"	$35-45	$45-60
jug, ice lip	8½", 72 oz.	$50-65	$75-95
mug, beer		$35-45	
parfait	5¾", 4½ oz.	$10-12	$12-16
plate	6"	$8-10	$10-12
plate	8"	$10-12	$12-15
shakers	3⅛"	$20-30 pr.	$35-50 pr.
sherbet	2⁹⁄₁₆", 3½ oz.	$8-10	$10-12
sherbet	2⅞", 4 oz.	$8 -10	$10-12
sherbet	2¾", 5 oz.	$10-12	$12-15
soda (new style)	6½", 12 oz.	$12-14	$16-18
soda, ftd.	4¹³⁄₁₆", 6 oz.	$10-12	$12-15
soda, ftd.	5⅜", 8 oz.	$12-15	$15-18
soda, ftd	5¾", 10 oz.	$14-16	$18-20
soda, ftd.	6¾", 12 oz.	$16-18	$20-22
soda, ftd., #154½	7³⁄₁₆", 12 oz.	$18-20	$22-24
soda, ftd.	8", 14 oz.	$20-22	$24-26
sugar	3¼", 7 oz.	$8-10	$10-12
sugar, hotel	2⅞", 11 oz.	$15-18	$20-24
sugar pourer	3¾", 2 oz.	$25-30	$35-50
sugar pourer	4½", 12 oz.	$40-50	$150-175
sundae	6¹⁄₁₆", 6½ oz.	$12-15	$15-20
sundae, tall	6¹⁄₁₆", 6½ oz.	$12-15	$15-20
sundae, tulip	4⅝", 4 oz.	$10-13	$14-16
sundae, tulip	5³⁄₁₆", 5 oz.	$12-15	$15-18
sundae, tulip, #154½	5¼", 7 oz.	$12-16	$15-20
tumbler	3¹³⁄₁₆", 7 oz.	$10-12	$12-14
tumbler	3¾", 9 oz.	$10-14	$14-16
weiss beer	8 ³⁄₁₆", 16 oz.	$18-22	$22-28
weiss beer	8³⁄₁₆", 20 oz.	$22-25	$24-26
weiss beer, shammed	8³⁄₁₆", 14 oz.	$15-20	$20-25

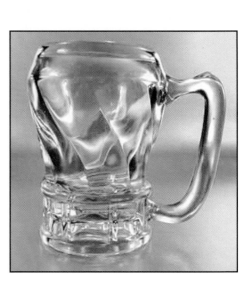

Crystal 2 oz. individual sugar shaker with pour top. $25.00 – 30.00.

Crystal 4½" sugar shaker with pour top. $40.00 – 50.00.

Crystal 6 oz. handled mug. $35.00 – 45.00.

Crystal salt and pepper. $20.00 – 30.00 (pair).

Green 2½ oz. oyster cocktail. $10.00 – 12.00.

Green salt shaker. $35.00 – 50.00 with pepper shaker.

Green sugar shaker with pour top. $150.00 – 175.00.

Green 4¾" 6 oz. footed soda. $12.00 – 15.00.

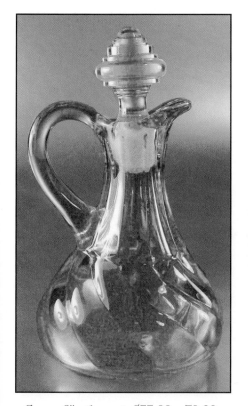

Cheriglo 6 oz. footed soda, $12.00 – 15.00, and 12 oz. Coca-Cola, $16.00 – 18.00.

Green 3¾"x 5¾" covered sugar bowl. $20.00 – 24.00.

Green 6" oil cruet. $55.00 – 70.00.

Cheriglo creamer. $10.00 – 14.00.

Cheriglo salt shaker. $35.00 – 50.00 with pepper shaker.

Cheriglo sugar shaker with pour top. $150.00 – 175.00.

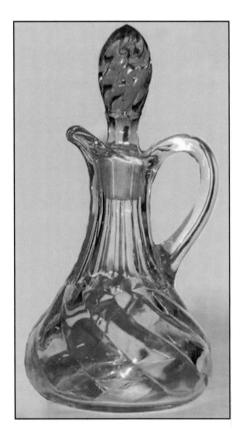

Cheriglo 7 oz. oil cruet; the stopper matches, but is not a known Paden City stopper. $55.00 – 70.00.

Cheriglo sugar. $10.00 – 12.00.

Cheriglo ice tub with 4 shot glasses. Ice tub $45.00 – 60.00, shot glasses $10.00 – 12.00 each.

Vale #444, a.k.a. Alexander

Line #444 is a late pattern that is very simple and elegant. The bowls in this pattern have very plain, round shapes and square bases. This design was also used by Cambridge, and I'm sure that there are some Paden City pieces in Cambridge collections. To make it even more confusing, both the single and the double candlesticks look just like Imperial's Candlewick pattern, and the candy boxes are very similar to some of Tiffin's candies. If this pattern is hard to find, it's because it is so easily confused with the products of other companies. If I needed a pattern to illustrate

Paden City's penchant to copy popular patterns, this would be it.

I'm uncertain as to whether the open comport should be here or included with the #900 items, but I think this is a smaller size than the #900 comport. Most of these pieces are found in crystal, but the candy boxes were made in green, Ruby, and Copen Blue, and were sometimes flashed with Ruby. Add 15% for flashed pieces. This plain pattern was also used for a lot of etchings.

Crystal 9½" wheel-cut footed candy. $30.00 – 35.00.

Ruby 9½" footed candy. $50.00 – 65.00.

Description	Size	Crystal	Ruby/Green/Blue
ashtray	3¾"	$4-6	
bowl, console	12½"	$22-25	
bowl, deep	8½"	$20-22	
bowl, handled	8½"	$24-26	
bowl, shallow	9"	$18-22	
bowl, shallow	12"	$22-25	
candlestick, single	6"	$25-30 ea.	
candlestick, double	5"	$25-30 ea.	
candy, flat	6"	$25-30	$45-50
candy, ftd	9½"	$30-35	$50-65
candy, sq. base	6"	$35-40	$50-65

Description	Size	Crystal	Ruby/Green/Blue
cheese & cracker	10½"	$40-50	
cheese & cracker, covered	12"	$50-65	
comport	7"	$18-22	$45-55
ice tub	5½"x8½"	$20-24	
plate	10½"	$18-20	
plate	15"	$18-20	
plate, handled	10½"	$20-24	
sherbet, cheese	5"	$12-15	

Ruby 6" flat candy. $45.00 – 50.00.

Ruby 6½" flared comport. $45.00 – 55.00.

Forest Green 6½" flared comport.
$45.00 – 55.00.

Specialty Items

Barware

The end of Prohibition brought about a golden era for glass factories. Suddenly, after all those years when no one needed fancy stemware, decanters, or cocktail shakers, booze was back and no one had those accessories in their homes. There was a rush to buy the glassware necessary for entertaining at cocktail parties and holidays, and the glass factories were in competition to produce the most original and beautiful sets. Paden City made some of their most beautiful glassware during this era.

Decanters

The decanters shown in the chrome holders are very similar, but the glass inserts were done by different companies. The Light Royal Blue decanter was made and etched by Paden City. The grape leaf has the same pattern as the leaf of the Vintager etching. I wasn't able to determine who made the green decanter, but it isn't a Paden City product. I'm including it only for identification value. The Eden Rose decanter is found in the same type holder and is priced in the Etchings section of this book.

The Penny Line decanter set is stunning. The bases of the tumblers and the decanter are covered with a thick silver overlay that makes that part of the glassware appear to be chrome to match the tray. Finding a matching set is very difficult.

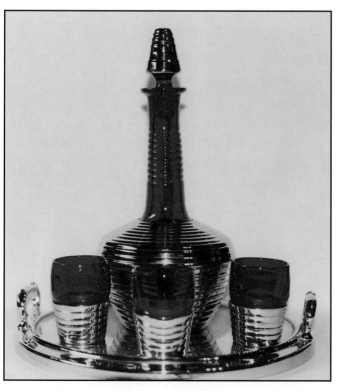

Penny Line decanter set Ruby with silver overlay.
$400.00 – 450.00.

Light Cobalt Blue Vintager wine decanter in metal frame. $125.00 – 150.00.

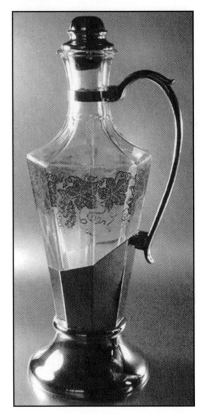

Close-up of the Paden City Vintager etching.

Close-up of the unknown vintage decanter etching.

Vintage green wine decanter in a metal frame; manufacturer is unknown.

Ruby #215½ tilt cordial decanter with silver overlay Poppy decoration. $50.00 – 65.00.

Ruby #211 12 oz. cordial decanter. $35.00 – 45.00.

Ruby #410 32 oz. decanter. $75.00 – 95.00.

Crystal #211 Spire horseshoe decanter with light Cranberry stain. $45.00 – 55.00.

Ruby #410 16 oz. decanter. $75.00 – 95.00.

Royal Blue #410 16 oz. decanter with silver overlay. $75.00 – 100.00.

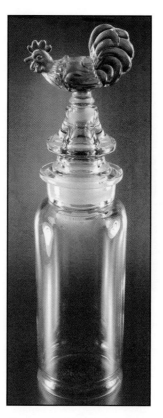

Ruby #215 9" flat-sided decanter. $75.00 – 95.00.

Crystal #902 3-piece decanter with rooster top. $75.00 – 100.00.

Crystal #902 3-piece decanter with a cutting and a rooster top. $125.00 – 150.00.

Green shot glass. $12.00 – 15.00.

Crystal #215 tilt cordial decanter with gold.
$18.00 – 22.00.

Crystal #902 3-piece decanter
with a cutting and a rooster top.
$125.00 – 150.00.

Green decanter tray that holds shot glasses and a narrow
decanter (see Ardith section for the decanter). $150.00 – 175.00
complete set, $20.00 – 24.00 tray only.

Crystal hobnail decanter with red paint.
$40.00 – 55.00.

Cocktail Shakers

There were some surprises in store for me when I looked through the union files at the Fenton factory. I found a company drawing for the Thirst Extinguisher cocktail shaker, a piece that I tried to attribute in the past but could not. Sold with it was a tumbler that is very much like the roly poly made by Macbeth Evans. It is certain that Paden City made these, because they have been found as part of the Crow's Foot punch set as well as the plain Ruby punch set. Paden City's roly poly is of a higher quality, but unless they are included with a recognized Paden City piece, it is hard to differentiate between the two.

Paden City made many more cocktail shakers, ice buckets, and matching glassware than shown here. Those can be found pictured, listed, and priced under their pattern categories.

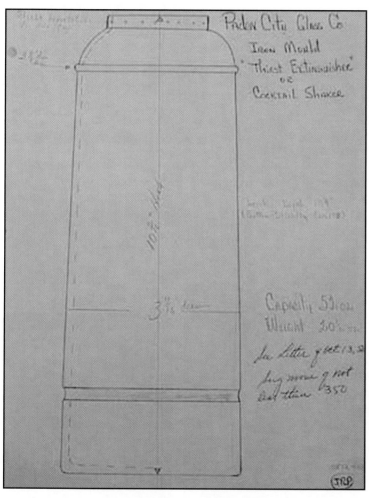

Drawing of Thirst Extinguisher.

Ruby Thirst Extinguisher cocktail shaker. $275.00 – 350.00.

Ruby roly poly used with cocktail shakers and punch sets. $8.00 – 10.00.

Green #191 cocktail shaker. $75.00 – 95.00.

Ruby #902 ice bucket with silver overlay. $35.00 – 40.00.

Royal Blue cocktail shaker, $100.00 – 125.00, and roly poly, $8.00 – 10.00.

Ruby #215 cocktail shaker with silver decoration, $100.00 – 125.00; #215 ice tub, $65.00 – 85.00, and #215 footed cocktail, $15.00 – 18.00.

Green #9 2" whiskey, 1 oz. $35.00 – 45.00.

Beverage Servers

No one knows for certain the companies responsible for samovars or wine decanters, but it is likely that both Paden City and Cambridge produced the glass for companies that supplied the metal parts and then marketed the decanters. In the case of the samovars, I think that Paden City made most, if not all, of the large tanks that have the same shape as the Cupid samovar. The tumbler sold with the pieces pictured here is definitely a Paden City piece. The colors, Ivory and Vaseline, must have been special order, because those are not typical Paden City colors.

The smaller samovar can be found with the Paden City etchings Cupid and Vintager. The Vintager etching on the samovar includes the grape arbor as well as the woman picking grapes. Because this example exists, I believe pieces with only the grapes to be Cambridge's Martha. With Paden City's penchant for duplicating other companys' patterns, it's entirely possible that these pieces are only copies of Martha, so I'm including them in the listing.

The Cherry Smash dispenser shown in this category was made by Paden City. I have a company drawing and a letter from the company to the union saying that it manufactured this piece. Paden City also made a Deluxe Dispenser, but I was unable to find one for a photo. I'm including a drawing of it so that you can identify it if you should have the good luck to find one.

Description & Etching	Size	Vaseline/Blue/Green	Painted Orange
samovar	large	$325–375	$250-275
samovar, Cupid	small	$450-575	$350-450
samovar, Cupid	large	$650-850	$400-475
samovar, grapes	small	$300-375	$250-300
samovar, urn, w/flowers	large	$350-375	
samovar, Vintager	small	$375-450	
tumbler, metal base		$18-22	$15-20

drink dispenser, Cherry Smash, Ruby, $375-500
drink dispenser, Deluxe, unknown color, $175-225

Vaseline #1000 blown satin tumbler and metal holder. $18.00 – 22.00.

Vaseline 13" satin samovar and #1000 blown tumblers. $325.00 – 375.00.

Ivory 13" samovar, $325.00 – 375.00, #1000 blown tumblers, $18.00 – 22.00 each.

Vaseline 13" etched samovar (probably Paden City's). $350.00 – 375.00.

Dark Aqua/Neptune Blue large samovar. $350.00 – 375.00.

Neptune Blue large Cupid samovar and #1000 blown tumblers. $650.00 – 750.00.

Neptune Blue Cupid flat samovar. $650.00 – 750.00.

Green Cupid samovar with no handles. $650.00 – 750.00.

Aqua samovar that was probably not made by Paden City. The metal work is exquisite, and the value, whether or not it is Paden City, is $300.00 – 350.00.

Crystal painted orange small Cupid samovar. $350.00 – 450.00.

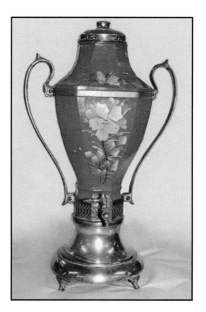

Crystal painted orange small floral-decorated samovar. $250.00 – 275.00.

Neptune Blue Vintager small samovar. $375.00 – 450.00.

Vaseline small samovar with a Vintage etching that may be either Cambridge's Martha or a similar etching done by Paden City. $300.00 – 375.00.

Cherry Smash dispenser. $375.00 – 500.00.

LIST ESTABLISHED

Paden City, W. Va.
City _____ State

September 19 1949
Month _____ Date

The Paden City Glass Company and Local Union No. 15
American Flint Glass Workers' Union, on the above date agreed to the following move and wages:

Name or number of article Cherry Smash Dispenser Move 200

Weight 11 1/2 lbs. Height 8 5/8 Ins. Width 7 1/8 Ins. Length _____

Capacity _____ Diameter _____ Depth _____ Shape Round

System worked Press Department
Pressed, Machine, Paste Mould, etc.

Finished or unfinished Finished

Shop composed of Three Men and Eight on Ruby 6 on crystal Boys

Joint or block mould Joint

Unlimited turn work Yes Unlimited piece work _____

Wages for each man on the shop:

Presser $ 7.85 $
Gatherer $ 6.73 $
Finished $ 7.11 $

Remarks: This article is made on a joint mould with a hole in the side for a spigot. Also with a peg on the bottom 1 5/8 long.

Signed for the Company:
J. E. Sullivan

Rough Sketch of Article Here
7 1/8"

Signed for the Local Union:
Edwin Slider
Arthur May

Russell Barker
Secretary Local Union No. 15

NOTICE—The blank space in this sheet must be properly filled out. Two copies should be presented to the company, one copy sent to National Vice-President Harry H. Cook, and one copy retained locally.

Union wages to be paid for the Cherry Smash dispenser.

PADEN CITY GLASS MANUFACTURING Co.
HAND MADE GLASSWARE OF QUALITY
PADEN CITY, W. VA.
September 4, 1947

J. Raymond Price, Sec'y
34 Conestoga Bldg.
Pittsburgh 22, Pa.

Dear Ray:

Refer to telephone conversation reference to Cherry Smash Dispenser.

Our Cherry Smash Dispenser is about the same size as the dimensions you gave the writer, which is diameter 7 1/4", the top 9" high over all, weight 5 lbs. Our production on this article is 125 pieces good.

While we haven't made this article for some years we do not believe that we could reach production of 125 pieces at the present time under existing conditions.

Yours very truly,
PADEN CITY GLASS MFG. COMPANY

Robt. E. McEldowney

Ray:-
A. B. Beaumont wanted to
quote a price to customer on
this item, so I phoned the info
REMG:RJ to him 9-5-47
GD

Letter sent from Robert E. McEldowney to J. Raymond Price, Secretary of the American Flint Glass Workers of America, regarding the Cherry Smash dispenser.

Sept. 3rd, 1947.

J. Ray Price:-

       Arthur B. Beaumont, Beaumont Co., Morgantown,
telephon ed to ask if we have any move and wage data on

Fowler's Cherry Smash Dispenser

It is a pressed article, cup shape,

    $7\frac{1}{4}$" Top Diameter,

    9" Deep

    A hole at side of bottom, to take metal outlet.
                                                Scant 3/4" diam.
    Weighs 5 pounds.

    Finished on top or open end

    Made of ruby glass & flashed.

Asked Mr. Beaumont if he had any idea who had made it. He said
    Kopp might have made it; perhaps, Corning...although
    the ruby looked too punk for Corning. I think he was
    merely mentioning some plants who might have made
    ruby glass.

I promised him YOU would look it up to see if our record

    divulged anything of value.

JRP called Paden City Glass Co
Thurs Sept. 4, 1947

R E McEldowney is to write up
move production on this article.
no moves set at P.C.

Check Dispenser file for best comparison.

Disp. Made At Paden City Same As Above.
See Letter From R.E.Mc Sept. 4, 1947
P.C.G.Co's Production Averaged 125 pcs. No
Move Est. Head Shop Wages.

More union correspondence for the Cherry Smash dispenser.

OFFICERS

E. J. BARRY, President
TOLEDO, OHIO

C. B. ROE, Vice President
MOUNDSVILLE, W. VA.

C. E. VOITLE, Secy.-Treas.
PITTSBURGH, PA.

GEORGE DOUGHERTY, Asst. Secy.
PITTSBURGH, PA.

PHONE 2681 COURT

NATIONAL ASSOCIATION OF MANUFACTURERS OF PRESSED AND BLOWN GLASSWARE

34 CONESTOGA BUILDING
PITTSBURGH, PA.

EXECUTIVE COMMITTEE

C. B. ROE - MOUNDSVILLE, W. VA.

C. M. RODEFER - BELLAIRE, OHIO

THOS. W. McCREARY - MONACA, PA.

C. W. GLEASON - BROOKLYN, N. Y.

M. A. SMITH - JEANNETTE, PA.

March 51, 1939.

Paden City Glass Mfg. Company,
Paden City, W. Va.

Gentlemen:-

We have your letter of March 30th wherein you advise that you manufacture a DeLuxe Dispenser on which the United States Glass Company have a move established of 250 with one mould, and 290 with two moulds, paying head shop wages.

This is to advise that under date of February 11, 1932, we informed you that your Premier Dispenser Cup, weight 36 ounces, was made at a move of 265 with one mould, paying head shop wages. The information we gave you at that time was just the same as was being made at the United States Glass Company at Glassport, Pa. when using one mould; but, when they use two moulds 10% additional is added to this move. This information was given to us by Mr. O. F. Murray when he was Superintendent of the United States Glass Company.

We have signed agreements from the Lancaster Glass Company on these Dispenser Bases and Cups, all of which are made at a move of 265 with one mould, and 10% additional when using two moulds. In other words, that would give you a move of 292 when working with two moulds. Evidently, the fellow that sent that information just dropped the two pieces making the move 290. The correct move is 265 with one mould and 10% additional with two moulds.

Very truly yours,

C. E. Voitle
Sec'y.-Treas.

CEV:LM

Correspondence regarding the Deluxe dispenser.

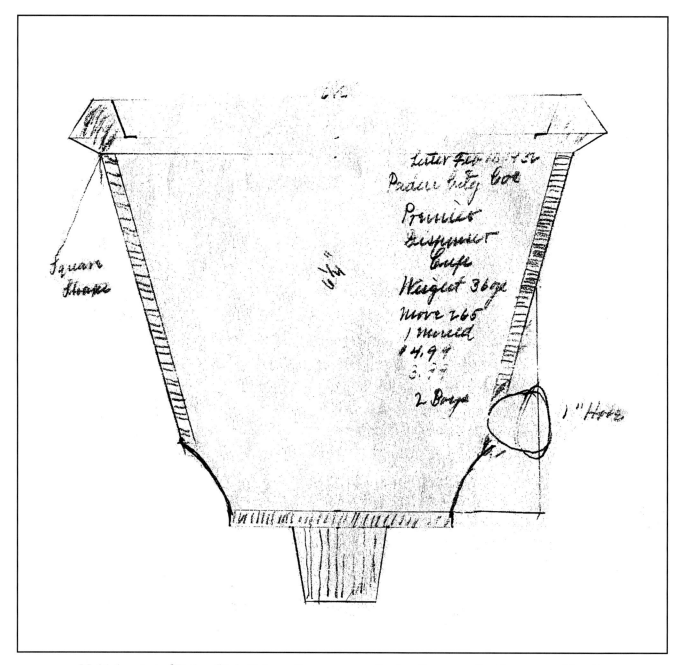

Mold drawing of Paden City's Deluxe dispenser mentioning the wages for the men making it.

Punch Sets

It wasn't long ago that the first Crow's Foot punch set was discovered. Usually, when a rare piece is found and documented, many others surface, but that is definitely not true of this set. They have been found in Ruby and Royal Blue, and may exist in other colors. You can see the detail in the Royal Blue punch set, but I photographed the Ruby set as it would have been used.

While I was going through the Union files, I found a drawing of a lamp base that was used to make the punch bowl for this set. It is very similar to the Crow's Foot set, but the glass bowl is unpatterned and sits completely in the metal base. Roly poly tumblers complete this set. It may exist in Royal Blue as well as Ruby.

Ruby Crow's Foot complete punch bowl set. $880.00 – 1,190.00 (includes 12 cups).

Royal Blue Crow's Foot punch bowl $750.00 – 950.00 and roly poly. $15.00 – 20.00.

Ruby unpatterned punch set. $300.00 – 350.00 cups $15.00 – 20.00 each.

Ruby glass insert, made from a lamp base mold and used for the unpatterned punch bowl.

Glass Animals

During the 1940s, Paden City and other companies produced a large variety of glass animal pieces either meant to be used as bookends or as purely decorative. Paden City also did private mold work for Barth Art Company, using Barth's animal designs. Other companies also made pieces from those molds, so it isn't certain which are Paden City. Some of those animals, such as the pelican, pouter pigeon, and rearing Horse, are so rare that no one cares that they may have been made by someone other than Paden City.

Paden City animals as well as the Barth Art examples have been found in both Copen Blue and in Crystal, but the long-tailed bird has also been found in Primrose. The crystal dragon swan shown below has been set in the sun to develop its lavender shading, or sun coloring. A few examples of all the animals have been found in a darker shade of Copen Blue. Add 20% to the value for this color. The Barth Art tall pony can be found in shades of yellow, Ebony, Amber, Aqua, and milk glass, but those colors were probably made by the Viking Glass Company after 1952. The flying geese relish is one of two figural relishes made by Paden City. The other is a duck that isn't divided. Both are hard to find, but the duck is more rare.

Crystal (sun-colored) dragon swan. $250.00 – 275.00.

Blue 9½" dragon swan. $275.00 – 325.00.

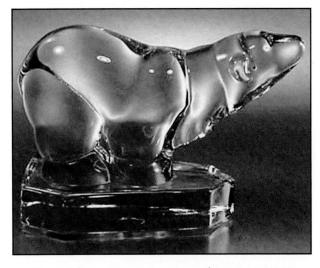

Blue 13½" Chinese pheasant. $200.00 – 250.00.

Crystal 4½" polar bear on ice. $75.00 – 100.00.

Description	Size	Crystal	Copen Blue
bird,* long tailed	5"	$50-75	$65-85
dragon swan	9½	$250-275	$275-325
eagle, bookends	7½"	$375-450 pr.	
duck, flying, relish	9"	$125-175	
geese, flying, relish	11¼"	$100-150	
goose	5"	$150-175	$175-225
horse,** rearing	10"	$250-300	
pelican,**	10"	$450-525	
pheasant, Chinese	13½"	$125-175	$200-250
pheasant, head turned	12"	$125-175	$200-250
pigeon,** pouter	6¼"	$125-175	
polar bear	4½"	$75-100	
pony, tall	11½"	$125-150	$175-225
ram's head, bookend	6½"	$275-350 pr.	
rooster,** barnyard	8¾"	$150-200	
rooster, chanticleer	9½"	$150-200	$200-250
rooster, elegant	11"	$200-250	$250-325
rooster,** head down	8¾"	$75-125	$150-225
sea horse	8⅜"	$75-125	
starfish, bookends	8"	$150-225 pr.	
squirrel**	5½"	$50-75	

*Primrose, $100.00-125.00
**Barth Art

Blue 9½" Chanticleer $200.00 – 250.00.

Crystal Chinese pheasant. $125.00 – 175.00.

Crystal satin Chanticleer. $150.00 – 200.00.

Dark Blue Chinese pheasant. $225.00 – 275.00.

Crystal Chanticleer lamp. $200.00 – 250.00.

Blue 13½" pheasant with head turned. $200.00 – 250.00.

Blue 11½" pony. $175.00 – 225.00.

Blue 11" elegant rooster.
$250.00 – 325.00.

Crystal 10" pelican. $450.00 – 525.00.

Crystal 7½" eagle bookends. $375.00 – 450.00 (pair).

Crystal 11¼" goose relish, $100.00 – 150.00, and spoons, $20.00 – 25.00 each.

Crystal ram's head bookends. $275.00 – 350.00 pair.

Crystal goose relish, top view.

Blue long-tailed bird. $65.00 – 75.00.

Primrose long-tailed bird on a stand. $100.00 – 125.00.

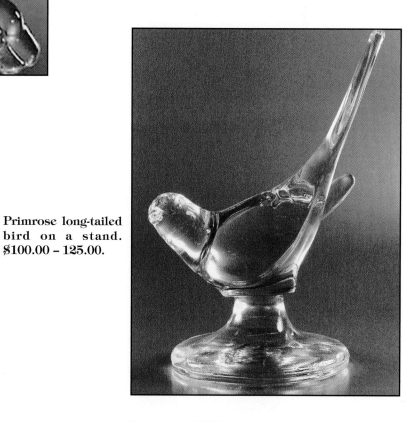

Blue goose. $175.00 – 225.00.

Blue rooster from Barth Art mold.
$150.00 – 225.00.

Kitchenware

Paden City was unsurpassed in the kitchenware business. The high quality of its reamers, batter sets, shakers, mixing bowls, and all the rest of the pieces that fall into this category made it a leader in the glass industry during the depression years.

Batter Sets

There are three sizes of pitchers that belong to the #11 batter sets. The 8" pitcher was meant for batter, the 7" for milk, and the 5¼" for syrup. Most of these sets came with Ebony lids, but they are sometimes found with matching lids. These pitchers had a popular shape for etchings like Black Forest, Trumpet Flower, Gothic Garden, Harvester, and — one that is very rare — Cupid. A Cupid syrup sold on eBay for more than $2,000, but I don't think we can count on such pitchers reaching those prices every day. The prices listed here are for unetched pieces. Look for prices for the etched examples under the listings for those etchings.

Description	Size	Crystal	Amber	Ebony	Pink
batter jug	8"	$50-60	$65-70	$70-75	$75-85
milk pitcher	7"	$45-50	$60-65	$65-75	$70-80
syrup	5¼"	$40-50	$50-65	$60-65	$65-75

Crystal pitchers with Ebony lids: 8" batter jug, $40.00 – 50.00; 7" milk jug, $45.00 – 50.00; 5½" syrup, $50.00 – 60.00.

Crystal and Ebony wheel-cut batter set.
$150.00 – 185.00.

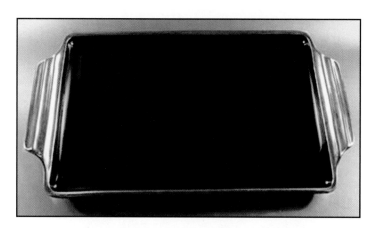

Ebony/Silver 10¼" tray. $40.00 – 55.00.

Cheriglo 8" batter jug. $75.00 – 85.00.

Crystal/Ebony batter set. $130.00 – 165.00.

Syrups & Marmalades

The Amber ranges from a deep shade to a light amber that is closer to yellow, and the color span of green is similar, ranging from a blue-green to a light apple green. Even though there is no real difference in the value of all these sizes, I want to list them so you will be aware of the variety made by Paden City over the years. Add 15% for cuttings or decorations.

Description	Line	Size	Crystal	Amber	Blue (Aqua)	Green/Cheriglo
syrup	89	20 oz.	$40-50			
syrup	181-0	12 oz.	$35-45	$40-50	$65-80	$50-65
syrup	185-0	12 oz.	$35-45	$45-50	$65-80	$50-65
syrup	198	8 oz.	$25-35	$35-40	$50-60	$40-55
syrup	198	10 oz.	$30-40	$40-45	$55-65	$45-65
syrup	198	12 oz.	$35-45	$40-50	$65-80	$65-70
syrup	404	16 oz.	$40-50	$45-55	$65-80	$65-75
syrup	405	12 oz.	$35-45	$40-50	$65-80	$50-65
Syrup	406	12 oz.	$35-45	$40-50	$65-80	$50-65
syrup, colonial	401	10 oz.	$40-50			
syrup, Georgian	69	12 oz.	$20-25	$35-45	$65-75	$50-65
syrup, nickel-plated top	191	8 oz.	$35-45	$40-50	$65-80	$65-70
syrup, molasses can	400		$40-50			
syrup, Party Line	191	12 oz.	$35-45	$40-50	$65-80	$65-70
syrup liner		5½"	$8-10	$10-12	$15-17	$12-15

Dark Aqua #185-0 syrup and plate. $80.00 – 95.00.

Amber #185-0 syrup and plate. $55.00 – 62.00.

Amber #185-0 marmalade and plate. $55.00 – 62.00.

Crystal/Amber #185-0 syrup. $35.00 – 45.00.

Green #191 syrup and plate. $75.00 – 85.00.

Green #191 syrup with nickle-plated top. $65.00 – 70.00.

SYRUP AND SUGAR SERVERS
Also furnished with Chrome Plated Tops

11—9 oz. Syrup Jug and Cover
(Also 20 oz. and 30 oz.)

89—20 oz. Syrup N. S. Top

90—12 oz. Large Sugar Server
N. P. Top   (Also 6 oz.)

91—6 oz. Ind. Sugar
Server N. P. Top

94—12 oz. Sugar Server
N. P. Base

198—12 oz. Syrup N. P. Top
(Also 8 oz.)

201—12 oz. Sugar Pourer
N. P. Top

401—6½ oz. Sugar
Shaker N. P. Top

404—16 oz. Syrup and N. P. Top

405—12 oz. Syrup and
N. P. Top

406—12 oz. Syrup and
N. P. Top

"A"—14 oz. Sugar Server
N. P. Top

"B"—3 oz. Sugar
Server N. P. Top

"C"—12 oz. Sugar
Server N. P. Top

"D"—12 oz. Sugar
Server N. P. Top

191—12 oz. Sugar
Server N. P. Top

No.		Height	Top Diameter	Bottom Diameter	Doz. in Ctn.	Doz. in Bbl.
11	9 oz. Syrup Jug and Cover	4- 5/16"	3-11/16"	2- 1/2"	3	10
11	20 oz. Jug and Cover	5- 3/4"	4- 5/8"	3- 1/8"	1½	5
11	30 oz. Jug and Cover	6- 3/4"	5- 3/8"	3- 1/2"	1	3½
89	20 oz. Syrup N. S. Top	6- 1/2"	3"	3- 3/4"	2	5
90	6 oz. Ind. Sugar N. P. Top	3- 3/4"	2- 3/8"	3"	4	15
90	12 oz. Large Sugar Server N. P. Top	5- 1/2"	2- 1/2"	3- 1/2"	3	11
91	6 oz. Ind. Sugar Server N. P. Top	4- 7/16"	2- 3/4"	3- 3/16"	4	15
94	12 oz. Sugar Server N. P. Base	5- 1/2"	2-15/16"	3"	3	10
198	12 oz. Syrup N. P. Top	5- 1/4"	2- 1/2"	3- 1/2"	3	9
198	8 oz. Syrup N. P. Top	4- 1/4"	2- 1/2"	3- 1/4"	4	12
201	12 oz. Sugar Pourer N. P. Top	5"	2- 7/8"	2- 3/4"	3	12
401	6½ oz. Sugar Shaker N. P. Top	4- 1/2"	2- 1/4"	3"	6	18
404	16 oz. Syrup and N. P. Top	6- 1/2"	2- 1/2"	4"	2	6
405	12 oz. Syrup and N. P. Top	5- 3/4"	2- 1/4"	3"	3	9
406	12 oz. Syrup and N. P. Top	5- 3/4"	2- 1/4"	3- 1/2"	3	9
"A"	14 oz. Sugar Server N. P. Top	4- 7/8"	2- 1/16"	3"	4	12
"B"	3 oz. Sugar Server N. P. Top	3- 1/4"	1-13/16"	2- 1/16"	6	30
"C"	12 oz. Sugar Server N. P. Top	4- 5/8"	2- 7/8"	3- 1/4"	4	12
"D"	12 oz. Sugar Server N. P. Top	4- 1/2"	2-13/16"	3- 3/8"	4	12
191	12 oz. Sugar Server N. P. Top	4- 3/8"	2- 3/4"	3- 3/8"	4	12

Paden City Glass Mfg. Co., Paden City, W. Va.

Syrups and sugar servers from 1920s catalog page.

Reamers

Reamers were so popular during the 1920s, 30s, and 40s that almost every company made them, but none made prettier or more useful reamers than Paden City. Some, such as all the Party Line styles, are common and are easily recognized as Paden City, but some are almost never seen and seldom correctly identified. There are two sizes of Regina #210 reamers, the shaker/reamer called Speak Easy and a lemon reamer shown in an old Paden City catalog. After talking with Mary Walker, author of *Many More Reamers,* I'm convinced that the small reamer was made from a Higgins mold that was used for only a short time by Paden City. I'm including photos of that reamer.

When I was going through the Paden City catalog pages, I noticed a #500 sugar bowl. It matches the base of a lemon reamer that has never been attributed to a manufacturer before now, and that reamer was made in Paden City colors. While I can't guarantee it beyond all doubt, I'm convinced these two pieces are a set made by Paden City.

Of all the #191 36 oz. reamers, crystal is the most rare and is only surpassed in value by the blue and the Ebony sets. Add 10% for cuttings and 25% for etchings.

Green #191 shaker/reamer.
$125.00 – 150.00.

Ebony #191 shaker/reamer.
$450.00 – 550.00.

Description	Line	Size	Crystal	Amber	Cheriglo/Green	Blue	Ebony
reamer	191	10 oz.	$75-100	$75-125	$100-125		
reamer	191	36 oz.	$500-650	$175-225	$175-225	$600-700	$700-800
reamer	210	36 oz.		$200-225	$225-275		$750-850
reamer, lemon	10		$35-45				
reamer, lemon	500		$65-75		$250-275		$450-500
shaker/reamer	156	18 oz.		$50-65	$75-85		
shaker/reamer	191	18 oz.	$100-125	$100-125	$125-150		$450-550
shaker/reamer	210	18 oz.		$100-125	$100-125		$450-550
Gothic Garden etched, $450-600.							

Green satin #191 shaker/reamer with Ebony border, $125.00 – 150.00, and 2½ oz. wine, $12.00 – 16.00.

Cheriglo #191 shaker/reamer. $125.00 – 150.00.

Cheriglo #191 shaker/ reamer with Cosmos border. $155.00 – 185.00.

Pink #191 shaker/reamer. $125.00 – 150.00.

Cheriglo #191 wheel-cut shaker/ reamer. $135.00 – 165.00.

Green #210 shaker/reamer with Gothic Garden etching. $225.00 – 300.00+.

Amber #156 shaker/reamer.
$50.00 – 65.00.

Amber #156 satin shaker/reamer.
$50.00 – 65.00.

Green #156 shaker/reamer.
$75.00 – 85.00.

Brown/Amber #156 shaker/
reamer. $50.00 – 65.00.

Green #156 wheel-cut shaker/reamer. $85.00 – 90.00.

#191 measuring cup/reamer base. $75.00 – 100.00.
$100.00 – 125.00 complete with top.

Amber #191 36 oz. pitcher/reamer.
$175.00 – 225.00.

Crystal #191 36 oz. pitcher/reamer.
$500.00 – 650.00.

Aqua #191 36 oz. pitcher/reamer.
$600.00 – 700.00.

Cheriglo #191 36 oz. wheel-cut pitcher/
reamer. $185.00 – 250.00.

Green #191 36 oz. pitcher/reamer.
$175.00 – 225.00.

Ebony #191 36 oz. pitcher/reamer.
$700.00 – 800.00.

Green #191 36 oz. wheel-cut pitcher/reamer. $185.00 – 250.00.

Ebony #210 36 oz. pitcher/reamer. $750.00 – 850.00.

#210 Cheriglo wheel-cut 36 oz. pitcher/reamer. $250.00 – 300.00.

Aqua #500 lemon reamer. $450.00 – 500.00.

Aqua #500 reamer base. $125.00 – 150.00.

Cheriglo #500 lemon reamer. $250.00 – 300.00.

Crystal Higgins reamer (Paden City's #10).
$35.00 – 45.00.

Crystal #500 "Baby's orange" reamer. $65.00 – 75.00.

Sugar Shakers

Green #90 5½" sugar shaker.
$250.00 – 275.00.

Amber and green #90 sugar shakers. $300.00 –
350.00 Amber, $250.00 – 275.00 green.

Description	Line	Size	Crystal	Amber	Cheriglo/Green	Blue	Ebony
A		14 oz.	$65-80	$150-175	$225-250		
B		3 oz.	$40-55	$175-200	$200-250		
bullet	94		$125-150	$350-400	$250-275		
C*		12 oz.	$40-50	$325-375	$300-350		$450-500
D*		12 oz.	$75-95	$200-225	$250-275		
indented sides	90	12 oz.	$100-125	$300-350	$250-275		
individual	91	6 oz.	$45-65		$65-85		

Description	Line	Size	Crystal	Amber	Cheriglo/Green	Blue	Ebony
narrow panels	201	12 oz.	$100-125	$300-350	$300-350	$800-1000	
narrow panels	210	8 oz.	$100-125	$300-350	$300-350		
Party Line, 6 rings	191		$125-150	$150-200	$275-325		
Party Line, rings at base	191		$100-125	$150-175	$150-175		
Rena	154		$55-75	$200-250	$250-300		
Rena, individual	154		$40-55				
wide panels**	401	6½ oz.	$75-100	$150-175	$225-250		

*Shown on catalog page on page 352.
**Opal, $100-125

#201 sugar shakers: Teal Green, $300.00 – 350.00; Royal Blue, $800.00 – 1,000.00. Amber, $300.00 – 350.00; and Light Green, $300.00 – 350.00.

Amber #94 sugar shaker. $350.00 – 400.00.

Shaker similar to one from line #94, but not Paden City. Shown for comparison only.

Green #94 sugar shaker. $250.00 – 275.00.

Cheriglo and Green #94 sugar shakers. $250.00 – 275.00 each. The yellow shaker is not Paden City.

Amber and Cheriglo #191 sugar shakers. $150.00 – 200.00 Amber, $275.00 – 325.00 Cheriglo.

Green and Cheriglo #154 sugar shakers. $250.00 – 300.00 each.

Cheriglo and green #191 sugar shakers. $150.00 – 175.00 each.

Opal, green, and green satin sugar shakers. $225.00 – 250.00 Opal and green satin, $100.00 – 125.00 green.

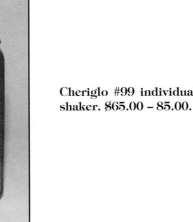

Cheriglo #99 individual sugar shaker. $65.00 – 85.00.

Cheriglo and Cheriglo satin #401 sugar shakers. $225.00 – 250.00 each.

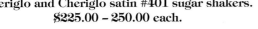

Ladles

Paden City made a least two different ladles for the mayonnaise sets or the marmalades. The #10 is the most common, but the #300 can also frequently be found. The crystal ladles (both styles) sell for $15 – 18. The colored pieces sell for $35 – 50.

Ruby #10 ladle. $35.00 – 50.00.

Aqua and Cheriglo #10 ladles. $35.00 – 50.00 each.

Green #300 Archaic ladle.
$35.00 – 50.00.

Salad Sets

This salad set has been identified as Cambridge for years, but with the information found in the Edward Paul catalog, we now know that it was made by Paden City. These sets have been found in Amber, $85 – 100; Ebony, $150 – 200; Copen Blue, $150 – 200; Ruby, $225 – 250; and green, $150 – 175.

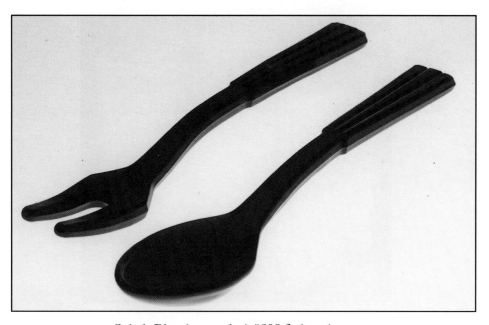

Cobalt Blue (rare color) #609 fork and spoon.

Napkin Holders

The #210 napkin holders were originally sold as stationery holders, but I'm listing them in the kitchen category because it seems that is how they are most often used today. These holders have some- times been mistakenly listed as Party Line, but the ridges on these are sharp, not rounded like the ridges found on Party Line items.

Opal	Ebony	Crystal	Green/Cheriglo
$65-75	$150-175	$65-85	$150-200

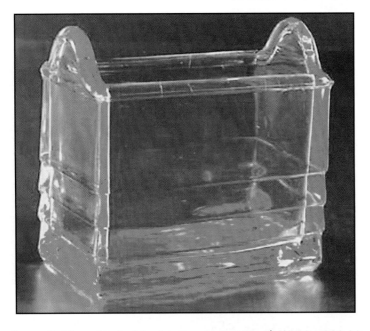

Green #210 napkin holder/stationery holder. $150.00 – 200.00.

Ebony #210 napkin holder/stationery holder. $200.00 – 225.00.

Crystal #210 napkin holder/stationery holder. $65.00 – 85.00.

Miscellaneous Kitchen Items

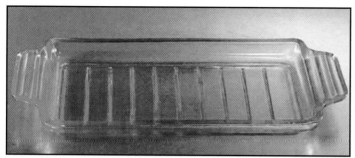

Green #210 10½" ribbed cream and sugar tray.
$30.00 – 45.00.

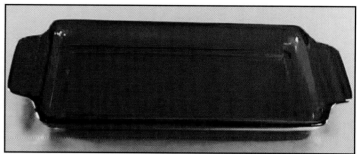

Ruby #210 10½" plain tray. $35.00 – 50.00.

Yellow #210 10½" ribbed cream and sugar tray.
$30.00 – 45.00.

Ebony #210 10½" tray used for batter sets as well as cream
and sugar sets. $35.00 – $50.00.

Green #108 7" dressing bottle,
12 oz. $45.00 – 65.00.

Cheriglo #405 5 oz. square oil. $55.00 – 65.00.

Cheriglo #205 5 oz. squat oil, $40.00 –
45.00, and green #204 5½" tall oil,
$40.00 – 50.00.

Green #402 banana split. $25.00 – 35.00.

Cheriglo #211 banana split. $35.00 – 40.00.

Amber #6 3-piece percolator. $175.00 – 225.00.

Mulberry #6 3-piece 15½" percolator. $250.00 – 300.00.

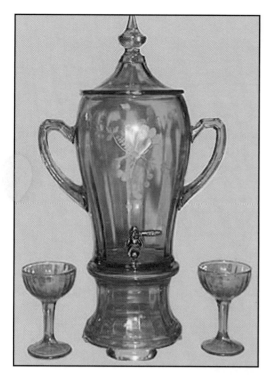

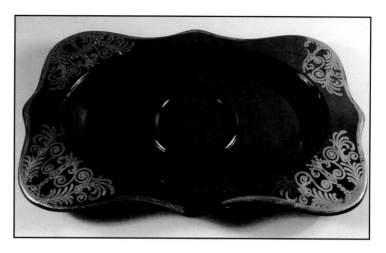

Ebony 9¾" gravy tray. $25.00 – 35.00.

Dark Aqua #6 wheel-cut percolator,
$250.00 – 325.00, and #841 cocktail,
$10.00 – 12.00.

Ebony macaroon jar/covered ice bucket.
$250.00 – 325.00.

Crystal/Gold casserole base with flowering urn etching.
$125.00 – 150.00

Dark Aqua #12 measuring cup, $100.00 – 135.00, and
unknown handled cup, $45.00 – 55.00.

Vanity Items

Paden City produced many items for the bedroom and bathroom. Included in that production was a whole group of perfumes, colognes, and trays that no one would guess was made by Paden City.

During the years of WWII, importers of giftware were not able to buy from the European sources, for obvious reasons. They had to turn to U.S. manufacturers for help in filling their orders. Many factories, such as Cambridge, Fenton, Imperial, and Paden City, agreed to make glassware for these giftware companies in hopes that, after the war, the importers would continue to give the American glass companies their business. But business is business, and when the war was over and prices for foreign goods were low, the giftware companies dropped the American factories and went back to their overseas sources.

Many of the vanity items can be found with etchings, color flashed, or cut. For etchings such as Black Forest, add 50% to the value of the item; for less collected etchings, add 25%. For color wash, flashing, or for pieces with cuttings, add 10%.

Perfumes/Colognes, Powders, and Trays

Crystal/Royal Blue moon set. $95.00 – 125.00.

Description	Line	Size	Crystal	Cheriglo/ Green/Amber	Aqua/Ruby/ Mulberry/Royal Blue	Ebony
perfume/cologne	499	1oz.	$50-65	$55-75	$75-100	$75-100
perfume/cologne	500	5 oz.	$55-75	$75-100	$100-120	$100-120
perfume/cologne	501	4 oz.	$50-65	$65-85	$75-95	$75- 95
perfume/cologne	502	5 oz.	$55-75	$75-100	$100-120	$100-120
perfume/cologne, atomizer			$45-65			
perfume/cologne, Glades	215		$45-65	$55-75	$65-95	$65-95
perfume/cologne, moon set			$35-55	$50-65	$65-95	
perfume/cologne, Party Line	191	1½ oz.	$50-65	$100-125	$100-125	
perfume/cologne, Regina	210		$55-75	$75-100	$100-125	$85-115
perfume/cologne, w/beehive stopper	503		$50-60	$65-75	$85-115	
powder	198		$30-40	$38-44	$60-80	$65-75
powder	201		$30-40	$40-45	$65-75	$70-75

Description	Line	Size	Crystal	Cheriglo/Green/Amber	Aqua/Ruby/Mulberry/Royal Blue	Ebony
powder	209		$30-40	$40-45	$65-75	$70-75
powder	503		$30-40	$38-44	$60-70	$65-75
powder	700		$35-40	$40-45	$65-75	$70-75
powder, flat	191	4½"	$35-45	$45-65	$70-90	
powder, ftd.	191		$35-45	$40-60	$65-85	
powder, Glades	215		$35-40	$40-45	$65-75	$75-85
powder, military hat			$35-45	$50-65	$65-85	
powder, moon set			$30-40			
tray	499		$18-22	$20-25	$25-30	$20-25
tray, Glades	215		$18-22			
tray, oval			$18-22	$20-25	$25-30	$20-25

Dark Aqua #191 colognes and powder and #499 tray.
$290.00 – 350.00.

Cheriglo #210 colognes, #503 powder, and #499 tray.
$210.00 – 270.00.

Cheriglo #503 perfume set. $195.00 – 225.00.

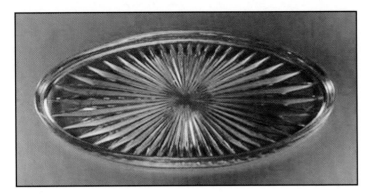

Cheriglo 9⅞" oval tray. $20.00 – 25.00.

Green #191 powder. $40.00 – 60.00.

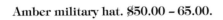

Mulberry #198 powder. $60.00 – 80.00.

Amber military hat. $50.00 – 65.00.

Crystal military hat with mirror top. $35.00 – 45.00.

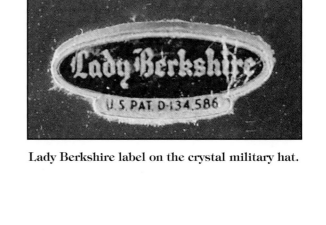

Lady Berkshire label on the crystal military hat.

Cheriglo military hat. $50.00 – 65.00.

Crystal Edward Paul oval tray. $25.00 – 45.00.

Green #500 perfumes, #198 powder, and #499 tray.
$200.00 – 265.00.

Dark Aqua #502 perfumes, #201 powder, and #499 tray.
$290.00 – 340.00.

Cheriglo #502 wheel-cut perfume set.

Dark Aqua #198 powder. $60.00 – 80.00.

Green #502 powder.

Crystal Edward Paul atomizer with unknown etching.

Ebony/Gold #210 Black Forest perfume, $200.00 – 225.00; Cheriglo #210 perfume, $75.00 – 100.00; Royal Blue #502 perfume, $100.00 – 120.00; Amber/Gold #502 Pansy-etched perfume, $175.00 – 200.00; crystal #502 wheel-cut perfume, $55.00 – 75.00.

Mulberry #191 perfumes, $100.00 – 125.00
each.

Blue #502 perfume. $100.00 – 120.00.

Green #502 perfume.
$75.00 – 100.00.

Crystal/Ruby #215 colognes. $55.00 – 65.00.

Cheriglo #503 perfume.
$65.00 – 75.00.

Ebony/Ruby and crystal/Ebony #215
colognes. $65.00 – 95.00 Ebony/Ruby,
$55.00 – 65.00 crystal/Ebony.

Crystal/Ebony #215 cologne set. $180.00 – 215.00.

Crystal/Ruby #215 cologne set. $180.00 – 215.00.

Guest Sets

Paden City made at least three different guest sets. Unfortunately, the #179 set is almost impossible to tell from the Cambridge #488 set. All of the Paden City sets come on a tray that has gently sloping handles, but so do many of the Cambridge sets. The Paden City tray measures 9" long and the Cambridge tray is 9½" long, but this is handmade glass, and these measurements may not always be consistent. (Cambridge made a second tray that is similar but has is a sharp, distinct rim where the edge begins to curve outward.) Even though the Cambridge #488 tray is the closest in size, 9½", it should be easy to tell the difference between it and the Paden City tray. I have included a photo of the Cambridge tray for comparison. But the problem doesn't end with identifying the tray; the pitchers of the two companies are also very similar, enough so to make

identification very difficult. Both companies used both smooth and ribbed handles. The Cambridge pitcher is 5" tall without the lid and 6" with it. The Paden City pitcher is also 5" tall by itself, but is 6¼" with the lid. The Cambridge tumbler is 3⅜" tall, the Paden City tumbler is 3⅛" tall.

The #179 guest set is also hard to tell from the Cambridge #726 set. According to Kenn and Margaret Whitmyer, whose information is always sound, the mold marks can easily be seen on the Paden City set but are hard to find on the Cambridge set.

I am listing these sets with prices for plain. Add 20% for cuttings. All the etched pieces will be priced on the pages for that etching, but I'm also listing those separately. This will avoid the need to go back to those pages to find the value.

Ebony #210 guest set. $200.00 – 225.00.

Dark Aqua #179 pitcher and tray. $160.00 – 200.00.

372

Description	Line	Crystal	Amber/Yellow	Cheriglo/Green	Aqua/Mulberry	Ebony
Black Forest	210			$600-750		$700-850
Eden Rose	179		$175-200	$175-225	$200-250	
Eden Rose	499		$175-200	$175-225	$200-250	
guest set	179	$125-150	$150-175	$175-200	$200-250	
guest set	210		$150-175	$175-200		$200-225
Peacock & Rose	499			$900-1000	$30-40	
pitcher	179	$90-110	$110-120	$127-140	$130-160	
tray	179	$18-20	$20-24	$24-30	$30-40	
tumbler	179	$18-20	$20-24	$24-30	$40-50	
tumble-up	499	$50-75	$100-125	$125-150	$150-175	

Mulberry #179 guest set. $200.00 – 250.00.

Cheriglo #179 wheel-cut guest set. $165.00 – 185.00.

Green #179 guest set. $175.00 – 200.00.

Crystal #179 pitcher. $90.00 – 110.00.

Light Green #179 guest set. $175.00 – 200.00.

Light Green #179 wheel-cut guest set. $200.00 – 225.00.

Amber #179 wheel-cut guest set. $200.00 – 225.00.

Cheriglo #499 Peacock and Rose guest set. $900.00 – 1,000.00.

Dark Aqua #499 Eden Rose guest set. $200.00 – 250.00.

Cheriglo #499 Peacock and Rose guest set.

374

Bunny Cotton Ball Holders

The bunny cotton ball holders are the last of the vanity items. These are a favorite of many collectors.

The ears-up bunny is quite rare. Add 15% for glossy pieces. The prices are for the satin finish.

Description	Size	Crystal	Cheriglo	Blue
bunny, ears down	5"	$100-125	$125-150	$150-175
bunny, ears up		$200-250	$250-300	$300-350

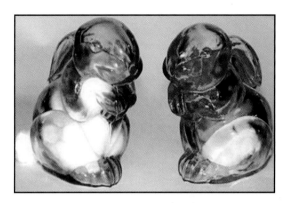

Glossy blue ears-down bunny, $165.00 – 200.00, and glossy Cheriglo ears-down bunny, $145.00 – 165.00.

Blue satin ears-down bunny. $150.00 – 175.00.

Cheriglo satin ears-down bunny.
$125.00 – 150.00.

Crystal ears-down bunny. $115.00 – 145.00.

Blue satin and Cheriglo satin ears-up bunnies.
$300.00 – 350.00 blue, $250.00 – 300.00 Cheriglo.

Edward Paul Company

One of the importers that bought from Paden City was the Edward Paul Company. When I was digging through the American Flint Glass Workers Union files at the Fenton factory, I found an Edward Paul catalog. In it, many perfumes, colognes, powders, and trays are pictured, and there is a notation, "all Paden City," that appears to have been put there by a union repre-

sentative. I was able to back up that Paden City identification with drawings submitted to the union to ascertain how the workers would be paid and how much they should produce in a turn.

The detail work done on the perfumes and stoppers is amazing and is certainly up to Paden City's standards. But these pieces are a far cry from the nor-

mal Paden City style; instead, they resemble the Czechoslovakian perfume sets that are so popular today. In fact, I'm certain most of these are sitting in collections of Czechoslovakian glassware, with the owners unaware of what they have.

All pieces in this catalog are rare, with the exception of the trays that resemble Imperial's Candlewick. They are much easier to find, and sell from $25 – 45, depending on size and condition. If a tray has the original mirror, increase this amount by 10%. All the per-

fumes, colognes, and powder jars were produced in crystal and in Copen Blue and may exist in Cheriglo. Cheriglo pieces would have the same value as Copen Blue. Until I have a better idea of pricing, I'm just averaging the amount I believe collectors might pay and dealers might sell at. For the elaborate pieces: in crystal, $125 – 175; in blue, $175 – 225. The swirl or ribbed pieces: in crystal, $50 – 75; in blue, $75 – 100. The powders: in crystal, $50 – 75; in blue, $75 – 100. The elaborate trays should sell for $100 – 125.

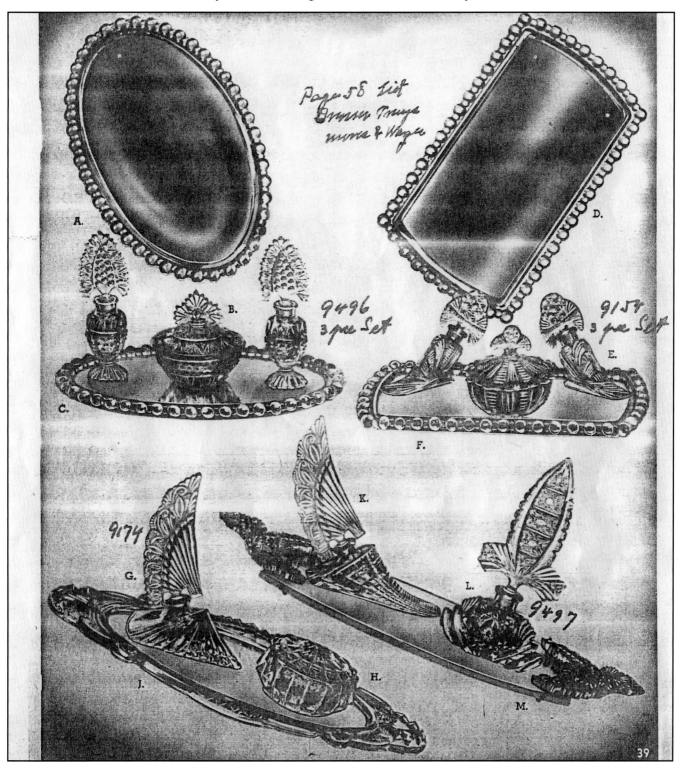

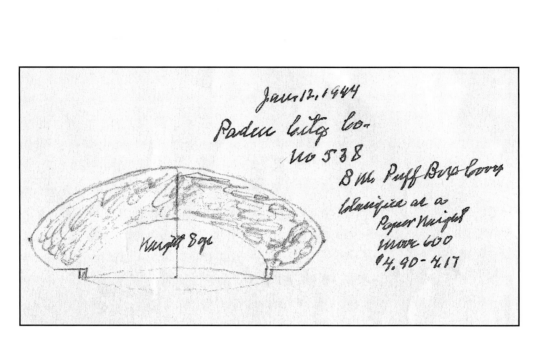

Paden City mold drawing for #538 puff box cover. 1/12/44.

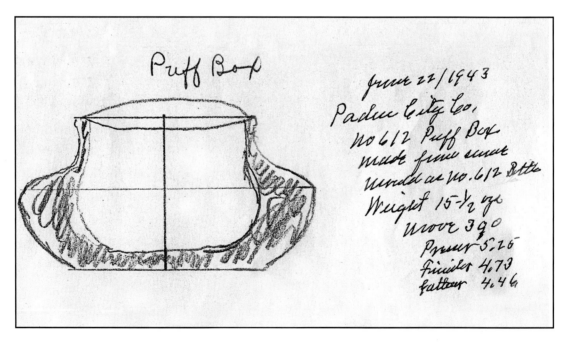

Paden City mold drawing for #612 puff box base. 6/22/43.

PADEN CITY GLASS MFG. COMPANY

NO. 9120 OVAL BOX WITH 8 TOES AND COVER

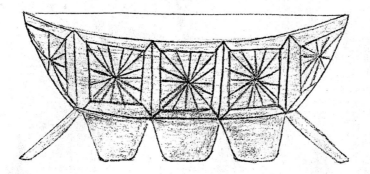

Diameter 4¼"
Height 1-3/4"
Weight 7 ozs.

Cover - 4-5/8" x 3-5/8".
Weight 5½ ozs.

Box showing 8 toes.

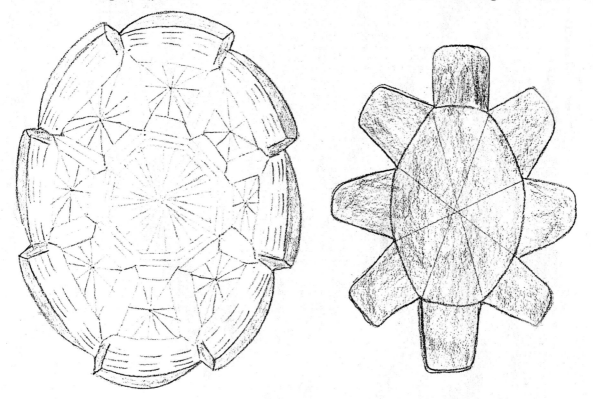

March 29, 1943 - Wrote R. E. McEldowney that set ware wages should apply
to this Box and Cover.

Paden City mold drawing for the #9120 powder made for the Edward Paul Company.

AUG 1 4 1945   AUG 1 4 1945

LIST ESTABLISHED

Paden City _____ W. Va.
City _____ State

Aug 6 _____ 19 45 —
Month _____ Date

The _Paden City_ _____ Glass Company and Local Union No. _15—_ ,
American Flint Glass Workers' Union, on the above date agreed to the following move and wages:

Name or number of article _#901 Cologne_ _____ Move _500_

Weight _1 oz_ Height _2 15/16 in_ Width _2 1/32 in_ Length _____

Capacity _1/4 oz_ Diameter _____ Depth _____ Shape _Round_

System worked _Pressed & Blown_
Pressed, Machine, Paste Mould, etc.

Finished or unfinished _Glazed_

Shop composed of _Two_ Men and _Three_ Boys

Joint or block mould _Joint_

Unlimited turn work _yes_ Unlimited piece work _____

Wages for each man on the shop:

Presser $ _5 00_ _____ $ _____
Gather $ _4 25_ _____ $ _____
_____ $ _____ _____ $ _____

Remarks: _____

Signed for the Company: | **Rough Sketch of Article Here** | Signed for the Local Union:
Theodore Schweig | | _Clarence Purdy_
| | _Mike McWilliams_

| | _Millard Tippins_
| | Secretary Local Union No. _15—_

NOTICE—The blank space in this sheet must be properly filled out. Two copies should be presented to the company, one copy sent to National 1st Vice-President Wm. G. Muhleman, and one copy retained locally.

Paden City wage and turn information for the #901 cologne made for the Edward Paul Company.

(Sent out June 1942).

NOV 29 1941

LIST ESTABLISHED

Paden City W. Va.
City / State

Oct. 3 _____ 19 41
Month / Date

The _____Paden City_____ Glass Company and Local Union No. 15 ,

American Flint Glass Workers' Union, on the above date agreed to the following move and wages:

Name or number of article B-10 Cologne bottle _____ Move 3.50

Weight 12 g. Height 6" when pressed _____ Length _____

Capacity _____ Diameter _____ Depth _____ Shape _____

System worked press. side lever
Pressed, Machine, Paste Mould, etc.

Finished or unfinished Patent tool

Shop composed of four Men and _____ Boys

Joint or block mould Joint mould

Unlimited turn work Yes Unlimited piece work _____

Wages for each man on the shop:

Presser $5.25   Gatherer $4.46

Finisher (Pat tool $6.00 $_____

Foot finisher $4.72 $_____

Remarks: This bottle is pressed through a joint and worked on a slide valve.

Presser Wm Powel

Signed for the Company:
Geo Dacier Sr

Rough Sketch of Article Here

Signed for the Local Union:
Mike McWilliamsS
Sherly Troyman
Roy Medley
Frank schultz
Robert Guthrie

Secretary Local Union No. 15

NOTICE—The blank space in this sheet must be properly filled out. Two copies should be presented to the company, one copy sent to National 1st Vice-President Wm. G. Muhleman, and one copy retained locally.

Paden City wage and turn information for the B-10 cologne bottle, possibly made for Edward Paul.

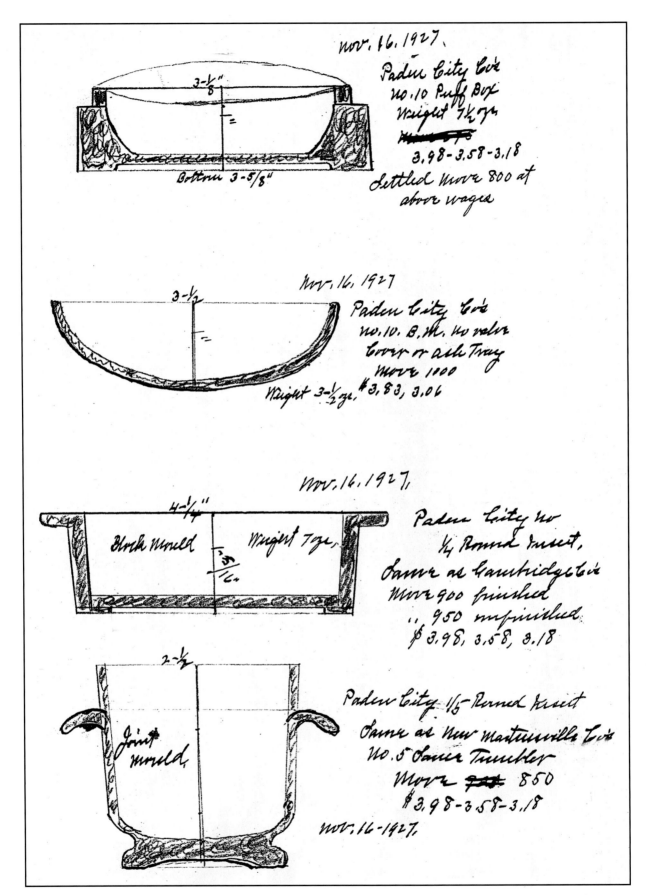

Nov. 16, 1927.
Paden City Co's
no. 10 Puff Box
Weight 7½ oz.
3.98 - 3.58 - 3.18
Settled Move 800 at
above wages

Nov. 16, 1927
Paden City Co's
no. 10. B. M. no valve
Cover or ash Tray
move 1000
Weight 3-½ oz. #3.83, 3.06

Nov. 16, 1927,
Paden City no
½ Round Insert.
Same as Cambridge Co's
move 900 finished
" 950 unfinished
#3.98, 3.58, 3.18

Block Mould   Weight 7oz.

Paden City 1/5 Round Insert
Same as New Martinsville Co's
no. 5 same Tumbler
Move 921 850
#3.98 - 3.58 - 3.18
nov. 16 - 1927,

Joint mould

Paden City mold drawing. The third piece down is the one used for the base of the lazy Susans made for Rubel.

Bibliography

Barnett, Jerry. "And Here's Cavendish." *Paden City Party Line,* September 1981.

_____. "Crow's Foot Square and Crow's Foot Round." *Paden City. Party Line,* March 1980.

_____. "The Nerva Pattern." *Paden City Party Line,* June 1980.

_____. *Paden City, the Color Company.* Privately published, 1982.

_____. "Paden City's Glades Pattern." *Paden City Party Line,* June 1982.

Bickenheuser Fred. *Tiffin Glassmasters, Book II.* OH: Glassmaster Publishers, 1981.

Bredehoft, Neila, and Dean Six, eds. *Paden City Glass, The Lost Plates: Prints from the Etching Plates.* Monograph no. 8 published as part of the glass study series of the West Virginia Museum of American Glass Ltd.

Brown, O.O. *Paden City Catalog Reprints from the 1920s.* Marietta, OH: Antique Publications, 2000.

Florence, Gene. *Collector's Encyclopedia of Depression Glass,* 13th ed. Paducah, Ky: Collector Books, 1998.

_____. *Kitchen Glassware of the Depression Years. Identification & Value,* 6th ed. Paducah, KY: Collector Books, 2001.

_____. *Elegant Glassware of the Depression Era: Identification & Value Guide,* 10th ed. Paducah, KY: Collector Books, 2002.

_____. *Very Rare Glassware of the Depression Years, Vol II.* Paducah, KY: Collector Books, 1991.

_____. *Very Rare Glassware of the Depression Years, Vol III.* Paducah, KY: Collector Books, 1993.

_____. *Very Rare Glassware of the Depression Years, Vol IV.* Paducah, KY: Collector Books, 1995.

_____. *Very Rare Glassware of the Depression Years, Vol V.* Paducah, KY: Collector Books, 1997.

_____. *Very Rare Glassware of the Depression Years, Vol VI.* Paducah, KY: Collector Books, 1999.

Garmon Lee and Dick Spencer. *Glass Animals of the Depression Era.* Paducah, KY: Collector Books, 1992.

Pina Leslie and Jerry Gallagher. *Tiffin Glass 1914 – 1940.* Atglen, PA: Schiffer Publishing, 2000.

Six, Dean. *West Virginia Glass Between the World Wars,* Atglen, PA: Schiffer Publishing, 2000.

Stender, Nancy. "Candlesticks, Out of the Homes of Paden City." *Paden City Glass Society Newsletter,* June 2002.

_____. "Crow's Foot." *Paden City Glass Society Newsletter,* June 2001.

_____. " Line 220 Largo and Line 221 Maya." *Paden City Glass Society Newsletter,* September 2002.

_____. "Line 555." *Paden City Glass Society Newsletter,* December 2001.

_____. "Paden City Animals." *Paden City Glass Society Newsletter,* September 2001.

Torsiello, Paul, Debora Torsiello, Tom Stillman, and Arlene Stillman. *Paden City Glassware.* Atglen, PA: Schiffer Publishing, 2002.

Walker, William, Joan Walker, and Melissa Bratkovich. *Paden City Glass Company.* Marietta, OH: The Glass Press, Inc., 2003.

Weatherman, Hazel Marie. *Colored Glassware of the Depression Era, Book 2.* Glassbooks, 1994.

_____. *Supplement and Price Trends 2: Colored Glassware of the Depression Era.* Glassbooks, 1982.

Whitmyer, Kenn, and Margaret Whitmyer. *Bedroom and Bathroom Glassware of the Depression Years.* Paducah, KY: Collector Books, 1989.

Associations:

Paden City Glass Society, Inc.
PO Box 139
Paden City, WV 26159
pcglasssociety@mailcity.com

Paden City Glass Collector's Guild
42 Aldine Rd.
Parsippany, NJ 07054

Index